W9-BVZ-311

MAKING M&A DEALS
HAPPEN

ROBERT STEFANOWSKI

McGraw-Hill

New York Chicago San Francisco Lisbon London Madrid
Mexico City Milan New Delhi San Juan Seoul
Singapore Sydney Toronto

1 2 3 4 5 6 7 8 9 0   DOC/DOC   0 9 8 7

ISBN-13: 978-0-07-144740-9
ISBN-10: 0-07-144740-7

This publication is designed to provide accurate and authoritative information in regard to the subject matter covered. It is sold with the understanding that the publisher is not engaged in rendering legal, accounting, or other professional service. If legal advice or other expert assistance is required, the services of a competent professional person should be sought.

> —*From a declaration of principles jointly adopted by a committee*
> *of the American Bar Association and a committee of publishers.*

McGraw-Hill books are available at special quantity discounts to use as premiums and sales promotions, or for use in corporate training programs. For more information, please write to the Director of Special Sales, Professional Publishing, McGraw-Hill, Two Penn Plaza, New York, NY 10121-2298. Or contact your local bookstore.

MAKING **M&A** DEALS
HAPPEN

Carol —

I really enjoyed meeting
you today. I look forward
to staying in touch!

Bus Stefan

To my parents, Bob Sr. and Eleanor, for realizing that a good education is one of the best gifts they could provide to their children, and to my sisters, Patty, Deb, and Sue for all of their support over the years. Finally, to Amy, Lauren, Rachel, and Megan for the love, under-standing, and fun they provide every day!

CONTENTS

This book is designed to give the reader a practical, businessperson's approach to M&A by providing a road map on how to source, negotiate, and close mergers, acquisitions, and joint ventures. We will discuss each stage of the typical deal process, highlighting the critical elements, risks, and opportunities of each. Whether you are a business professional in the M&A field, an investment banker, a chief executive officer with overall business responsibility, or a student who has an interest in learning about the deal process, this text should help to make you more effective in your work.

America's fascination with the stock market and the continued pressure on corporations to grow has resulted in a proliferation of M&A activity in recent years, both in the United States and abroad. As a result, the ability to understand M&A and get deals done has become a critical skill in corporate America. Whether someone is directly or indirectly involved in the deal process, a basic understanding of business combinations is essential to success in business today. Although this book is written from the perspective of a deal principal (i.e., a corporation that is contemplating some type of business combination: merger, acquisition, joint venture, and so on), the information is useful to a variety of constituencies including the following:

> *Corporate business development groups.* The term *business development* will be used throughout the text to indicate those corporate professionals whose primary responsibility is to grow their companies by purchasing or merging with other firms. In some organizations, these efforts are referred to as the Strategic Development, Corporate Development, or simply M&A Department.

> *Related corporate roles.* Although they are not directly responsible for M&A activity, it is essential that people in various senior corporate roles, such as chief executive officer, chief financial officer, and chief operating officer, have a working understanding of the M&A process and its risks and oppor-

tunities. As we will see in Chapter 1, failure of company managers to understand this process can have a dramatic effect, both on their companies and on their individual careers.

Investment banks. For larger or more complicated transactions, both the buyer and the seller generally hire investment bankers. Having a working understanding of the process and the issues facing the principals in these transactions is essential to the effectiveness of any investment banking professional. By guiding the reader through the M&A process and its potential pitfalls, this book will enable the current or future investment banker to be much better prepared to serve his or her clients.

Private equity professionals/LBO groups/hedge funds. The 1990s and 2000s have seen a proliferation of private equity groups and, more recently, hedge funds that have an interest in equity investing. The legendary firms such as Kolhberg, Kravis, and Roberts (KKR), with its hostile takeover of Nabisco (as popularized in the book/movie *Barbarians at the Gate*) have evolved into an extensive network of private funds focused on buying companies for their own account. These partnerships are generally formed by investment professionals financed by a group of wealthy investors, pension funds, or other institutions. The purpose of these equity funds is to locate attractive companies for purchase, run the companies for a period of time, and, hopefully, sell the company for a profit at some point in the future to provide a return on capital to the investors. As we will discuss later, the billions of dollars in capital raised by these funds have had a dramatic impact on the dynamics of the M&A industry. Most, if not all, of the issues faced by M&A professionals in a corporate environment are identical to those faced by private equity groups arranged to buy and run companies.

Other advisors. Employees of a wide variety of other players, including legal and tax advisors, appraisal firms, public relations firms, and other such organizations, need to understand the M&A process. Having an adequate understanding of the process can be critical to the success or failure of these individuals.

COMMON DEFINITIONS

"M&A" is a generic term that can have a variety of meanings, depending on the context. The discussion in this text is applicable to all forms of M&A transactions, as outlined here:

- *Acquisition.* The 100 percent purchase by one company of another. The target company is normally absorbed by the acquirer and no longer exists as a separate entity after the deal closes.
- *Merger.* The combination of two companies/legal entities into one. This normally occurs in situations where two companies of similar size and characteristics agree to combine their efforts.
- *Minority equity investment.* Something less than a 100 percent purchase. A minority equity investment provides the buyer with a portion of the equity value in the target without having operating control of the firm.
- *Joint venture/strategic alliance.* The process whereby two companies decide to work together on some portion of their existing or future business. For example, Dow

EXHIBIT I-1

The Dow Corning Joint Venture

Dow Corning Corporation (Dow Corning) was incorporated in 1943 by Corning Glass Works (now Corning Incorporated) and The Dow Chemical Company (Dow Chemical) for the purpose of developing and producing polymers and other materials based on silicon chemistry. Corning Incorporated provided the basic silicone technology and Dow Chemical supplied the chemical processing and manufacturing know-how. Both companies contributed key employees to the venture, while maintaining their own separate, distinct operating companies. Dow Corning became a wholly owned subsidiary, owned 50 percent by Dow Chemical and 50 percent by Corning, Inc. Dow Corning currently manufactures over 10,000 products and serves approximately 50,000 customers worldwide.

Discussion Questions

1. What are the benefits of this joint venture combination as opposed to a 100 percent purchase of one company by the other?

2. What are some issues that could arise from such a structure (that is, 50/50 ownership)?

3. Is there anything unique about this situation that lends itself to a joint venture arrangement?

Chemical and Corning Incorporated formed a joint venture called Dow Corning to develop new products that leveraged the core competency of each business. The joint venture structure allowed the firms to work together on new product development, while still leaving the core operations of each business unit separate. (See Exhibit I-1, "The Dow Corning Joint Venture.")

We will also frequently refer to the concept of "due diligence" throughout the course of this book. Due diligence represents the financial, operational, and strategic analysis that a buyer undertakes when evaluating (1) whether to purchase a target company, (2) how to structure the deal, and (3) how much to pay. A detailed description of the due diligence process is provided in Chapters 4 and 5.

NOTES

Bryan Bullough and John Helyar, *Barbarians at the Gate: The Fall of RJR Nabisco* (New York: Harper Perennial Press,).

ACKNOWLEDGMENTS

I would like to thank the following people who were critical to the development of this book: Irene McGeachy, my outstanding assistant who helped in production; Pattie Amoroso at McGraw-Hill, for her editing and production expertise; Mark O'Leary, who "volunteered" to read the entire text and made great suggestions; and Dave Wente, Carl Lobell, Jane McDonald, and Bill Gutowitz, who taught me all I know about M&A.

The M&A Environment

Merger and acquisition activity has historically been cyclical, based upon certain macro factors involving

- The overall state of the economy in the United States and abroad
- Public stock prices
- Levels of liquidity in the financial markets
- The extent of antitrust pressure on mergers and acquisitions
- The amount of regulatory scrutiny of certain industries, such as airlines, telecommunications, banking, and other financial services
- Whether "conglomerates" (single corporations with multiple business lines, such as United Technologies, which has divisions producing jet engines, elevators, helicopters, and automotive parts) or "pure play" companies (firms like Wal-Mart, Kodak, and Exxon that are mainly in one line of business) are in favor among analysts and market "experts"

While there always seems to be a minimum amount of core activity in M&A, the number of companies bought and sold, as well as the prices paid for these deals, has varied widely over time.

THE ROARING NINETIES

Take the case of Conseco Finance, which was trading near its highest level at $50 per share in June 1998. The company's CEO, Stephen

Hilbert, and the public markets were very confident about the company's prospects. However, that same month, Hilbert announced the acquisition of Green Tree Financial, a subprime mortgage and consumer lending company, for a whopping $7.6 billion. The price was seven times the net worth of Green Tree, or a $6.6 billion premium to tangible book value. Over the next two years, Conseco's stock price dropped from $50 a share to below $10 (see Exhibit 1-1); the company ultimately filed for bankruptcy in the spring of 2003. Analysts attributed the company's long, painful downfall directly to its overpayment for the Green Tree assets and the subsequent adverse impact of that purchase on Conseco's operations. This ill-advised acquisition not only cost Hilbert his job, but drove a very successful company out of business.

The popular press has reported many examples of acquisitions that have performed poorly because of a faulty business strategy or an overpayment for assets purchased in a merger or acquisition. In many cases, the overall financial and stock performance of the combined company is significantly worse after the acquisition. In fact, there appears to be a fairly strong negative correlation between the announcement of a major acquisition and an acquiring firm's stock performance after the acquisition.[1] Studies have shown that over 50

EXHIBIT 1-1

Conseco Stock Price, 1998 to 2001

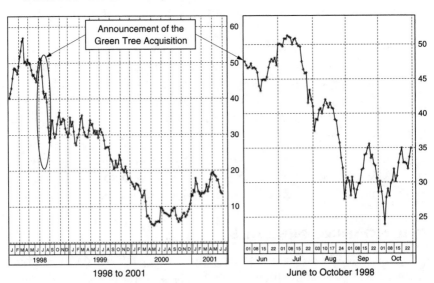

percent of M&A transactions actually dilute the total shareholder value of the acquiring company within one year of closing.

A second example can be seen in the consolidation of the U.S. banking sector in the heyday of M&A activity, the late 1990s (see Exhibit 1-2). Despite the subpar returns realized on acquisitions, deal activity kept increasing at a faster and faster rate (see Exhibit 1-3). In many cases, overly aggressive M&A strategies actually reduced the acquirer's stock price.

Historically, neither the company's senior management team nor the board of directors has been held accountable for making faulty acquisitions. Firms essentially had a "free option"; if a particular deal worked, senior management and the company took all of the credit. If the deal failed, the company's poor postmerger performance was blamed on subpar operations, a bad market, or some other factor.

As we will see later, the twenty-first century has held senior executives more accountable when they fail to deliver on their deals. So, the logical question that arises is, why are CEOs and their boards of directors willing to put themselves and their companies at risk for a strategy that has so many potential pitfalls, as evidenced by historical data?

The largest single factor driving the growth in M&A activity in the twenty-first century is the increasing pressure on private and pub-

EXHIBIT 1-2

Excess Returns after Announcement for Largest U.S. Bank Deals

	Acquirer	Target	Weighted Avgerage
FirstStar/US BanCorp	(10%)	8%	0%
Travellers/CitiCorp	26%	18%	23%
NationsBank/BankAmerica	6%	5%	6%
Norwest/Wells	(7%)	1%	(3%)
BancOne/First Chicago	(1%)	2%	0%
Wamu/Ahmanson	2%	19%	7%
First Union/CoreStates	(3%)	10%	0%
NationsBank/Barnett	(5%)	25%	2%
Wells/First Interstate	0%	32%	14%
Chemical/Chase	11%	13%	12%
NationsBank/Boatman's	(7%)	25%	4%

Source: Robert Townsend, Jill Ferguson, and Craig Williams, "The US Is Growing Wary of Mega-mergers," Salomon Smith Barney Equity Research, October 6, 2000, pp. 13.

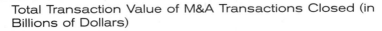

EXHIBIT 1-3

Total Transaction Value of M&A Transactions Closed (in Billions of Dollars)

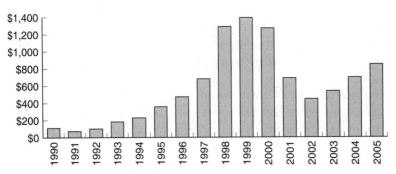

Source: Bloomberg Professional M&A Statistics.

lic companies to produce asset and income growth to feed investors' expectations. In most markets, the growth demanded by investors cannot be achieved with their existing lines of business. Chief executive officers have become increasingly dependent on acquisitions to increase their penetration of their existing markets, enter new markets, and produce the incremental income needed to meet investors' expectations. However, the ever-increasing pressure by investors has thrown the risk/reward equation out of balance. Although they fluctuate with economic cycles, M&A premiums consistently exceed 20 percent of the book value of assets acquired (see Exhibit 1-4). In other words, in order to induce a seller to sell, buyers consistently have to pay 20 percent more than the assets are"worth."These high premiums leave little margin for error and put enormous pressure on the operating results of a company postacquisition, forcing management to grow assets and income aggressively to achieve pro forma projections.

Other factors leading to the proliferation of M&A activity include the following.

Stock-for-Stock Acquisitions

The large P/E multiples of publicly traded companies in the late 1990s accelerated the use of stock as an acquisition currency and made some deals look relatively inexpensive compared to a cash purchase funded through debt issued by the purchaser. Take Webvan's acquisition of Homegrocer.com in September 2000. Webvan issued 138 million shares of common stock to retire all Homegrocer shares and recorded over $900

E X H I B I T   1-4

Premium over Target Book Value

Average Premium Offered (in percents)

Source: Thompson Financial

million in goodwill. Although the issuance of common stock diluted current Webvan equity holders' positions, this was a very efficient form of merger because the company did not have to pay any cash, or issue any incremental debt to complete the deal. However, from an investor's perspective, the true cost of the acquisition was not reflected in Webvan's financial statements. In fact, the stock ultimately proved to be worthless, as Webvan filed for bankruptcy in the second quarter of 2001.

Sellers' Market

The constant pressure for corporate growth at any cost has kept the demand for acquisitions high. The result has been a deal climate in which there are more "buyers" than there are companies willing to sell. In addition to driving up prices, this has resulted in a very cavalier approach by the investment bankers that are marketing companies. Even in major, multibillion-dollar acquisitions, the amount of time allowed for buyers to complete their due diligence on target companies has been compressed.

Shorter due diligence periods work to the advantage of the seller for a variety of reasons:

- Only one of the bidders completing due diligence will actually purchase the company. Therefore, sellers are motivated to release the least amount of information possible to protect the confidentiality of information.
- Better-educated buyers are usually smarter buyers. If the amount of information available is limited, the advantage in negotiations goes to the seller.

- Sellers can limit the amount of disruption to their management teams and employees by limiting the amount of due diligence offered to potential buyers. Having multiple potential buyers come in for extended due diligence periods can have a very disrupting influence on the seller's company.

A third trend seen in the 1990s was a "roll-up" strategy, which many companies engaged in to accelerate asset and income growth. Management teams were established not as operating units, but rather to consolidate many smaller companies in fragmented industries and build immediate scale. These public firms used their own stock as acquisition currency to consolidate smaller, privately held firms. The managers of the target exchanged their equity for stock in the larger public entity. These roll-ups were used to consolidate many disparate private companies into one large public company in such industries as waste management, equipment rental, video rental, and health-care services.

This aggressive acquisition strategy put a lot of pressure on the acquirer's balance sheet because of the significant amount of goodwill needed to close these deals. Parent companies struggled to integrate the diverse cultures, operating systems, and management teams of the firms that had been rolled up. Although this strategy was initially hyped as the wave of the future, many of these deals ended up with a significant dilution of value for all the firms invested.

ACQUISITION TRENDS IN THE TWENTY-FIRST CENTURY

The depressed stock values and slowing economy in the first few years of the twenty-first century intensified the scrutiny of the activities of management in the M&A arena by the public markets and boards of directors. CEOs of well-known, Fortune 500 companies such as First Union, Aetna, and Tyco have been asked to resign because of their failure to produce the acquisition results promised to investors. The continued proliferation of investment information available to the general public made possible by the Internet, more stringent accounting rules surrounding M&A, and heightened regulatory oversight under Sarbanes-Oxley have also intensified the scrutiny of management activities. Investors and analysts are holding deal professionals accountable for actually performing on the promises made at the time the acquisition was proposed.

Even successful deals are viewed with skepticism today. Rating agencies and other shareholder interest groups are becoming increasingly concerned with the quality of earnings as well as the "quantity". Some firms have been criticized for not having enough growth from continuing operations, but instead relying too heavily on deals outside of their core competencies for growth. Some public companies have been challenged to grow their assets and net income while maintaining a high return on invested capital after the deals close.

All of these trends make it even more imperative that deal professionals, corporate senior management, investment bankers, and other advisors understand how to get deals done and, perhaps more importantly, what deals not to do. The remainder of this book is devoted to educating the reader on how to avoid the pitfalls. Corporate America has learned the hard way that a mistake can cost you your job—or even worse.

CHAPTER 1 SUMMARY

1. The level of M&A activity has been cyclical over time based on the state of the economy, world stock markets, and the macroeconomic environment.

2. Over 50 percent of M&A transactions fail; that is, the addition of the target's operations is dilutive to overall shareholder value.

3. As investors become more and more informed via the Internet and other sources, companies will come under increasing pressure to grow. Acquisitions provide an immediate way to build scale and show growth. However, management needs to be careful when contemplating deals to ensure that only the right deals are done. A bad deal can have a very negative impact on a good company and its senior management.

4. The first part of the twenty-first century has seen a more cautious approach to deals as a result of depressed stock values, heightened sensitivity on the part of regulatory agencies, and increased awareness of potential problems, brought about by several large, public M&A failures.

5. Senior management in all functions needs to be knowledgeable about the fundamentals of M&A to ensure that the

right deals are pursued and, just as important, bad deals are
avoided.

NOTES

1. Robert Townsend, Jill Ferguson, and Craig Williams, "The US Is Growing Wary of
   Mega-mergers," Salomon Smith Barney Equity Research, October 6, 2000, pp.
   1–3.

Sourcing the Deal

The old question, "Which came first, the chicken or the egg?" rephrased as, "Which came first, the strategy or the opportunity?" can be especially true in an M&A context. Most academics recommend a top-down approach to M&A, with senior management going through the following steps sequentially:

1. Establish an overall company strategy concerning acquisitions, that is, do we want to acquire, how much do we want to acquire, how soon, what part of the firm's growth will come from acquisition, and so on?
2. Select strategic markets to play in—what new industries would be a good complement to where we currently have a presence?
3. Find solid companies to target within those industries.
4. Focus the company's M&A resources on those firms first.

A strategic approach to M&A is logical, orderly, and driven from the highest levels of management in the corporation (see Exhibit 2-1). Unfortunately, this nice, orderly process is rarely followed in practice. It is only through years of hard work and experience that M&A professionals are able to adapt to the multiple situations and pressures that their profession requires.

EXHIBIT 2-1

Strategic Approach to M&A

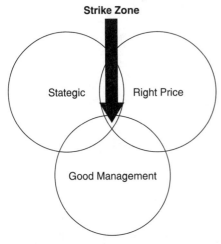

Created by Rachel Stefanowski.

1. STRATEGIC APPROACH TO M&A

A company's long-range strategic plan should provide a road map for how the firm can grow its customer base, revenue, and earnings. It is the bridge from where a company is today to where it wants to be three to five years out. A sound M&A strategy provides a means of accelerating this development plan by expanding the company's presence in existing markets or by enabling it to enter new markets, technologies, or geographies.

For example, assume that a U.S.-based home security company, Katie, Inc., decides that European expansion is critical to its long-range strategic plan. Trying to start a U.K.-based home security company could be extremely difficult and time-consuming. Katie would have to (1) become familiar with U.K. laws and customs, (2) analyze the dynamics of the U.K. market, (3) determine a pricing strategy, (4) hire European locals to staff the function, (5) develop accounting and reporting systems, (6) find a location for a home office and branch facilities, and (7) enter into agreements to support its supply chain. Building such a business can be a very time-consuming task and could distract management from its existing U.S. operations. However, an acquisition of an existing U.K. security company would provide Katie with immediate scale and a management team that understands the U.K. market. This could be much more efficient than trying to build a company from scratch.

2. LEVERAGING STRATEGIC MARKETING GROUPS

In some organizations, the strategic marketing function is combined with the business development role (groups or individuals responsible for buying and selling companies), and in others it is a stand-alone function. In either case, a good strategic marketing group can add huge value to the M&A process. Business development is normally focused more on the execution of ideas that have been generated and are deemed to be worthwhile. Strategic marketing is focused more on "big-picture thinking" and long-term strategies for the firm. These marketing personnel often have a very good understanding of the broader issues facing an organization and its growth prospects. They can identify trends in the industries they serve as well as potential areas for expansion. This can form the basis for a useful dialogue with business development professionals on what market sectors it might make sense to expand into and what companies to begin a dialogue with. As we will discuss later, this can form the basis for strategic alliances, joint ventures, or outright purchases, depending on the interests of the respective parties.

Business development professionals must ensure that the organization will support their ideas before they expend too much time and effort on them. The worst situation, which actually occurs quite frequently, is where a business development team expends a huge amount of time and effort exploring a strategic opportunity with a third party, only to learn that their own company senior management has little or no interest in the project once it is brought forward. Not only is this an unwise use of resources, but it can damage a company's industry reputation when the potential acquisition target/strategic partner learns that all of this effort has been spent on a project that never had the support of senior management.

Vetting ideas early with both the strategic management group and senior management is critical. Most strategic marketing functions have frequent access to the CEO and his or her senior management team. These groups can serve as a great sounding board for ideas, especially unique, out-of-the-box ideas, before engaging the potential target in discussions.

3. IDENTIFYING DEAL FLOW

Once the overall strategic marketing and acquisition plan has been developed, it is time to find real opportunities. The key challenge is to narrow the broad range of opportunities at any point in time to those situations where (1) the target has a real interest in selling, (2) the buyer's senior management has an interest in buying, and (3) terms and conditions, including price, can be agreed upon between buyer and seller. As outlined in Exhibit 2-2, various targets are eliminated at each stage of this process until eventually one deal out of the huge population is closed. This trial-and-error operation is a fundamental part of the M&A process and a main focus of this book.

4. OPPORTUNISTIC APPROACH

Going back to our earlier example, what would Katie do if no U.K. security firms were interested in selling, or if the premium that firms required became cost prohibitive? Katie may have spent a lot of time developing a very logical and well-supported European M&A strategy, only to be frustrated by market conditions that prevent this strategy from being carried out. Senior management and deal teams should certainly put thought into what industries are attractive and complementary to their current portfolio of businesses. However, even the best strategy will be foiled if no companies are available for sale at the time the strategy is developed. This is precisely why, in practice, most acquisitions are driven by the opportunity *first* and the strategy *second*.

Consider Tyco's June 2001 purchase of the financial services giant CIT. Did Tyco senior executives strategize about getting into the financial services business to complement their existing operations in health care, fire protection, security, and electronics? Or did Tyco realize that a large group of assets ($9.2 billion) that could generate substantial net income was available, and then go to the board of directors and public shareholders and try to rationalize the transaction? Unless you were a member of the deal team, you can't be sure. However, one driver of this "financial services strategy" could have been the availability of a large company, CIT, that could provide immediate incremental net income to Tyco.

EXHIBIT 2-2

The Deal Funnel

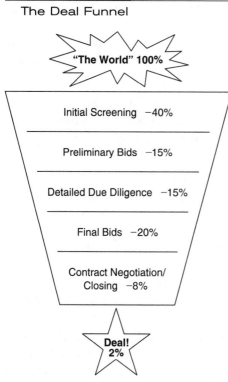

"The World" 100%

Initial Screening −40%

Preliminary Bids −15%

Detailed Due Diligence −15%

Final Bids −20%

Contract Negotiation/
Closing −8%

Deal!
2%

Created by Lauren Stefanowski.

Some companies have employed a strategic approach to M&A effectively, producing very compelling combinations. For example, FedEx's $2.4 billion purchase of Kinko's copy centers in the first half of 2004 seemed very strategic. The purchase allowed FedEx to leverage Kinko's retail branch network to provide a more complete range of document and shipping services. By setting up FedEx kiosks at Kinko's retail locations, FedEx was able to drive immediate incremental shipping traffic without that much incremental cost. This is the type of "strategic acquisition" that most consultants dream about—instant, relatively easy to realize synergies.

5. ENTERING COMPETITIVE AUCTIONS

Most companies for sale will hire an investment bank to run an auction process in order to maximize their value by selling to the highest bidder. Deal professionals need to be in close contact with the investment banks running these processes. Senior company management should be familiar with the investment banking professionals in their industry segments or those segments that they would like to penetrate, to make sure that they are aware of all new opportunities. Investment banks are a very efficient way to source transactions; however, they do come with certain disadvantages:

1. The winner of a competitive auction is almost always the party that was willing to pay the highest price—which makes realizing the required return levels especially difficult.
2. It is easy to get caught up in the hype of an auction and overpay for the target, particularly when the deal team has spent a lot of time analyzing the company and its outlook.
3. Investment bankers working for the seller often present a very optimistic view of the company's prospects and future financial performance. This can cause purchasers to overbid in cases where these financial results do not materialize.
4. In most cases, investment bankers will limit buyers' access to company management, financial information, and forecast support. Sellers are very careful not to disclose important information like customer lists, patents, or pricing to those bidding on the deal. Although this is immoral and in some cases illegal, potential buyers have been known to enter the bid process just to see the inner workings of their competitors, with no desire to ultimately go through with the transaction. Because of this, investment bankers are extremely reluctant to release data, in some cases data that are critical to developing an informed bid for the company.

   For example, in the hot M&A market of the mid-1990s, many banking transactions were consummated based on publicly available information (10-Ks, 10-Qs, and so on) alone. Acquirers were not allowed to meet with the management of the target or to ask questions about the target's operations or financial results. Despite this, huge premiums were paid to acquire banks with little substantiation of the underlying value.

6. PROPRIETARY DEAL FLOW—HOW TO FIND IT

A much better, and much more difficult, way to get a "bargain" is to find proprietary deal flow. In an M&A context, the word *proprietary* means that your team is the only one looking at the target company at the current time. The seller has not yet engaged an investment banker to create a competitive auction situation with multiple potential bidders; your team is the only one trying to negotiate a transaction. There are several big advantages to calling on a company directly:

- Buyers can often avoid a competitive auction situation, where prices are normally driven up by multiple bidders.
- Buyers receive better access to company senior management, financial data, and strategic plans without having to work through investment bank intermediaries.
- Buyers can often customize the terms of the transaction with respect to form of payment, timing of closing, retention of senior management, and other items to facilitate the transfer of ownership.

Several methods can be pursued to avoid competitive auction situations:

Cold Calling

Cold calling involves developing a list of companies related to the acquiring firm through industry journals, word of mouth, industry SIC codes, or competitor lists. The list is then distributed to sales personnel, who call on each company directly and attempt to find a person of authority in the finance or treasury function. After a brief explanation of their own firm, the salespeople attempt to determine whether the company has any interest in being acquired or forming a strategic alliance.

Pros

- This is a great source of proprietary deal flow.
- The buyer gets to know the target's senior management early in the process.
- Calling all SIC codes or competitors provides broad market coverage.

- It can be an efficient way to find new leads if the actual cold calling effort is outsourced.

Cons

- This method has an extremely low success rate. Normally less than 5 percent of the firms contacted have any interest in even entering into discussions. This can also be a very inefficient use of salespeople's time to the extent that they are involved in other sourcing activities.
- It is hard to get to the decision maker. Decision makers are usually fairly high up in the management chain and do not normally take unsolicited calls. Administrative assistants can be very good gatekeepers, preventing access unless the reason for the call is known.
- It is difficult work. Cold calling is the least desirable aspect of most salespeople's activities. With the frequent negative reaction and rejection, it is difficult to sustain a positive attitude while conducting a cold calling program.
- The approach is impersonal. Callers may not have a great understanding of the buyer's operations.

Engage a Third-Party Caller

An industry has developed in which independent contractors will perform cold calling and other search techniques for a fee. Normally, either this fee is based on the number of contacts made or a larger, contingent fee is paid only if the search is successful. Periodic reports are generated that show the companies contacted, their level of interest, and follow-up items for each prospect. The buyer can then engage its sales or M&A staff to follow up only on real prospects, as opposed to sorting through multiple companies that may or may not be interested in discussing a combination.

Pros

- Using a third party frees up resources at the acquiring firm to provide more value-added functions than merely cold calling.
- Third-party employees have been trained in and are efficient at making these calls. Over time, they have developed

an approach that is more likely to get through the road-blocks and reach the decision maker.

- These third-party services can appear to be more independent, serving the role of matchmaker between buyer and seller. This can be less threatening to the seller and may thus be more successful.

Cons

- Third parties do not know the buyer's business or its acquisition "strike zone" as well as the acquirer's own staff would. This can sometimes cause confusion if a potential target wants answers to detailed questions before it agrees to engage in further discussions.
- The buyer's reputation is at risk if there is any inappropriate behavior on the part of the third-party caller. Callers often have to be relatively aggressive to get through to the decision maker. However, there is a fine line between being aggressive and being too pushy, particularly if the third-party caller is paid only on a contingent basis. This is of particular concern because the calls are usually made to competitors and other participants in the buyer's industry, who will not always distinguish between the third-party caller and the buyer who hired her or him.

Use Deal Brokers

In many industries, independent deal brokers can be found to source transactions on behalf of buyers. These brokers are usually former industry players who are very well networked and have decided to go out on their own to broker deals for others. Brokers are normally paid on a commission basis only if their introduction leads to a successful transaction.

Pros

- This can be a good source of proprietary deal flow.
- Brokers normally have very broad market coverage.
- Brokers are familiar with a wide range of buyers and the qualities essential to a successful transaction.

Cons

- This is not normally a regulated profession. Buyers and sellers need to ensure that they are dealing with a reputable broker. Many brokers are one-person shops with little history.
- There is a divergence of interests. Brokers get paid only if they are successful in arranging a transaction that both sides are willing to consummate. This creates a tendency for brokers to provide a very positive outlook to both buyer and seller—even when it is not warranted.
- Many brokers are "guns for hire" that will show a potential transaction to multiple buyers in hopes of earning a commission. This can turn supposedly proprietary deal flow into a competitive situation.

Engage Investment Banks on the Buy Side

Hiring one or more investment banks to find suitable acquisition candidates can be a very efficient way to locate proprietary deal flow. Banks will generally have a few areas of expertise in which they have relationships with many players in the industry through their corporate finance, research, and M&A advisory departments. Because they are constantly in the market, they often hear about potential acquisition candidates before they become widely known. Developing a close working relationship with several investment banks in the buyer's industry can lead to interesting M&A opportunities.

Pros

- This is an efficient method of finding new deal flow. Rather than tying up firm resources, the investment bank brings only relevant opportunities to the buyer.
- Investment banks may have broader coverage of the industry than a buyer has.
- Because they are also paid on commission, investment banks will often find unique transactions in industries that are different from but related to those of the buyer, giving the buyer the opportunity to diversify its holdings.
- Investment banks are very adept at structuring transactions. Through the use of earn-outs, contingent payment

structures, asset/stock sales, and so on, investment banks can often find ways to bridge the gap between the expectations of buyers and sellers to make a deal happen.

■ If there is a deal, the buyer can engage the investment bank to help with the negotiation, due diligence, and closing of the transaction. The banker's knowledge of the target and the target's industry can be very valuable in evaluating the seller's projections and the appropriate amount to pay for the company.

Cons

■ *Proprietary* is a relative term. Most investment banks will show opportunities to multiple buyers in hopes of earning their commission. This can quickly turn a proprietary deal into a competitive situation and drive up the price.

■ Investment banks don't get paid unless there is a deal, causing a potential conflict of interest between them and the buyer.

■ Investment banks usually demand a very high commission on transactions that they source. This can add a material amount to the buyer's cost of the deal.

Finally, discussions at the CEO or board of directors level can be one of the most efficient ways to develop transactions. Close industry competitors are often in contact at customer events, industry seminars, and trade shows. This can lead to informal discussions about acquisitions or strategic alliances that ultimately come true. The $58 billion merger of JP Morgan and Banc One in January 2004 started with a meeting between the CEOs of the two companies, William Harrison of JP Morgan and Jamie Dimon of Banc One. Through a long "courting period," Dimon and Harrison developed a level of trust and mutual agreement about the benefits of a combination of their two organizations. Although investment bankers were involved at a later stage to structure, price, and negotiate the transaction, the leaders of the two companies had agreed to the core elements of the deal. This is a very efficient way to get a deal done—and to keep it private while discussions are under way. However, not many M&A transactions have the luxury of the two CEOs creating an early bond.

7. SCREENING DEALS

Most professionals do not realize the extremely low success rate of
M&A transactions. In fact, on average less than 5 percent of deals
that are sourced ultimately make it through due diligence,
approval, and negotiation to the ultimate closing of a transaction.
This puts extreme pressure on M&A professionals to be efficient
with resources. Whether you are buying companies in the corporate sector or advising at an investment bank, weeks, months, and
in some cases years can be invested in a particular transaction, only
to have the deal die because of a variety of events that, in many
cases, are outside the control of the deal team. These include a failure to agree on purchase price, issues discovered in due diligence,
regulatory changes having an impact on the target's operations,
legal issues, culture clashes, and so on.

It is absolutely critical that any issues be uncovered as quickly
as possible, before resources are committed to a deal that will not
get done. To make matters more complicated, acquisition professionals can often get emotionally attached to transactions. After
working on a target for months, it can be very hard to let go and
realize that all of that effort was in vain. Management of the deal
team must make quick assessments about whether the issues can
be overcome and what steps to take to get there.

Alternatively, deal teams must guard against abandoning
transactions for the wrong reasons. The typical due diligence team
is cross-functional, with representatives from human resources,
risk, legal, finance, and so on, who generally have full-time responsibilities in addition to M&A representation. These professionals
do not have as much of a vested interest in getting a deal done as
the business development professionals do; it is not their primary
job. Therefore, being asked to "volunteer" for a due diligence team
is time-consuming and adds stress to an already very busy work
schedule. As a result, some of the "issues" raised are often not sub-
stantive, but rather are raised to try to slow down the deal. Deal
team management must be disciplined to try to balance the concerns raised by team members. Is the issue a real one that should
prevent the deal from getting done, one way or another? Or is it a
marginal problem that can be structured around or handled in
some other manner? Only with experience does the business development professional learn to strike a balance, not getting bogged
down in the details, while still highlighting those issues that can
have a material impact on the deal.

8. TOOLS TO BE/STAY EFFICIENT

Get Early Buy-In

Maintaining close contact with corporate senior management is a critical element of efficiency. As stated earlier, a large number of ideas must be generated to get a few deals that close. Often, a very quick discussion with senior management will root out big issues or disclose an emotionally adverse reaction to a given opportunity.

Most efficient corporations have an "early read" process for deals. This involves preparing a document of at most three to four pages that summarizes the key items in a proposed deal. It is done very early, at the preliminary discussion stage with the target. This allows company senior management to express its views on the deal, the likelihood of the deal's closing, and key issues to investigate during the due diligence process. See Exhibit 2-3 for an example. This 15- to 30-minute quick review can save a company millions of dollars in due diligence expenses. Once a deal team gets going, the outside banking costs, attorney fees, consultants, appraisers, and so on used to support the analysis can quickly run up the tab. These outside firms must be paid regardless of whether the transaction closes.

Alternatively, if the CEO and/or the senior management team likes the deal, this can be a huge benefit to the deal team. With high-level support, allocation of key resources becomes easier and the mindset of the people engaged on the project improves. If a particular department head knows that the CEO is "hot on the deal," he or she is likely to be more constructive and supportive during the deal process. By knowing and addressing any key issues disclosed in the early read, the deal team is much better prepared for the ultimate approval meeting on the deal. Senior management often knows some or all of the target's management team. These relationships can be leveraged at the appropriate times in the deal process to get over deal-breaking issues. Finally, senior management can provide insights into synergies or cost takeouts that can make the projected financial returns much more accretive.

Link to Strategic Marketing/Corporate Strategy

As discussed earlier, the strategic marketing group can also be helpful in determining which opportunities might be the most appealing, given the current direction of the corporation. Whether a deal

EXHIBIT 2-3

"Early Read" Memorandum

Wilson Boatworks Acquisition   Executive Summary

Background

- Opportunity to Purchase #4 U.S. boat manufacturer

- Family-Controlled/Run LLC — Noah Wilson CEO, Age 58, 30 years in industry. COO and CFO in mid 40s, likely to stay with operation

- Solid reputation for high-quality, top-tier boat production

- Sold through independent dealers throughout North America. Primary production facility in Madison, CT

- $10 million EBITDA trailing 12 months

Current Situation

- Aging owner seeks a liquidity event and efficient tax planning

- IDI Investment Bank engaged to run a "limited" auction (three players); our company has been invited to bid

- First-round bids due December 1; limited info available

- Second-round due diligence scheduled on CT site second week of January

- Binding letters of intent due February 15

Financials (in millions)

	04 act	05 act	06 est	07 est	08 est
Revenue	$120	$131	$140	$145	$160
EBITDA	$8	$10	$13	$15	$18
Net Income	$3	$4	$6	$8	$9
ROE	12%	13%	15%	18%	20%

Assumptions:
- 10x TTM EBITDA = $100 million purchase price
- Transaction levered 9:1

Rationale/Issues

- We are #1 U.S. boat manufacturer when combined

- Nice overlap of product types, markets, customers

- Can take cost out of Madison manufacturing facility

- Issues;
  - Loss of CEO upon deal
  - Family issues complicate tax structure
  - Need to retain COO and CFO
  - Lack of information on company performance

is opportunistic or strategic, the strategic marketing group can help to gain consensus around the deal, given this group's access to senior management and its credibility. The strategic marketing group can also appear more objective than a business development team that clearly has a vested interested in getting deals done.

Assess Chances of Winning

An early read of a deal with your investment banker can also make good sense at times. Bankers can provide a feeling for how competitive a particular situation might be and how much of a premium it will require for the seller to sell. The deal team can then weigh this information against the firm's view of the transaction and required rates of return to see if the deal will be competitive once it goes to market. This can save a lot of time and expense.

Many M&A teams will undertake a huge amount of due diligence, internal discussion, and expense, only to find out that they are not even close to being competitive on price. It could be the perfect deal, in the perfect industry, at just the right time. However, if the price gets bid out of a range where you will be competitive, all of this time and effort is wasted. This not only hurts the deal team's credibility on the current deal, but might make the organization less willing to allocate resources for the next big deal that comes to market.

Look for Early Warning Signs

Every organization has different sensitivities and hot buttons to watch out for. The absolute worst case for a deal team is to go through an expensive due diligence process, only to turn the deal down because of a factor that should have been obvious at the start of the deal. Consider the merger of Hewlett-Packard and Compaq, which was consummated in May 2002. This deal was hotly contested by Walter Hewlett, son of the company's founder, and by many of the large shareholders of both companies. In fact, the final shareholder count was 48.6 percent against and 51.4 percent in favor, approving the deal by the smallest of margins. Hewlett and other shareholders feared that the large cost synergies forecast by management would never materialize.

To make this situation worse, it appears that many of the issues that caused the combined company's subpar performance were known before the deal closed. The *New York Times* reported, "Hewlett produced internal documents from Hewlett Packard and Compaq describing both companies as 'deteriorating,' something that was unsaid in the executives sales pitches."[1] Lawrence J. White, professor of economics at New York University Stern School of Business, said that Hewlett-Packard's acquisition of Compaq was a prime example of why shareholders should be suspicious of mergers. "As you look at what seems to be going wrong for the company, it's the stuff that is most closely associated with the Compaq acquisition."[2]

Not only are these situations a very inefficient use of resources, but there can be other collateral damage:

- Running a process with little chance of closure reflects poorly on the M&A team.
- There can be a lot of hard feelings on both the buyer's and the seller's side when the deal does not happen.
- The worst potential outcome is that a deal closes when in reality it should not have. In some cases, the efforts expended and the fear of reprisal will cause a deal team to close a transaction that it should not and suffer the consequences later. As was seen with Compaq and Hewlett-Packard, this can be a recipe for disaster. The combined entity has yet to recover. In mid-2005, newly appointed CEO Carly Fiorina was dismissed for poor integration efforts and subpar postmerger company financial performance.

9. USING SPEED FOR COMPETITIVE ADVANTAGE

Strangely enough, an effective deal-screening system not only prevents bad deals from being done, but also provides a big competitive advantage on deals that you decide to pursue, namely speed. If a deal team has early access to strategic marketing and senior management, the organization can often be more responsive and its actions more timely than an organization in which the deal is buried within middle management. Sellers are evaluating bidders not only on price, but on how likely it is that a particular buyer will actually execute the deal. Early, high-level management involvement provides huge credibility to the process that often can be the difference between winning and losing a deal. Having the decision makers available also provides for a level of responsiveness that sellers will appreciate.

Deal teams must make every effort to act professional and responsive early in the deal. These first impressions will normally be retained throughout the deal process. For example, a well-timed call from the buyer's CEO to the seller's CEO to express his or her interest can make a seller much more comfortable with a potential buyer. This kind of gesture is not possible unless the M&A team has early and frequent contact with the buyer's senior management. The decisions made by the buyer as to who to invite to due diligence should be made partially on fact and partially on emotion. Early senior management involvement can often be the difference between being invited back for a second round of due diligence versus exiting the process.

CHAPTER 2 SUMMARY

1. Most M&A transactions do not follow a logical pattern from setting the strategy to locating a target and closing the deal. The level of experience of the deal people and functional areas is a critical element for the success of a transaction.

2. Every company's long-range strategic planning should include a component on acquisition opportunities.

3. The strategic marketing and business development groups must work together to set the strategy and develop a tactical game plan to attract targets.

4. This trial-and-error process weeds out bad candidates and focuses the deal teams on transactions where the buyer and seller are motivated to close.

5. In an opportunistic approach to M&A, the strategy represented by the deal or industry is normally based on targets that are first identified as being available.

6. Competitive auctions are situations in which the seller sets up a process for multiple bidders to examine its property, normally engaging the help of an investment bank to maximize the value received.

7. Proprietary deal flow is a situation in which a small number of buyers, often just one buyer, is engaged in negotiations with the seller. This is generally a good situation for the buyer, as it can leverage its purchasing power to drive the price and terms and conditions in its favor.

8. Proprietary deal flow can be lucrative but hard to develop. Cold calling, third-party calling agencies, deal brokers, investment banks, and discussions at the board of directors/CEO level are all methods used to identify proprietary deal flow.

9. Early screening of deal flow is critical to maximize the efficiency of deal teams and prevent the expenditure of needless effort on unattractive deals.

10. Executive summaries and informal discussions with senior management can be deployed to screen out bad deals early in the process and to start to build momentum around attractive targets. Deal teams need to be conscious of early warning signs about deals so as not to disappoint internal and external constituencies later.

11. Speed in completing due diligence, signing agreements, closing, and funding can be used by sophisticated buyers to provide a competitive advantage.

NOTES

1. Gretchen Morgenson,"Just Don't Say Synergies to a Hewlett Investor," *New York Times,* August 15, 2004.
2. Morgenson.

The First Round

The first round of the M&A process begins once a seller has decided to put itself up for sale and a buyer has indicated some level of interest in moving forward. It is somewhat of a "beauty contest" where the buyer and seller are each evaluating the other before they enter into a binding agreement. This does not mean that the seller has committed to sell or the buyer has committed to purchase; it merely indicates that there is enough interest on each side to take the next step and learn more.

In this chapter, we will discuss several fairly standard steps that are common to all transactions. However, each particular deal will have a life of its own depending on some of the following attributes:

- Form of the transaction—asset or stock purchase, strategic alliance, minority investment, and so on
- Public or private company
- Level of investment bank involvement
- Size of the deal and the companies involved
- Proprietary versus auction situation
- Required time frame for the transaction
- Relationship/level of trust among the principals to the transaction
- Amount of regulatory oversight

The potential impact of each of these elements will be high-lighted as we discuss the various steps of the first round of the M&A process.

1. CONFIDENTIALITY AGREEMENTS

Most sellers are understandably very sensitive about releasing financial or other proprietary information to the multiple buyers who may be interested in their firm. Confidentiality or nondisclosure agreements (NDAs) are designed to mitigate this risk. See Exhibit 3-1. They normally include protections against hiring the seller's employees, restrictions on the use of proprietary product information, and requirements that all data—both written and verbal—discussed throughout the deal process be kept confidential. The terms of these agreements are heavily negotiated, but the time period involved normally ranges from 24 to 48 months. The scope of the agreement is also normally negotiated—for example, which employees at the potential buyer's firm will be bound by the agreement. There is a constant tension between a potential buyer's need to operate whether a deal happens or not and the seller's understandable concerns around confidentiality. This is a particularly difficult issue when one division of a large, diversified company is involved in a transaction. Potential buyers may not have the ability to bind nonkey employees at other divisions to the agreement that the seller wants them to sign. As a result, business development professionals need to seek the advice of senior management and the company's legal staff at this stage of the process.

2. DECIDING WHETHER TO USE INVESTMENT BANKERS

An entire chapter could be devoted to dealing with investment bankers in an M&A context. We will separate our discussion into three parts: (1) considerations in deciding to use a banker, (2) what to look out for if you do, and (3) steps to take if you are going it alone, without a banker's assistance.

Seller Considerations

There are several distinct advantages that investment bankers can bring to a seller:

Sample Nondisclosure Agreement

PLEASE NOTE THAT THIS IS AN EXAMPLE ONLY. ANY ACTUAL BID AGREEMENT SHOULD BE REVIEWED AND APPROVED BY YOUR COMPANY'S LEGAL COUNSEL.

Dear _____ :

Potential Buyer ("Buyer") is interested in entering into discussions with *Potential Seller ("Seller")* concerning a possible purchase of seller operations. To allow buyer to evaluate seller operations, seller has agreed to make certain disclosures to buyer. In order for buyer and seller to have free and open communication, it is necessary to reach an understanding now as to how any "Confidential Information" (as defined below) shall be treated.

"Confidential Information" as defined in this agreement means any written or oral information provided before or after the date of this agreement by or through the seller in connection with possible M&A transaction relating to the business, finances, operations, or affairs of buyer. Buyer will use efforts to maintain as confidential any information as outlined below:

• Keep confidential information on a "need-to-know" basis to its employees, officers, directors, agents, consultants, attorneys, and accountants ("Representatives"). Buyer shall inform each Representative receiving Confidential Information of the confidential nature of the material disclosed and shall direct them to treat it confidential.
• In the event that a final transaction is not consummated, buyer agrees not to solicit any of the seller's employees met during the due diligence process for a period of three years after the date of this agreement.
• In the event that a final transaction is not consummated, any Confidential Information shall be, upon the seller's request, either returned or destroyed.

Except for confidentiality as outline above, the commencement of discussions shall not create any other obligation for either the seller or buyer, and no such obligation can be created except by a duly authorized, executed, and delivered written agreement.

This agreement shall remain effective for a term of 36 months from the date hereof. This agreement shall be superceded by the final documents if an M&A transaction is consummated. If the foregoing terms are satisfactory, please indicate your acceptance below and return this letter, the attached copy is provided for your files.

Very truly yours,
Potential Buyer.
By: _____
Title: _____

Accepted and agreed to by:
this _____ day of _____ , 200__:
Potential Seller.
By: _____
Title: _____

- *Sophistication.* Bankers can give a professional air to a sale by assigning qualified, smart associates to guide potential buyers through the process. They also provide a nice buffer between buyer and seller that can effectively mediate issues without affecting the relationship between the two principal parties that may ultimately have to work together.

- *Contacts.* Bankers normally have a large network of contacts in their specialized industry area. This can help to bring more parties into the process and create an auction environment with multiple bidders. The sale price will go up as potential buyers bid against each other to win the property.

- *Data accumulation and control.* Sellers must provide some level of information to potential buyers to enable them to evaluate their companies. Bankers can be very useful in determining the appropriate data, cataloguing the data, and controlling distribution. In most cases, a formal "data room" containing all of the documents available to potential buyers is set up. A junior associate from the seller's investment bank will be assigned as a sort of librarian to control data distribution and make copies of pertinent documents for buyers.

- *Advice.* As we will see later in the book, the negotiation of terms and prices is one of the most critical elements of the M&A process. Investment bankers can be invaluable in this stage. Having been through multiple deals, bankers know what terms are standard and customary and when buyers are reaching for something that is not normally allowed. Most sellers will go through an M&A process only once in their lifetime and do not have a frame of reference to negotiate these terms effectively.

Buyer Considerations

The decision to hire a banker on the buy side is a little trickier. Although the benefits for the buyer are not as obvious, there are certain advantages:

- Bankers can provide expertise and assistance in financial modeling of the target and due diligence assistance.

- Bankers can provide guidance on structuring the transaction so that it best meets the needs of both the seller and the buyer.
- Bankers can provide data on comparable acquisitions recently completed in the market as a benchmark for the amount the buyer is paying.
- Perhaps the most valuable element that bankers provide is market "intelligence," or inside information about what is driving the seller's sale process. For example, a buy-side banker can talk with the seller and get a feel for where the first-round bid needs to be in order to keep her or his client in the process. The investment bankers for the buyer and the seller will often know each other and travel in the same circles. A buy-side banker can sometimes get information that might not be available otherwise about key issues the seller has with a buyer's bid. This gives the buyer the chance to alter its bid to try to accommodate these issues.
- Having an "independent" banker advise a buyer will normally make the buyer's senior management more comfortable with the process. Parties to the buyer's transaction may feel better having the experts review and supervise the process.

3. FAIRNESS OPINIONS

In many public deals, the buyer's investment bank will be engaged to provide a *fairness opinion* on the transaction. This is essentially a letter to the buyer's board of directors stating that the company is paying a fair price for the target and is not grossly overpaying. Although the letters are more form than substance, they do provide some insurance in the case of a failed acquisition and subsequent lawsuit by shareholders for the loss in company value.

However, the fairness opinion *does not guarantee* that a proposed deal is good. It merely compares the valuation of a deal to other similar recent deals in the marketplace. Users of the opinion also need to be aware of potential conflicts of interest when investment bankers on the advisory side of the deal also provide the fairness opinion. For example, Goldman Sachs and UBS were criticized for the 2005 fairness opinion that they prepared for the merger of Gillette and Procter & Gamble. These same banks were also advising on the M&A deal itself and stood to make massive fees should the deal close. The inherent risk was that Goldman and UBS would have an incentive to say that the deal was fair in order to collect the contingent M&A fee on the deal closing.

For these reasons, users of fairness opinions (whether buyers or sellers) should keep the following in mind:

1. Fairness opinions analyze the valuation of your deal as compared to other similar market transactions; they are not a guarantee that you are paying the right price.
2. Readers should evaluate who prepared the opinion and the preparer's level of independence with respect to the M&A transaction.
3. Merely getting a third-party opinion does not eliminate your fiduciary obligation as a member of the board of directors or senior management to evaluate the terms of the deal on your own.
4. As regulatory scrutiny of companies and their advisors continues to increase, the cost of opinions might go up, and some banks may be less willing to complete fairness opinion work based on the potential liability associated with the service.

4. SIMPLE FINANCIAL MODELS

The biggest challenge at this early deal stage is the tension between the buyer's desire for more information and the seller's reluctance to provide any information until it has narrowed the list of bidders. This tension manifests itself nowhere better than in the financial modeling process. Senior management of the buyer will often ask, "How can I deliver a purchase price number when I have little or no financial information on which to evaluate the target?"

Putting a detailed financial model together at this point in the process is very difficult. Until buyers are committed, the seller is very reluctant to release too much information. At the same time, the buyer's senior managers will be pushing for some indication of what the returns might be before they commit the resources necessary for detailed due diligence. It is the business development professional's job to bridge the gap between the expectations of the buyer's senior management and the information made available at this early stage of the deal.

Creating the Model

The steps in the process are as follows:

1. Obtain historical financial information on the target from company management, the seller's investment bank, public SEC filings, or any other source available.

2. Adjust this financial information to make it look "as if" the buyer owned the company from day one, pro forma. The primary adjustments relate to changing the debt/equity ratio and weighted average cost of capital from that of the seller to that of the buyer, that is, to make it look as if the buyer owned the company during this historical period.

3. Project financial information out into the future. A three- to five-year window is usually applied to projections. A longer period generally is not useful because of the lack of validity of assumptions going out more than five years. As indicated earlier, this is where the majority of the discussion on the due diligence team occurs. Getting an accurate, but conservative view of how the target company will perform postacquisition is critical to determining the appropriate purchase price.

4. Determine the expected returns based on an assumed purchase price and the pro forma projections developed. Most firms will use an internal rate of return or return on equity calculation to make this evaluation.

5. Run sensitivities and determine whether to proceed. This is another step in the process that generates much discussion on the due diligence team. As we will see later, small changes in assumptions concerning expected growth rates, margins, expense levels, and so on, can have a dramatic effect on the projected financial results and returns, and ultimately on the decision as to whether to proceed with the deal. Do not be overly conservative at this stage of the process.

Exhibit 3-2 shows an example of an early-stage financial model based on very limited financial data.

Preliminary Deal Model

	Holly Corporation *Income Statement (in millions of dollars)*					

Holly Corporation
Income Statement (in millions of dollars)

	Historical			*Forecast*		
	2003	**2004**	**2005**	**2006**	**2007**	**2008**
Revenues	$21.2	$24.5	$29.7	$39.6	$46.9	$52.7
% Growth	12%	15%	21%	33%	18%	12%
Cost of Goods Sold	15.8	17.2	19.2	26.5	30.0	32.2
% Revenues	74%	70%	64%	67%	64%	61%
Gross Profit	5.4	7.3	10.5	13.1	16.9	20.5
% Revenues	25%	30%	35%	33%	36%	39%
EBITDA	3.2	3.5	3.8	5.9	8.8	11.3
% Revenues	15%	14%	13%	15%	19%	21%
EBT	2.5	2.7	3.0	4.3	6.9	8.8
% Revenues	12%	11%	10%	11%	15%	17%
Net Income	1.5	1.7	1.8	2.6	4.1	5.3
% Revenues	7%	7%	6%	7%	9%	10%

Holly Corporation
Balance Sheet (in millions of dollars)

	Historical			*Forecast*		
	2003	**2004**	**2005**	**2006**	**2007**	**2008**
Current Assets	$5.0	$5.3	$5.6	$5.7	$5.8	$5.7
Fixed Assets	13.5	13.7	13.9	14.0	14.5	14.3
Goodwill/Intangibles	0	0	0	5.0	4.9	4.7
Total	18.5	19.0	19.5	24.7	25.2	24.7
Nondebt Liabilities	2.0	2.3	2.5	2.7	2.8	2.7
Net Investment	16.5	16.7	17.0	22.0	22.4	22.0
Debt	8.3	8.4	8.5	12.1	12.3	12.1
Equity	8.2	8.3	8.5	9.9	10.1	9.9
Key Ratios						
Debt to Percent	50%	50%	50%	55%	55%	55%
Return on Investment	9%	10%	11%	12%	18%	24%
Return on Equity	18%	20%	21%	26%	41%	54%

COPING WITH LIMITED DATA

Business development professionals must work with their CFO to develop a pro forma forecast for the target company. Pro forma models take the target's historical financial results, adjust the results for how they will look in the buyer's company, and project the balances out into the future on a basis consistent with the historical presentation. Adjustments need to be made for such items as leverage (i.e., balances must be adjusted to reflect the debt/equity ratio of the buyer), different accounting conventions (e.g., capitalizing versus expensing costs, amortization periods for intangible assets, and so on), cost of capital (the cost of debt used to finance the company), and the premium to be paid by the buyer.

Evaluating Seller Projections

Buyers need to take extreme care when evaluating seller projections. Sellers are obviously trying to put their best foot forward to maximize the ultimate purchase price. There can be a tendency for sellers to overstate how well their markets and their own performance in those markets will perform postclosing. Buyers are often presented with "hockey stick" projections that bear little resemblance to reality. A hockey stick projection is one in which a target has achieved, say, $10 million of annual net income consistently for the past three years; however, for the first 12 months after the acquisition date, it suddenly projects net income of $20 million. This is normally based on very optimistic "assumptions" about improvement in margins, expansion of product sales, expense cuts, and so on. Business development professionals need to take extreme caution here and make an independent evaluation of the achievability of the numbers forecasted. See Exhibit 3-3.

E X H I B I T   3-3

"Hockey Stick" Financial Projections

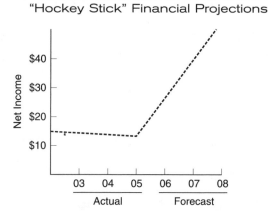

Functional representatives on the due diligence team can play a valuable role here by providing a sanity check. For example, the buyer's head of sales can review the seller's assumptions about market growth, margin improvement, and other such factors, based upon his or her knowledge of the buyer's current market conditions. With this feedback, aggressive assumptions made by the seller can be discounted in the buyer's pro forma financial model to arrive at a more reasonable forecast. The buyer's sales managers will probably be more conservative than the seller's because they will be the ones ultimately responsible for delivering these returns should the deal close.

Leveraging Public Information

The proliferation of information on the Internet has provided another great way to get objective data on target companies. The U.S. Securities and Exchange Commission provides access to all filings for public companies in its EDGAR database. Information about historical financial performance, trends in the industry, material significant events, composition of the board of directors, major shareholder groups, and the backgrounds of management can all be found by reviewing 10-Ks, 10-Qs, and other public filings.

Company Web sites, industry groups, and trade associations are all a great source of information for private companies. Private companies with public bond offerings may also have data listed on the SEC's EDGAR site. In any case, it is very worthwhile to have an analyst attempt to find such information in addition to preparing the information requests for due diligence. These sources can provide an independent check on the data produced by the target and also can be used to prepare the members of the deal team before they visit the company location for due diligence.

All of these procedures become much more difficult in a private-company sale. Buyers cannot go to the SEC's public Web sites to get information on the target. They are almost 100 percent percent reliant on the seller and the seller's investment bankers to provide the necessary financial information to evaluate the target. However, at this early stage in the process, private sellers are particularly reluctant to release sensitive information. The seller's desire is to give out as little information as possible to get first-round bids in because many of the sales processes will ultimately fail. Even in successful auctions, only *one* of the bidders ultimately wins the property. It is obviously in the seller's best interest to release as little information as possible to bidders at this early stage, particularly when some of the bidders may be competitors of the seller.

Even though all buyers have been required to sign a confidentiality agreement, having private company information in the hands of potential competitors is not a comforting thought. In addition, less than honest buyers have been known to enter the due diligence process of a competitor in order to learn about the company's operations and best practices, with little intention of actually buying the company. Investment bankers' representatives can be helpful at this point in the process by bridging the gap. Having been through multiple deals, the bankers know what level of information is customary at this early stage of the deal process. Remember that all models should be presented on a pro forma basis, that is, showing how the seller would look under the buyer's accounting and reporting routines. This ensures that calculations of cash flow, net income, and return on investment match what the buyer will actually experience if the deal closes.

5. PRELIMINARY BIDS

Once confidentiality terms have been agreed to and information has been exchanged, potential buyers begin the process of analyzing these data in order to come up with a preliminary bid price for the seller's company. Preliminary bids are just that—preliminary. Normally based on very limited financial information, they are used by the seller to screen out parties that it doesn't want in the process. This can be for competitive reasons (i.e., an unwillingness to allow a direct competitor into the process) or because the seller's preliminary indication of value is too low. The bids normally are not legally binding and provide multiple "outs" for the buyer to walk away from the transaction.

Bidding Strategies—Getting to the Next Round

As a buyer, your main objective at this stage is to decide whether you are interested in going forward and, if so, how to get invited back for the next round of due diligence. You want to bid just enough to be

invited back by the seller and nothing more. Once a number has
been put forward, it will set a benchmark for all future price discussions. Detailed analysis normally does not make a lot of sense at this
point, given the limited amount of information available. An investment bank representative can be particularly helpful here in finding
out where the bid needs to be to get the seller interested.

One strategy is to provide a range of values rather than one
specific bid price for the target. This gives the buyer some flexibility
to alter its purchase price based on what is discovered in the
detailed due diligence. However, sellers will invariably default to
the high end of the range as the probable outcome. Therefore, buyers need to be careful about managing expectations while still providing a good enough offer to get invited back.

There are a variety of other factors that a buyer can use to gain
an advantage over others in the process. They should be noted in
the preliminary bid letter if they are available to the buyer and provide a competitive advantage.

- *Speed.* Sellers are often under time pressure to close a deal
  fast. Buyers who can act quickly to close will normally be
  looked at more favorably than those requiring a long
  process to close.
- *Financing.* Buyers who can bid without a financing contingency usually have a distinct advantage. A financing contingency gives a buyer the ability to walk away if it cannot
  arrange the financing to complete the deal. This provides
  another element of uncertainty that is not viewed favorably
  by a seller. All other things being equal, a seller will pick
  the buyer with financing already lined up and ready to go.
- *Due diligence requirement.* Deal teams must strike a fine balance between asking for sufficient information to evaluate a
  target and overreaching for information in a sensitive situation. For example, in many cases, the most logical buyer of a
  property is a close competitor of the seller's firm. This obviously increases the seller's reluctance to release sensitive
  data. Sellers will assess the amount of effort they need to go
  through to satisfy each buyer's due diligence requirement.
  Buyers who appear to have an efficient, streamlined due diligence approach will be viewed more favorably. However,
  buyers must take extreme care to ensure that they get adequate information to assess the target and avoid mistakes.

Legal Issues—Letter of Intent

Exhibit 3-4 shows a typical letter of intent for a first-round bid. Letters at this stage will normally include

- A range of potential purchase prices.
- An outline of the information that will be required to adequately assess the target.
- Timing—how quickly a buyer can close the deal and what steps are involved.
- Internal, external, and regulatory approvals that will be required to close the deal.
- Financing, legal, or other contingencies.
- A preliminary view on the target's employees—whether they will remain in place, be consolidated into the buyer, or somewhere in between.
- A final clause, for legal purposes, stating that the letter at this stage of the process is "not binding and does not create a legally enforceable obligation for the buyer to buy or for the seller to sell." This is an extremely important clause at this stage of the diligence process, given the limited amount of information provided to the buyer so far.

A list of elements to be included in the letter of intent is often provided to buyers in larger deals run by investment banks. This ensures that the seller gets all the relevant information required to adequately assess each bid and decide whom to invite back to the next round.

Strategies for Getting Invited Back

In most acquisitions, the "softer" issues matter as much as, or more than, the purchase price offered. In fact, in some cases, the highest bidder does not win the auction because of seller concerns that are unrelated to price. Buyers have a variety of ways to influence the auction process to better position themselves as the winner:

- *Spend time with target management.* Buyers should capitalize on all opportunities to spend time with the target's senior management team. Relationships developed at this stage can help a buyer's chance of winning and also be leveraged after the deal closes to get the combination off to a

E X H I B I T   3-4

First-Round Bid: Preliminary Letter of Intent

PLEASE NOTE THAT THIS IS AN EXAMPLE ONLY. ANY ACTUAL BID LETTER SHOULD BE REVIEWED AND APPROVED BY YOUR ACTUAL COMPANY'S LEGAL COUNSEL.

Dear (Seller):

In accordance with your instructions, dated xxxx, we are pleased to submit to Seller a preliminary nonbinding letter of intent for the purchase of the business operations of Target. The purchase price is based on data provided by you in your offering memorandum dated xxx. We have relied on your representations about the company, both written and verbal, to arrive at a preliminary indication value in the range of xxx to xxx for all assets, employees, and operations of the xxxx company. A more definitive commitment agreement could be provided after we have access to company management, financial records, and key locations—attached is a detailed information request by functional area.

We are prepared to commence our due diligence procedures immediately on execution of this agreement. This letter is not meant to create any legally binding obligation on the part of the buyer or seller. Any such obligation would be based on a detailed review and documentation of the assets purchased, consideration amounts and obligations, and rights of the buyer and seller with respect to this transaction. We look forward to working with you toward a mutually agreeable transaction. Your response to this offer should be communicated directly to:

John Doe
XXX Company and Address

---

quick start. The "feel" that the seller has about who is about to own it will have a huge impact on its decision on whom to invite back.

- *Consider the size and approach of the due diligence team.* Just as the buyer is evaluating the target during the due diligence process, the seller is evaluating potential buyers. Typical sellers have a variety of concerns:
  - Who will have a job when the deal goes through?

- Will the culture/identity of the company survive?
- Will they have to relocate?
- Will they like their new owner and the new colleagues that they interact with on a daily basis?
- Will the new owner's culture be a good fit with the existing company personality?

Business development professionals need to be aware of these concerns and manage them properly to ensure that their company has the best chance of winning. Due diligence team members must be "managed" to ensure that they are empathetic and don't take too aggressive an approach to the target and its employees. The size of the due diligence team must also be managed so not to overwhelm the target company.

Other Considerations

Deal teams need to guard against being overly conservative at this stage of the process. They must keep in mind that the letter of intent is generally nonbinding at this stage. With the limited information available, it is very easy to reach a decision not to proceed. Given that they already have full-time jobs, cross-functional members of the deal team may not be overly excited about a pending due diligence process and all the work involved in integrating a new company. This can result in a tendency to avoid a new situation/opportunity/company and to point out all of the potential issues without focusing on the potential upside. This can be a critical time for business development professionals. They may have to objectively champion the deal over the inertia of a deal team to keep a deal alive. On the other hand, M&A professionals must not waste valuable company resources chasing deals that are not a good fit and/or have a low likelihood of getting done. This can be a very inefficient use of resources and make due diligence participants less likely to cooperate when a more legitimate deal arises. Striking the proper balance between aggressive deal advocate and conservative business executive sets great M&A professionals apart from the pack.

6. FIRST-ROUND BID SUBMISSION

Buyers will normally schedule a final meeting with their senior management team prior to submitting a bid. For larger, high-profile deals, a special meeting of the board of directors might be arranged; however, such a high-level meeting is normally delayed until due diligence is completed and a binding offer is being issued. Final strategies such as range of value to bid, timing of the process, any major issues noted at this point, or other potential issues are discussed at length. Once a final price range has been agreed to, the attorneys step in. Both inside and outside counsel will perform a detailed analysis of the terms and conditions outlined in the letter. They will attempt to strike a balance, showing a commitment to move forward, but not binding the buyer too severely at this early stage. Attorneys will ensure that any desired "outs" to the contract—that is, issues that would result in the buyer's not proceeding—are well documented and provide adequate protection to the buyer.

The first-round bid can be submitted either as a written document (that is, the bid letter is e-mailed over to the sellers) or at a formal meeting to discuss the bid. The approach depends on the size of the deal, whether the seller has an investment bank, and the number of parties involved as bidders. Larger, more complicated deals usually will require a more formal sales process to control the flow of information. Particularly when investment banks are involved, the flow of data is more tightly controlled and managed in a centralized fashion. Information is doled out on a "need to know" basis.

Generally, getting in front of the company to discuss the bid is a great thing for buyers. It allows them to outline the specific terms and conditions of the bid, discuss their plans for the company, and address any questions that the seller may have about the buyer, its management, or its bid. If this is not practical, buyers should attempt to reach out to the seller to get feedback on their bid as soon as possible. In some cases, sellers can misinterpret what a buyer really means. Items that appear to be major issues can sometimes be taken care of quickly if there is a positive dialogue between buyer and seller. In larger deals, this discussion may take place between the buyer and seller's investment bank representatives, respectively. If this is the case, the buyer needs to ensure that its banker has a thorough understanding of the bid and of the areas where the buyer is willing to compromise in order to keep the deal process moving forward. In any case, it is critical that the lines of communication remain open to prevent misunderstandings later.

CHAPTER 3 SUMMARY

1. The first round of the M&A process begins when the seller has decided to put itself up for sale and a buyer is interested in looking.

2. Confidentiality agreements are used by the seller to protect against the disclosure of proprietary information given to the buyer as part of the due diligence process.

3. Both buyer and seller need to decide whether to hire an investment bank to help their side of the process. Bankers can provide significant advantages in the form of data analysis, contacts, financial modeling, deal structuring, and market intelligence.

4. Fairness opinions are often prepared by investment bankers to compare the price, terms, and conditions of the current deal with other, similar market transactions.

5. Simple financial models are normally prepared in the first round to give the buyer a feel for a potential purchase price and the resulting economics of the deal.

6. Through the use of historical data, management forecasts, and sensitivity analysis, the buyer attempts to estimate how the target company would perform if it were purchased. These pro forma financial models are reviewed with the buyer's senior management to determine if the target can generate the buyer's required rates of return.

7. There is often a tension at this point in the process because of a lack of data. Sellers are reluctant to release too much information too soon, and buyers are desperate for information to arrive at a range of purchase values.

8. Seller projections must be critically evaluated for reasonableness. Many sellers are overly aggressive in their forecasts and make projections that can never be achieved. This is done to make the target look better than it is and drive up the purchase price.

9. The buyer's functional personnel, public information, and common sense can all be leveraged to help evaluate the target's projections.

10. Preliminary bids are normally nonbinding first indications of value for the target or a range of values. They are used by the seller to weed out those buyers that will not be competitive, resulting in a smaller population of buyers that can be brought back for a second round of more detailed discussions.

11. Interested buyers can use a variety of techniques to help their chances of getting invited back, including a more aggressive bid, speed, flexible terms, limited due diligence, and financing lined up in advance.

12. The letter of intent lays out preliminary terms on which a transaction might be based. It includes the purchase price, timing, approvals or other contingencies, and other relevant terms of a transaction.

13. First-round bids can be delivered by e-mail or in person. Deal teams must be careful not to bid either too aggressively or too conservatively at this stage. Often the goal is simply to get invited back so that more information can be obtained and a more informed, and binding, bid submitted in the second round.

Due Diligence: The Internal Side

In the first round of the M&A process, the buyer and the seller are feeling each other out, without a high level of commitment by either party. If you are a buyer and you are fortunate enough to be invited back for a second round, now the work really begins. At this point in the process, the buyer and the seller are starting to form both an implicit and an explicit agreement to ultimately commit to some form of transaction. This is a very difficult stage of the M&A process, in which business development professionals need to coordinate the buyer's resources to evaluate the transaction efficiently and effectively and keep the entire team, as well as the overall process, on track.

DUE DILIGENCE

Due diligence is a generic term for the financial, operational, and strategic analysis that a buyer completes when evaluating (1) whether to purchase a target company and (2) how much to pay. It is undertaken when two parties are considering a purchase/sale, strategic alliance, joint venture, or some other form of partnership. The process can take many forms, cover different time periods, and include a variety of players from internal employees of the buyer and seller to outside consultants.

Due diligence is one of the *most critical* of all the elements in a transaction for the following reasons:

- If done properly, it can provide an early warning that a deal should not get done, saving a huge amount of time and resources that could be directed toward other projects of the buyer.
- It is the single most important factor that, when overlooked or underappreciated, can result in doing a deal that does not meet expectations.
- It can be a great mechanism to get buy-in and a sense of ownership from the various constituencies (both internal and external) working on a transaction. People on the deal team will feel a sense of ownership if they are actively involved in the decision-making process. The due diligence process is a great opportunity for the different functional areas of a corporation—tax, finance, legal, risk, and so on—to get together and work toward a common goal. Alternatively, due diligence is a unique opportunity for third-party consultants— investment bankers, tax experts, legal firms, and so on—to build relationships with their clients (both buyer and seller) that can lead to future business engagements.
- Due diligence is generally the first time that employees of the buyer and the seller get the chance to interact. This provides a great opportunity to start forming working relationships between the buyer and the seller that can be leveraged should the transaction be completed.
- It is a great professional development tool for the buyer's management team. By interacting with one another to solve problems, team members can form bonds that carry over into their daily responsibilities.

Unfortunately, many acquirers do not take the due diligence phase seriously enough. In too many cases, surprises happen after the due diligence phase has been completed. At this point, both buyer and seller have often become emotionally attached to the deal, and it becomes progressively harder to reverse course. Rather than disappoint their investors and themselves, management will frequently push on with a deal that might not be optimal. For these reasons, breakups are less likely once the due diligence process has been completed and contracts are started. However, if issues are uncovered early, it is not as difficult to back out—indeed, studies estimate that as many as 20 percent of deals die during the due diligence phase.[1]

STEPS IN THE DUE DILIGENCE PROCESS

Selecting the Due Diligence Team

Think about this situation. You are the chief risk officer of a Fortune 500 company; let's call it Sparky, Inc., based in Trenton, New Jersey. You come in on a Monday morning, and you have 25 e-mails to respond to, back-to-back meetings all day, seven phone messages, and an urgent message from Sparky's CEO that you need to prepare for a board meeting in two weeks. Then the head of business development, John Wilson, calls you with "great news." Your major competitor, Jack, Inc., is up for sale and can be purchased if you move quickly. A due diligence trip is scheduled for Tuesday through Friday of this week in Seattle, and you need to leave this afternoon for a flight out west.

As chief risk officer, you could react in two different ways to this request, depending on your perspective. On the one hand, this seems like a great opportunity for Sparky, Inc., to grow its business and enhance the prospects for all who work there. However, the truth is that you have a full-time job, family responsibilities, and personal interests that make a 3,000-mile trip on such short notice not the most desirable event right now.

This illustrates a theme that we'll look at throughout the book: the value of the interpersonal skills of the deal professional in getting transactions accomplished. Hopefully, the head of M&A for Sparky, Inc., had taken the time to build a personal relationship with the chief risk officer well before the Jack transaction surfaced. It is much easier to call someone and ask him or her to drop everything to join a difficult transaction if a solid relationship has previously been established. It is essential that deal professionals network and build relationships with all of the functional areas of a corporation to ensure support, adequate reserves, and a quick response when it is really needed. Adept business development professionals lay the groundwork for these relationships well before an "urgent" deal surfaces.

Managing the Internal Side

One of a business development professional's most critical tasks is to manage the internal due diligence and approval process in the buyer's corporation. This includes everything from establishing the initial due diligence team to keeping team members informed to coordinating with the seller or its investment bankers. Business development professionals need to constantly balance the multiple, and at times conflicting, priorities of the members of the due diligence team and the seller's representatives.

Establishing/Managing a Cross-Functional Due Diligence Team

A typical due diligence team will generally include representatives from the following groups:

- Tax
- Legal
- Risk
- Operations/Information Technology
- Finance
- Environmental/Regulatory
- Human Resources
- Strategic Marketing
- Sales
- Integration

A critical, and often overlooked, function at this stage is integration. Too many companies wait until the end of the deal process to get integration teams involved. The best acquirers have separate integration groups that focus only on integrating deals. The due diligence phase is a great opportunity for these individuals to get to know the target's management and to evaluate the compatibility of systems, benefits plans, cultures, and other such elements in order to ensure a more streamlined integration process. In fact, some firms require that the integration team be present at the senior management meeting for final approval of the transaction. Team members will lay out a detailed integration plan with milestones and accountability for each step. We will discuss the integration process further in Chapter 10.

The business development leader should initiate an organizational meeting for the various functional heads to introduce the deal and outline the due diligence timeline. It helps to have the firm's CEO kick off this meeting to express the importance of the deal to the firm's success and request that all functional areas provide their undivided support and attention to the process. The

M&A head should then give an outline of the transaction, provide background information on the company, and open up a discussion on concerns or questions. The timing and logistics of the due diligence process should be laid out clearly so that everyone understands her or his responsibilities over the coming weeks. Each functional head should be asked for a representative dedicated to the deal team for the duration of the project. This ensures accountability throughout the deal and provides the continuity necessary for an efficient process. Solid project management skills are an integral part of this stage of the process to keep everyone engaged and on track.

How Large Should the Due Diligence Team Be?

A frequent issue is the size of the due diligence team. There are two teams that need to be formed for most deals. One is a smaller group of senior executives to attend a kick-off meeting and other senior-level meetings run by the target management. The problem is that *everyone* wants to be on this team. People want to feel part of senior management and mingle with their firm's CEO. Limiting the size of this team to a manageable number again requires considerable interpersonal skills and tact.

The second, larger group is dedicated to performing a detailed analysis of data provided by the target in a controlled data room. In general, *no one* wants to be part of this team. This is the long, tedious analysis that is generally delegated by the department heads to people working in their groups. Again, the size of the team becomes an issue. Functional heads want to be confident that every issue has been uncovered so that they do not get embarrassed. This normally results in each group wanting multiple people to join the data room team.

When you add up the number of different functional areas and include multiple members from each group, plus the senior executive team, the size of the due diligence team can quickly get out of hand. In some cases, deal teams have grown to 100 people or more, making the process very inefficient. If the seller is using an investment bank, it will usually place a hard limit on the number of people it allows to visit, often based on the size and complexity of the selling firm. Teams that grow to more than 25 to 30 members start to become unwieldy and difficult to manage. Again, the interpersonal skills of the business development professional come into

play. Telling an individual that he is not on the on-site due diligence deal team, but is an essential part of the deal team or that she
can go to the data room but not to the senior management presentations, can be a tricky proposition at best.

Preparing Information Requests

The due diligence information request provides an outline of what
the buyer needs in order to assess the value of the target firm and
make a bid. The lists are normally prepared by each of the functional areas and contain a request for documentation, meetings
with management, review of financial results, and, in some cases,
meetings with outside advisors such as the target's law firms, outside accountants, and so on. It is essential that these lists be as comprehensive as possible, in order to ensure that an adequate amount
of information is available to assess the target and uncover any
problem areas. Appendix B contains sample due diligence lists
organized by functional area. Although these lists can be used as a
guideline, they are not comprehensive. It is essential that they be
tailored to the specific industry and size of the company that you
are examining. The information requests need to be living documents that are updated based on experience with other mergers
and the unique circumstances of the deal at hand.

Despite putting together a detailed list, it is very unusual for
a buyer to get all or nearly all of the information that it requests for
a variety of reasons:

- *Confidentiality.* Even with a signed confidentiality agreement, sellers are reluctant to release too much information
  to prospective buyers. They fear that this information may
  be misused if the buyer backs out of the process, particularly if the buyer and seller compete in the same industry.
- *Availability.* Target firms often have trouble finding and
  summarizing the litany of data required by the various
  bidders. They will normally consolidate the requests of all
  the bidders and provide one list of common information
  that they make available to everyone.
- *Investment banks.* Access is normally most limited when a
  seller engages an investment bank to manage the sale
  process. Most times, investment bankers furnish a standard list of data that are provided to all buyers. In many

cases, the investment banks will ignore specific requests by potential buyers and provide data that they consider "customary" based on other engagements they have worked on. They will assemble a data room, which may not even be at a target's location, but rather at a nearby hotel or conference center. All data are tightly controlled, with a checkout system based on cross-reference to a complete inventory. No copies of documents, working papers, or other data are allowed without consent from the investment bank running the process. Access to management is very tightly controlled. Any discussions with target management must be coordinated through the investment banker, who normally attends the session to make sure that no confidential discussions take place. This level of control can make it very difficult for the buyer to get an adequate sense of the risks and issues of the deal contemplated.

- *Competitiveness of the situation/desire to sell.* A target that must sell and has a limited population of potential buyers will be much more willing to open up access than one with a more attractive property. For example, in the late 1990s to early 2000s, the U.S. banking sector saw a great wave of consolidation. Because there were so many buyers, sellers were much more able to dictate the terms upon which they would sell. In many cases, buyers were making decisions based on two-day due diligence sessions or, even worse, only on publicly available information (10-Ks, 10-Qs, and so on), without any input from the target management. This is an extremely risky way to do business. The dramatic failures of many large corporations, as discussed in Chapter 1, exemplify the potential disasters that can result from not getting enough information and making a bad decision.

- *Location of information.* With the complexity of today's multinational corporations, it is unusual for a company's operations to be focused in one geographical area only. However, in order to control the process, sellers rarely allow buyers to visit satellite office locations. This puts additional limitations on a buyer's ability to adequately assess the operations of the seller and to identify issues out in the field.

FIRE DRILLS AND DEAL KILLERS

A major focus of any due diligence process is to quickly determine any critical issues that cannot be overcome. Discovering major obstacles early prevents deal teams from wasting valuable resources that could be better applied in other areas of the buyer's business. It also helps protect the buyer's reputation in the market for future transactions that may be achievable. However, care should also be taken not to kill deals too early or for the wrong reasons. In many cases, "deal killer" issues can be surmounted if the team takes the time to understand the risk and how to structure around it. The various functional heads participating in the due diligence process often raise these issues as deal killers, and they need to be thought through and analyzed further.

Depending on the situation, many members of the deal team may not have actually been through an M&A transaction before. This unfamiliarity with the process often causes functional heads to be very conservative in their assessment of the target's operations. For example, it is much "safer" for the legal team member to highlight all potential issues in the company and document them in a memo, rather than to sort through the issues and point out only the truly meaningful points.

Functional heads also may not have an overall perspective on the risks and rewards of the deal; instead, they are looking at the issues from their unique frame of reference. Once again, the business development leader needs to be objective and to listen carefully to the concerns of all due diligence team members. However, business development leaders cannot let immaterial issues derail the internal approval process. This is a very tricky part of the deal for business development professionals, but one in which they can add significant value. They need to calm the deal team, trying to find solutions to the issues raised while still paying close attention to, and highlighting, any issues that can't be overcome.

UPPER MANAGEMENT INVOLVEMENT

Upper management involvement at the due diligence stage is critical for a well-functioning deal team and an orderly process. Active participation by the buyer's senior management provides the following benefits:

- *Motivates the deal team.* If the due diligence team knows that senior management supports the deal, its members will be more likely to put in the effort required to evaluate the target and think creatively about how to win the transaction. If the team members get the sense that the deal has lost the support of management, they will be less likely to stretch to get it done.
- *Shows support to seller.* Sellers get a feel for how serious potential buyers are by the level and frequency of their contact with the buyer's senior management.
- *Helps to iron out issues that arise during due diligence.* Senior management can provide an appeal process on "deal breaker" issues raised by the functional members of the due diligence team. Senior management has a broader perspective and more authority to waive issues that should not stop the deal process.
- *Facilitates ultimate deal approval.* At the due diligence phase, the buyer is still making a decision about whether to proceed with the deal. However, active senior management involvement makes it easier when it comes time for ultimate deal approval. Management is not hit with the deal cold and has a perspective on what the issues are and, more importantly, what the deal team has done to mitigate these issues. It is also more familiar and comfortable with the target company and its management.

CHAPTER 4 SUMMARY

1. Due diligence is a generic term for the financial, operational, and strategic analysis that a buyer completes when evaluating (a) whether to purchase the target company and (b) how much to pay.
2. Due diligence is one of the most critical stages of the M&A process. Done correctly, it provides an early warning that certain deals should not get done, saving considerable time and labor later. It is also a great opportunity for buyer and seller management to get to know each other and build lasting relationships.
3. Managing the cross-functional due diligence process is one of the business development professional's primary

obligations. It takes considerable interpersonal and project
management skills to keep the team focused and working
toward closing the deal.

4. Integration is a critical part of the process that should be
   initiated early in the due diligence phase, not after the
   deal closes. Involving the integration team early drives a
   more efficient integration of the target should the deal
   move forward.

5. Managing the size of due diligence teams and buyer
   information requests is also critical to maintaining a
   healthy relationship with the seller.

6. Sellers will often be reluctant to release too much information because of confidentiality issues, competitive secrets,
   availability of data, or concerns that the deal will not ultimately close.

7. Discovering big issues early is critical to a team's efficiency. However, care must also be taken to keep issues in
   perspective. The business development professional needs
   to avoid letting minor issues raised by the functional
   areas derail the M&A process, while maintaining an objective view toward real issues raised by the team.

8. Early and frequent upper management involvement in
   the due diligence process can help deal teams stay
   focused and on track.

CHAPTER 4 CASE STUDIES

CASE STUDY 4–1

DUE DILIGENCE "SURPRISES"

Adapted from American Institute of Certified Public Accountants Case Study
Project in July 2002. Case study authored by Robert Stefanowski on July 12, 2002.

INTRODUCTION

Jane Samson, controller of Apex Corporation, looked out the window of
her office in Chicago on a cold, rainy day. Her manufacturing company
was in serious trouble; it had less than six months of cash left and was in
an industry that was very much out of favor with investors. Fire
Corporation of America (FCA) was completing the final stages of its due
diligence to acquire 100 percent of the stock of Apex and infuse $30 mil-
lion in cash to keep the operations going. Surprisingly, FCA was very bull-

ish on Apex's prospects and seemed ready to move ahead with the transaction and save Apex from certain bankruptcy. There was only one problem: Jane knew that the pro forma financial projections prepared by Implus Partners, Apex's investment bank, were severely overstated. Jane realized that there was no way that Apex could come close to the revenues and income estimated, but somehow FCA had not figured this out. To make matters worse, Jane was aware of certain material liabilities that were not adequately disclosed on the closing balance sheet and that FCA had not discovered in its due diligence. In her heart, Jane knew that she should speak up and educate FCA. However, she could not forget her limited job prospects in the current industry, the employment of her colleagues, and her two young daughters at home.

FEBRUARY 10

It had all started innocently enough. Fred Thompson, Apex's chief financial officer, had called a meeting of his finance staff on February 10. He started the meeting with, "I have a great Valentine's Day present for you and your significant others . . . our firm is saved." Samson and her colleagues could not believe it. With the recent downturn in the economy, Apex had seen a dramatic fall-off in demand for its products, and it was almost out of cash. There were daily discussions about when Apex would be formally shut down and people displaced from their jobs.

Thompson explained that Fire Corporation of America was interested in various Apex products and had made a preliminary bid to purchase the company. FCA planned to (1) maintain the existing operations of Apex, (2) keep all employees, and (3) infuse $30 million of cash to finish the development of major products.

Thompson stated that the only contingency left was "due diligence" to be completed by FCA. This due diligence was a one-week process in which FCA was to get to know Apex by reviewing its accounting records, analyzing its financial performance, and having discussions with key Apex personnel. Thompson went on to explain, "We must make the best possible impression on FCA. Be optimistic, friendly, and supportive to FCA over the next seven days. This is our last chance to avoid bankruptcy and save our jobs."

FEBRUARY 12

The management team from FCA arrived on site, along with FCA's investment bankers, Implus Partners. FCA had prepared a list of required information (see Attachment 1) and had requested "informal interviews" with all of the finance staff. In fact, Robert Stanley, FCA's chief financial officer, requested a meeting with Samson and her accounting manager, Bob Quest, for that afternoon.

When Stanley arrived, he passed out copies of a financial model that he was using for the following (see Attachment 2):

- Help determine what to pay for Apex.

- Develop reasonable assumptions about the future of the business, including revenues, expenses, losses, and any other material facts.

- Based on these forecasted returns, determine the return on investment expected on the acquisition. Stanley indicated that FCA's "hurdle rate" on new investments was at least 20 percent; that is, if a proposed acquisition did not provide a 20 percent return on investment, then FCA would not proceed with the deal.

The first thing that Jane noticed on the model was that the planned return came out at approximately 21 percent. She thought to herself that this did not leave much of a cushion before FCA would walk away from the deal. She then realized that sales growth for the Trycon product line was 20 percent per year for the forecasted period. Jane knew that a major, very profitable customer for this product had recently threatened to move its business overseas because of its recent dissatisfaction with the quality of Apex's product and the poor timeliness of deliveries. Although the impact had not shown up in the historical financials yet, Jane suspected that future results for this product line would be neutral to down, and certainly not the 20 percent growth that FCA had projected.

Stanley asked Samson and Quest to look at these models and let him know whether anything seemed "out of the ordinary" based on their knowledge of the business. As he started to leave, Jane asked, "Who prepared these models, anyway?" Stanley replied that his investment bankers had put the projections together. Unfortunately, because of the secrecy surrounding the transaction, the bankers had had no access to company personnel and therefore had to make their own assumptions about revenue, income, and expense growth.

After Stanley left the room Jane said, "Do you believe these projections for Trycon? There is no way this will happen." Quest replied, "I agree. I also noticed that there is a formula error in this row of the spreadsheet. Advertising expenses are not being picked up in the total expense line; therefore, gross margins and net income are overstated in all of the forecasted periods presented."

FEBRUARY 13

Jane was asked to attend a meeting with Joe Crabb, FCA's chief legal counsel, to discuss the status of all litigation surrounding the company. Jane knew that Crabb had not bothered to send out legal letters to outside Apex legal counsel asking for the current status of all pending, threatened, or other litigation. Instead, Crabb produced a list of pending or threatened litigation that he had developed in a four-hour meeting with the internal Apex legal department that morning. Jane scanned the list and did not see any mention of Bailey Corporation. Jane knew that just last week, Bailey had called threatening a $10 million suit because of downtime that its factory had incurred when Apex was late in a delivery from its troubled Trycon line. Although it was very early in the process, based on what she knew, Jane felt that Bailey had a reasonable basis for a claim. However, she decided to check with her legal group before mentioning it to Crabb. She told Crabb that she would "review the list and get back to him."

FEBRUARY 15

Just as she was leaving for the day, Bob Quest came running into her office, looking worried. He had just received a call from the state Department of Environmental Protection indicating that it was sending in a team next week for a complete analysis of the manufacturing processes at Apex. This review resulted from a complaint by several residents downstream from Apex's main production plant in town. Bob's first thought was, thank goodness, FCA would be gone by then. He did not know whether there was anything to this, as Apex was frequently subjected to environmental reviews in various forms. Fortunately, they had all turned out well to date. However, he also knew that FCA had not asked any questions about environmental liability at Apex. FCA had not visited all of the company's locations or completed Phase I environmental reviews on any of the manufacturing sites.

FEBRUARY 16

Fred Thompson called a meeting of everyone involved in the due diligence process with FCA. Along with Sampson and Quest were representatives from Apex's legal, tax, business development, and credit departments. Thompson stated that FCA had requested a full-day meeting with the group on February 17 to get answers to all outstanding questions and conclude its due diligence. Thompson thanked the group for its participation to date and indicted that FCA had not found anything "out of the ordinary" and was ready to close the deal, pending a good meeting the next day. Thompson congratulated everyone on a "job well done."

Samson raised her hand and said, "I don't know about the others in the group, but I think FCA has missed some critical issues in its due diligence. For example, its financial projections of what this business can do are crazy. I am not sure how to handle this in the meeting tomorrow." Joe Bliss, Apex's chief credit officer, chimed in, "I agree. FCA has been overly optimistic in its assumptions regarding the amount of credit losses we will sustain in this business. I wanted to check with you first, Fred, but don't we need to make them aware of these issues?"

Fred stood up and addressed the group. "Listen, we all want this deal to close, right? Just to remind you all, if FCA goes away, we file for bankruptcy and you are all out of work within two weeks. FCA has hired a nationally recognized investment bank to calculate these projections . . . they are not stupid. We have provided every bit of information that FCA requested. We have opened up our company and answered all of FCA's questions for an entire week. I don't know what else we can do. This is still a great company, and I am sure that, even with the minor issues you have, FCA will make this deal a huge success. My advice for tomorrow is to be positive and not get bogged down with any minor issues you might have."

At this point, the meeting was adjourned. Jane went back to her office to reflect on her next steps.

Discussion Questions

1. Assume that you are Jane Samson. What are your moral and legal obligations to disclose the issues you know of to FCA?

2. What steps did FCA miss as part of its due diligence?

ATTACHMENT 1

FCA Due Diligence—Apex
Detailed Information Request

Finance

1. Audited financial statements for the past three years
2. Independent audit work papers for the past three years
3. Calculation of Reserve for Doubtful Accounts
4. Accounting policy manual
5. Internal audit work papers for the past three years
6. Sales backlog report
7. Support for financial statement footnotes

Legal

1. List of existing, threatened, and pending litigation
2. Major legal settlements over the past five years

Tax

1. Tax returns for the past five years
2. Calculations of effective tax rate for the last five years
3. Status of any IRS audits currently under way

Human Resources

1. Employee lists, including years of service, background, and compensation history
2. Documentation of compensation, benefit, and incentive plans
3. Key person life insurance plans
4. All union agreements
5. Status of unfunded or underfunded pension plans

Risk

1. Write-off activity for the last five years
2. Major credit issues currently outstanding
3. Recoveries of bad debts over the last five years
4. List of top ten customer accounts

Business Development

1. Major contract proposals outstanding
2. Any acquisition activity planned
3. Status of relations with top ten customers

Information Technology

1. Flowchart of major systems—accounting and other
2. Disaster recovery plan
3. IT initiatives/upgrades currently in process

Other

1. Minutes of board of directors meetings over the past five years

ATTACHMENT 2

Apex Corporation FCA Due Diligence
Pro Forma Financials
(in millions of dollars)

	Historical			Projected		
	2003	**2004**	**2005**	**2006**	**2007**	**2008**
Trycon Sales	$12.9	$13.0	$12.5	$15.0	$18.0	$21.6
Bliston Sales	4.0	5.0	6.5	7.5	7.9	8.5
Scott Sales	2.0	3.2	1.9	2.0	2.5	2.9
Total	18.9	21.2	20.9	24.5	28.4	33.0
Cost of Goods Sold	10.0	11.0	10.9	12.1	13.2	14.0
Gross Margin	8.9	10.2	10.0	12.4	15.2	19.0
SG&A						
Salaries	1.0	1.2	1.3	1.2	1.3	1.4
Administrative	0.9	1.0	1.1	0.8	0.9	1.0
Advertising	0.5	0.6	0.7	0.9	0.9	0.9
Legal	0.2	0.3	0.4	0.3	0.3	0.3
Other	0.8	1.8	0.7	0.2	0.2	0.2
Total	2.9	4.3	3.5	2.5	2.7	2.9
Pretax Income	6.0	5.9	6.5	9.9	12.5	16.1
Taxes	2.4	2.4	2.6	4.0	5.0	6.5
Net Income	**$3.6**	**$3.5**	**$3.9**	**$5.9**	**$7.5**	**$9.6**
Cash	$2.0	$2.0	$2.1	$1.5	$1.5	$1.5
A/R	25.0	25.2	18.0	24.0	25.0	26.5
Inventories	12.0	11.0	13.0	15.0	15.5	16.0
PP&E	15.0	15.4	16.5	17.0	17.4	17.9
Other	5.0	4.0	3.5	5.5	6.0	7.0
Total	59.0	57.6	53.1	63.0	65.4	68.9
Liabilities	31.5	29.6	23.5	34.5	31.4	22.4
Net Investment	27.5	28.0	29.6	28.5	34.0	46.5
Return on Investment				**20.7%**	**22.0%**	**20.6%**

NOTES

1. Pyle, Alexander, Foley Hoag, LLP, Boston, as quoted in *CFO Magazine*, July 2004, Roy Harris author.

Due Diligence:
The External Side

Relations with target management during the due diligence phase are very tricky and extremely important. It is a great opportunity for buyers to assess the target senior managers and to evaluate how they would run the company after the acquisition. Through management presentations, data analysis, and question and answer sessions, members of the buyer's team can assess how target management performs, particularly in a time of stress. However, at the same time, the target's managers are assessing whether they want to be part of the buyer's team after the acquisition. In a hotly contested auction for a company, target management's views on the various suitors can have a significant bearing on who wins the auction. In summary, the due diligence phase is a great opportunity to start building relationships with the target's team that can be used to create an efficient organization postacquisition.

PUSHING THE TARGET FOR INFORMATION

As noted earlier, there is a natural tension between the amount of information that a buyer needs in order to assess the target and the willingness of the seller to release proprietary data. Business development professionals need to bridge this gap between buyer and seller. Functional members of the deal team will immediately turn to the business development person when data are lacking. The deal team's usual reaction is, "Until I get more data, I can't give you any opinion on this target." Due diligence team members are often tense, out of their normal job scope, and traveling out of town, heightening their panic about data availability. All of the functional areas get concerned that there will be major issues that will subsequently make them look bad. Once again, interpersonal skills are critical. The business development professional needs to prioritize the multiple requests made by the deal team, sort through them for relevance, and push the seller for this information without disadvantaging his company's chances of winning the auction.

GETTING QUESTIONS ANSWERED

This is a very similar situation to closing information gaps. Business development professionals must get answers to all of the material questions the deal team has, while at the same time not pushing so hard that the seller gets frustrated with the process and moves on to another buyer. This can be an informal process in smaller deals or a formal process if an investment banker is involved. Bankers will often ask for a written list of questions, which they review with the seller to ensure that (1) appropriate thought is put into the answers, (2) inappropriate questions are thrown out, and (3) consistent answers are provided to multiple buyers. Most questions that are considered inappropriate are those that ask for either too much detail or highly sensitive data at this early stage of the process. Sellers may want to withhold such confidential information until they narrow the field down to a few serious buyers.

KEY STEPS IN THE DILIGENCE PROCESS

Every due diligence process will be different, depending on the size of the target and the industry it participates in. Outlined here are some general steps by functional area that are present in most deals. The main focus of the business development professional leading the deal team is to keep all of the functional areas on track, get them the information they need, and try to manage an efficient and comprehensive due diligence process. At the same time, the team is trying to make a positive impression on the target to enhance the chance that a deal will happen.

General

The business development leader is responsible for keeping a broad perspective on the overall company, as compared to the narrow, functional view that each of the functional members of the due diligence team will apply. This approach should include overall observations on the company, its management, and how the different parts of the organization interact with one another. It is imperative that the due diligence cover all major elements of the company that need to be evaluated to arrive at a purchase price.

A variety of methods are normally applied to get this information, including discussions with management, reading the minutes of board of directors meetings, visits to major company locations, and observations at the corporate headquarters. Each of the functional teams, as outlined here, will review its area of expertise at the target and generate a report of its findings at the completion of the due diligence period.

Human Resources

HR professionals must be actively evaluating the target personnel throughout the due diligence period. As we will see in Chapter 10, "The Importance of Integration," the culture of the target firm is an often overlooked, but very critical element of the process. As a result, HR professionals should spend as much time as offered at the target location to get a sense for the cultural or other issues that might be faced once the contracts are signed. By spending time on site, they can learn about the culture and working style of the target and how that may fit with the buyer's culture. Tactical plans can be created for central issues that are identified early. These often include differences in philosophy, work environment, standards of integrity, work/life balance, diversity of the workforce, and other such issues. Although often overlooked, these areas can be more critical to the venture's success than all of the hard data analysis and financial modeling.

Other, more mechanical steps for HR to take include the following:

- A review of the benefit plans of the target for cost and consistency with the buyer's plans. In many cases, a target's plan is dramatically different in terms of the types of coverages offered for insurance, 401(k), defined-benefit plans, vacation time, sick time, and so on. These issues may seem minor during due diligence, but they can have a dramatic impact on the morale of both the buyer's and the target's employees postacquisition. They can also have a dramatic impact on the cost structure of the target postacquisition. The funding status of defined-benefit compensation plans should also be analyzed. Fluctuations in the stock market can have a dramatic effect on the value of plan assets available for distribution to plan participants. Any shortage in these plans that is not picked up by the seller would represent an incremental cost to the buyer.

- Provisions for the senior leadership team of the target need to be reviewed in detail. Long-term incentive compensation, severance, guaranteed employment contracts, and so on can impose a significant liability on the seller that would not necessarily be apparent in the target's financial statements.

- In most due diligences, access to the "rank and file" of the target is somewhat limited by the seller. However, the buyer's HR representative needs to form an opinion concerning the target's senior management team and the plans for each individual postacquisition.

- Employment agreements need to be negotiated for those senior managers that the target wants to keep. This can be a difficult and time-consuming process, and it should be started as early in the due diligence process as possible. In many situations, a buyer's bid will be made contingent on its ability to lock in senior management to an employment agreement before the deal is closed. Once the deal has closed, all leverage shifts to the seller and target management. However, if these discussions happen preclose, the seller can be engaged to help sign up key managers, or a purchase price reduction can be proposed if the buyer can't get key managers to sign on. You don't want to wait until after the deal closes to learn that a key target employee is not coming along. By this time, it is too late, and you have paid a premium for management that is no longer there.

Risk

Risk professionals can play a large part in preventing bad deals from being done. They should approach the deal with a healthy skepticism, unlike marketing, sales, and business development professionals, who will often take an optimistic view of what can be done with the target. Good risk people will take an interest in trying to structure around issues or get protections in the contract for issues that have been identified, while still protecting the integrity of the process. They want to do deals to help their company grow, avoid deals that would adversely affect the value of their company, and get the appropriate protections in the process. In many cases, risk personnel are viewed as the "protectors" of the buyer's business, ensuring that bad deals don't get closed.

Areas to be analyzed in the risk process include the following:

- The credit quality of major customers, including an aging of accounts receivable and analysis of customer financial statements. Due diligence team members need to assess the adequacy of the provision for bad debts to ensure that the amounts paid for receivables can be collected from customers after the transaction closes. Particular attention needs to be paid to large delinquent balances identified in the target accounts.

- The major supplier/subcontractor agreements need to be analyzed for potential price escalations, cancellation clauses, or other elements that would affect the supply of goods and services to the target. Many contracts have "change in control" provisions that allow for modification or cancellation of a contract should majority ownership in the target change hands. Also, large, unfavorable contracts with suppliers that can't be cancelled should be identified early and their cost factored into the purchase model.

- Review the customer base for any major customer concentrations. A loss of a significant customer at or after closing of the transaction can have a dramatic effect on the financial results of the target postclose. A change in company control can cause many customers to rethink their relationship and send contracts out for competitive bidding.

The risk representative will often be at the heart of the major due diligence issues. The approach that this individual takes can make the difference between doing a bad deal, walking away from a bad deal, or moving forward with adequate protections in the contract for the issues raised. Business development professionals need to develop a level of trust with the risk team to ensure that the appropriate level of skepticism is applied to the target while attempting to find a way to make good deals happen.

Finance

Financial representatives are primarily responsible for coming up with the amount to be paid for the acquisition and an estimate of what the target company can generate postacquisition. In addition, they review the financial records of the target, assess the target's projections of future financial performance, and review the internal controls that are in place at the target's facility. Finally, the finance representative is normally the "keeper" of the detailed acquisition model. He or she will interface with the business development leader throughout the deal to reflect the various assumptions and findings of the due diligence team. This model will ultimately be used to derive a purchase price for the target and to calculate the returns expected to be achieved on the acquisition for the buyer's board of directors.

A variety of methods are employed for this review, including discussions with the target's finance personnel; review of independent audit work papers; review of the 10-K, 10-Q, and annual reports if the target company is public; and discussions with the target's internal audit group. Through these discussions, finance professionals can get a sense for the reasonableness of the amounts recorded on the financial statements that will be used to value the target.

In the final purchase agreement, the seller will normally represent that the financial statements were prepared in accordance with generally accepted accounting principles (GAAP) and fairly represent the financial position of the target. However, even within GAAP, there are judgments concerning things like depreciation lives for fixed assets, value of intangible assets like patents or trademarks, revenue recognition, costing of inventories (LIFO, FIFO, average), and so on. Treatment of these items can have a very material effect on the value of the target if the buyer takes a different view of the estimates or judgments.

As a result, the purchase agreement will often include a more detailed description of how the balance sheet and income statement accounts are calculated. An independent auditor, selected jointly by buyer and seller, will come in after the deal closes to audit the closing date income statement and balance sheet items versus the contractual definitions. Major changes in the balances presented will be posted as an adjustment to the purchase price if the buyer and seller agree. If they do not agree, contracts will generally contain dispute resolution mechanisms to resolve the difference.

Tax

Tax representatives are responsible for reviewing the adequacy of the target's prior year returns, any ongoing audits or disputes between the target and the IRS or state agencies, and the propriety of deferred tax balances and other tax accounts to be transferred to the buyer. Tax professionals are also heavily involved in structuring the "acquisition vehicle," the entity formed to purchase the target's operations. Efficient tax planning can often save the buyer or seller significant incremental tax liability resulting from the purchase of assets.

One major consideration is the form of company (partnership, corporation, limited liability corporation, and so on) that is selling the assets. As we will see in Chapter 8, "Final Bid Strategies/Structuring the Deal," depending on the seller's tax basis (the value of the assets recorded by the seller for tax purposes), a sale of assets can generate a significant tax liability. However, by structuring around these issues, the buyers' tax professionals can help mitigate the adverse consequences to the seller, making the overall bid much more competitive.

Legal/Environmental

Legal deal team members start to get more heavily involved in the deal process at this point. They ultimately have to give an opinion on whether the seller owns and has the ability to sell the assets represented. This analysis is made by a review of the articles of incorporation, board of directors meeting minutes, and other legal documentation provided by the seller. Merger and acquisition law is a specialized subject, in which most in-house legal staffs do not have expertise. As a result, outside legal counsel is often engaged to assist the in-house lawyers in their review.

The second major function of the legal staff is to ensure that no significant unrecorded exposures exist at the target at the time of purchase. These would include areas like poison pills or other antitakeover measures, pending or threatened litigation, or environmental and employee exposures that are too new to be recorded on the financial statements but could produce significant unreserved exposure depending on the outcome of the proceedings. The business development leader can deal with these issues via purchase accounting adjustments or contractual protection if they are uncovered early. However, once the agreements are signed and money changes hands, it is normally too late. Therefore, a detailed analysis of legal and regulatory correspondence, discussions with target legal personnel, and close review of the footnotes to the financial statements is a prudent due diligence step.

Third, the buyer will normally request a report on all pending, threatened, or actual litigation involving the target. Through a review of this report and discussions with the target's legal counsel, the buyer's attorneys assess the probability and amount of damages likely to be incurred. For larger exposures, this may include a discussion with outside counsel handling the case. Large expected exposures are normally reserved in the purchase price or are indemnified by the seller, that is, the seller picks up the cost that is ultimately paid out as a result of litigation.

Finally, both internal and external counsel are responsible for drafting the asset purchase agreement with the seller. There should be a direct relationship between the findings of the deal team and the negotiation of this purchase agreement. For example, assume that the HR deal team representative discovered an employee discrimination claim that was made 60 days prior to the buyer's due diligence. The facts and validity of the case may not have been clear at the time of the target's last quarterly financial statements; therefore, no estimate of liability was recorded. However, there could well be significant exposure to this case once all the facts are analyzed. In this instance, the buyer's counsel would normally request an indemnification, or protection, from the seller that shields the buyer from this liability after closing. Since this event happened while the seller still owned the company, it should be responsible for exposure to the event, even if the actual expense does not hit until after closing. Both internal and external legal counsel are a critical part of the due diligence process, given the sensitivity and the wide range of potential legal issues and their related exposure.

Compliance

An examination of compliance procedures is an essential part of *every* due diligence process. The buyer or target's type of industry will influence the amount and nature of the compliance review that will be necessary. The target's compliance with laws, regulations, and local policies can be extremely important to the success of the company postacquisition. For example, assume the target is in the drug manufacturing business. In this instance, proper regulatory approval of drugs before they go to market would clearly be an important part of the target's profile. Failure to receive such approval could significantly impair the revenues associated with these drugs going forward and introduce the possibility of penalties from regulators, lawsuits from customers, and similar problems. An important part of the buyer's diligence would be to verify that the target has all the necessary approvals to produce and deliver the products safely.

Another example is the review of target legal requirements to do business in a particular industry or jurisdiction. Buyers need to be confident that the licenses essential to the normal operations of the target are valid and in good standing. A failure to meet these requirements and subsequent loss of license after closing could have a very material impact on the success of the company. As we will see in Chapter 10, "The Importance of Integration," Sarbanes-Oxley has introduced another set of requirements on individuals and the firms they work for that are extremely important as well. Business Development professionals need to work very closely with their internal legal/compliance departments and external counsel, as necessary, to put together a comprehensive audit plan of compliance procedures to be completed during the due diligence process.

Sales/Marketing

Acquirers must make assumptions about how well the target can perform under new ownership. This is where the sales and strategic marketing functions come into play—to assess the reasonableness of the revenue and margin projections used in the purchase accounting model to price the deal. These assessments are made by a review of the historical performance and revenue growth of the target and by evaluating how robust the existing markets appear to be going forward. In some cases, incremental revenue and earnings are forecast from new markets, products, or customers that the buyer plans to introduce to the seller after the deal closes. Sales and marketing personnel will be asked to review these plans for reasonableness and to discuss the integration or other issues that will be faced in trying to implement these strategies.

Salespeople will be reluctant to commit to unreasonable performance goals based on a set of aggressive forecasts by the target.

The more aggressive these projections are, the harder it will be for sales personnel to achieve them and hit their bonus targets. Business development professionals have to watch out for over-conservatism and make sure the projections contain numbers that are within the range that the salespeople can achieve.

On the other hand, too many acquisitions are entered into with overly aggressive assumptions about what can be accomplished when the two companies are combined. For example, a target that has experienced gradually declining revenue levels and margins is likely to have trouble turning this around immediately upon being purchased by someone else. However, a surprising number of due diligence teams are overly aggressive and feel that things can be turned around quickly and without risk. Once again, sales personnel will be asked to give an opinion on the forecasts presented to senior management.

The buyer's head of sales will also have to form a preliminary view of what the target's sales force should look like after the deal closes. Will the target's sales force remain intact, or will it be merged into the buyer's sales force? There may well be overlap in geographies or markets covered by the two sales forces. This is an area where cost synergies can be achieved by redeploying redundant personnel or consolidating duplicate branch offices. At the same time, the due diligence team has to keep the bigger picture in mind. The target company was attractive to the buyer for some reason, usually a different approach, different markets, a different customer base, different geographies, or a combination of all of these. Care must be taken not to mold the target into the buyer's style and routines. The independence and value that the target brings with it should be maintained and promoted as it is integrated into the seller's operations.

Strategic marketing personnel can help explain why it makes sense to pursue a particular acquisition. There must be revenue synergies, new markets, complementary products, or other capabilities that the buyer does not currently have. In addition, the deal team has to convince senior management that the best way to get these capabilities is by buying another company, rather than trying to develop them in-house. One large advantage of a buy strategy is that the acquisition begins to provide benefits immediately after the deal closes. (See Exhibit 5-1.) It takes most companies a longer time to try to build a market or product specialty in-house. With Wall Street's increasing focus on quarterly earnings growth, it may make

EXHIBIT 5-1

Buy versus Build

Pros to Buy	Pros to Build
Immediate scale	Cheaper
Immediate income	One culture
New skills acquired	Fewer integration issues
Cons to Buy	**Cons to Build**
Premium paid	Takes time
Integration issues	Lose focus on core
Cultural differences	Execution risk

sense to buy rather than build as long as the price of buying is not prohibitive. To make a decision, buyers will compare the premium required to purchase the business to the delay in earnings in trying to build it themselves.

Operations/Information Technology

The operations area is a frequently overlooked, but very important, part of the due diligence process. Operations are the nuts and bolts of how the company will run after it is acquired. In some situations, functions at the target (payroll, tax services, legal, financial reporting, internal audit, and so on) may have been part of the target and therefore come over in the acquisition. However, in many cases, the target's parent company (the seller) has performed many of these services on behalf of the target subsidiary. In these situations, the buyer needs to make plans for who will perform these services postclose to avert a significant disruption of the target's business. M&A "war stories" abound about target personnel who don't get paid until weeks after closing because no provision had been made for payroll services that had previously been provided by the target's parent.

A transition services agreement is normally negotiated between buyer and seller to help deal with these areas. This agreement stipulates that the sellers will continue to provide these basic services for a short period (usually 90 days), until the buyer has the chance to get all the employees, customers, and target data on to its operating systems. In most cases, there is not enough time during due diligence for the buyer's operations representative to fully analyze every one of the target's operating systems and translate it to the buyer's system. A transition services agreement gives the buyer time to make the transition over a logical period, while still getting the services provided by the former parent. A monthly fee will normally be paid to the seller throughout the term of this agreement.

For purposes of due diligence, the operations representative will prepare an outline of the target's existing systems and how they will interface with the buyer's. A systems integration plan is developed, outlining a schedule and timeline for these systems to be converted. In some cases, the target's system applications may actually be better than the buyer's, so that the buyer's data are integrated into the seller's system. In either case, a logical and orderly plan must be developed to prevent any disruption to the normal operations or interface with customers.

Integration

Integration can be the single most important and most often overlooked aspect of the due diligence process. In fact, integration teams historically have not even joined the deal team until contract signing, well after due diligence. Frequent acquirers are getting smarter and now are engaging a team of integration professionals that is embedded in the due diligence team. This allows the integration team to get a feel for the operations, people, and culture of the target, and to help it be more effective in its job if the deal closes. Many acquirers will now require a separate report on the integration plan and the issues to be faced as part of the board of directors deal approval discussion.

Chapter 10 provides a detailed discussion of integration and the issues to be aware of. However, some main focuses in due diligence need to be

- *Target culture.* Particularly in international deals, the corporate culture of the target may be very different from that of the buyer. Buyers need to be sensitive to these issues and adapt their approach accordingly.
- *Employee attitude.* Is this acquisition viewed as a good thing by the target's employees? Most people don't like change, and the thought of being owned by a new parent company can be very unsettling. Frequent, open, and honest com-

munication is the best way to put employees more at ease with their company's new owners.

- *Integration plan.* What steps will need to be accomplished to properly integrate the target into the parent company's operations? How can/should employees be handled to prevent any unwanted attrition?
- *Unique deal issues.* Integration professionals have a better understanding of and sensitivity to deal-specific issues if they have been part of the due diligence team. They are not hit with the deal cold once the contracts are signed. Rather, they have the perspective and time to consider various solutions to the inevitable problems that will arise once the contracts have been signed.

CHAPTER 5 SUMMARY

1. Relations with target management during due diligence are tricky, but can be critical. Business development professionals must strike a balance between getting all critical information necessary and maintaining good relations with target management.
2. Interpersonal skills are important to keep the due diligence team calm and focused on finding ways to solve problems.
3. Due diligence team members will be asked to review their areas of expertise and produce a report of their findings at the end of the process.
4. Human resources can be helpful in evaluating target management and looking for cultural differences that need to be addressed in integration. Employment agreements should be negotiated for key employees to ensure that they stay on postacquisition.
5. Risk personnel need to provide an objective assessment of any issues that they see at the target. These issues are addressed with the seller or dealt with in the final purchase agreement to ensure that the buyer is adequately protected.
6. Financial representation is critical to review the books and records of the target for reasonableness and to help assess the legitimacy of the financial projections.

Financial personnel will also coordinate an acquisition model showing the expected performance of the company postacquisition and the returns expected given a particular purchase price.

7. Members of the buyer's tax department should review the target's tax accounts for the proper accounting and reserve levels. Tax professionals can also help to evaluate alternative structures that the buyer might want to use to acquire the target.

8. The buyer's attorneys should give an opinion on the legitimacy of the target's books and records, ownership structure, and ability to transfer title to the buyer. The legal review should also include an analysis of recorded and unrecorded pending litigation to ensure that there are proper reserves.

9. The buyer's legal counsel also assists in the drafting and negotiation of the purchase agreement, along with representations and indemnities made by the seller and buyer.

10. Sales/marketing personnel can be deployed to review the reasonableness of the financial projections submitted by the seller and the markets that the target desires to pursue.

11. Operations personnel are critical to ensuring that the buyer can run the company after the deal closes. Often a transitions services agreement is negotiated to allow the seller to continue to perform normal operations (payroll, accounts payable, and so on) for a 60- to 90-day period until the buyer can get its systems in place.

12. Integration is one of the *most important* elements of the deal team, but it is often overlooked. The right culture and attitude of the target will be critical to the success of the acquired entity. By putting integration on the deal team early, anticipated problems can be dealt with and corrected in real time.

Financial Modeling and Final Valuation

As stated earlier, the "level of commitment" of both parties to the transaction is much higher in the second round. The seller has narrowed down the field of potential buyers and has provided substantial information about the target in the due diligence process. The buyer now needs to refine the purchase price valuation range presented in the first round and ultimately commit to a specific price. In order to do this, the preliminary financial model developed in Phase 1 needs to be refined for due diligence findings and expanded to reflect the buyer's thoughts on what it can do with the company postacquisition.

The financial modeling process is normally run by a person on the finance staff who has been loaned to the due diligence team, facilitated by discussions with each of the functional areas represented on the deal team. Issues brought to the surface in due diligence need to be either resolved with the seller or included in the buyer's purchase price calculation. The actual price to bid can be calculated in one of four ways:

1. Discounted cash flow analysis
2. Market-based method
3. Asset-oriented methods
4. Generally accepted accounting principles (GAAP) income approach

In practice, some combination of two or more of these methods will be employed to try to narrow in on a purchase price to bid.

In each case, the first step is to try to forecast the results of oper-ations and cash flows that the bidder expects after the deal has closed. Although each deal is somewhat different, the following steps are generally taken to forecast these results:

1. Expand the preliminary financial model to reflect a more complete listing of balance sheet and income statement accounts.

2. Using the financial projections provided by management as a basis, project the target's financial performance for-ward. These projections need to be adjusted for areas that the buyer thinks are overly aggressive or unattainable. As indicated in Chapter 5, business development profession-als need to be extremely careful here. Management pro-jections are normally too aggressive, particularly if the seller's investment banker has helped put them together. Sellers are inclined to exaggerate their pro forma results because (1) they are forecasts only, with many assump-tions, (2) people tend to be optimistic about what they can accomplish, (3) the forecasts are hard to verify or dispute, and (4) higher projections will normally result in a higher purchase price. Business development professionals have to manage the process to ensure that they take sellers' biases into account without being overly conservative and developing an uncompetitive acquisition bid.

3. Calculate any revenue synergies that will add value to the combined entity. Revenue synergies represent incre-mental sources of revenue that can be generated by the target company through its association with the buyer, including

   a. Sharing of customer lists. The companies can share information on customers and cross-sell the target's products to this new combined, larger customer base.

   b. Leveraging the larger, combined sales force. By work-ing together, the buyer's and seller's sales groups can be more efficient in covering their markets to drive more business.

   c. Product development. Sharing R&D and technology between buyer and seller can often produce powerful new ideas that drive new product offerings and stim-ulate sales for the new combined entity.

    d. Share marketing strategies. The best marketing prac-
tices of each party can be combined to drive more
efficient results postacquisition.

4. Calculate synergies that will reduce the costs of the
combined entity postacquisition. Examples include

    a. Reduction or elimination of common facilities. A con-
solidation of duplicate corporate and field office locations can produce significant cost savings for the
combined entity postacquisition. In many cases, the
target firm may have negotiated more favorable lease
terms or may have better locations.

    b. Streamline operations. Dealing with duplicate person-
nel is one of the most difficult parts of the M&A
process. However, working with human resources,
the deal team needs to make an assessment of how
many and what people should be kept in the combined entity. Eliminating the salary and benefit costs
of those people that are redundant to the new organization can generate a large cost savings over time

    c. Access to supplier agreements. The target or seller may
have more favorable terms from vendors and suppliers.
Cost savings can be found by leveraging the best of
each.

    d. Economies of scale. Simple things like FedEx agree-
ments can be maximized by having more volume
pass through the service agreements. Leverage can be
used with major supplies to take advantage of quantity discounts and other economies of scale.

    e. Cost of capital. A large purchaser will often consoli-
date the operations of a smaller target. The purchaser
may have a better debt rating (Moody's, S&P, and so
on), allowing it access to a lower cost of capital—both
debt and equity. These savings can have a material
impact on performance when they are passed on to
the target company after the deal has closed.

    f. Control and discipline. A larger, more developed pur-
chaser may have better reporting routines and procedures than the company being acquired. Productivity
can be increased by applying these disciplines to a
more informal target once the deal has closed.

Although this is not true 100 percent of the time, cost synergies are normally easier to achieve than revenue synergies because they are more controllable by management postacquisition. For example, it is much easier to consolidate the home offices of the buyer and the seller to reduce cost immediately than to drive incremental revenue from sharing customer lists. Business development professionals need to closely review the assumptions underlying revenue synergies and when they are to be realized. In many M&A deals, either the synergies are never realized or they take much longer than expected. (See Exhibit 6-1.)

Financial modeling needs to be an iterative process based on the stage of the deal and the findings of the due diligence team. All of these issues are interrelated. For example, suppose

E X H I B I T   6-1

The Difficulty of Revenue Synergies

AOL TIME WARNER

The merger of AOL and Time Warner was supposed to be the perfect combination of an old-economy "bricks-and-mortar" business (Time Warner) and a new-age Internet company (AOL). Growth targets of 30 percent or more were forecast based on potential sharing of customer lists and selling of Time Warner products over the Internet. Large operating synergies were forecast from sharing of the music and publishing networks. However, company management vastly underestimated the cultural differences between the two firms. Time Warner's old-style conservatism clashed with the freewheeling entrepreneurship of the new-economy AOL. Each of the companies took a very parochial view of its business. They were reluctant to share customer lists and make introductions for fear of losing key customers. As a result, the forecast revenue synergies were never achieved. The company was saddled with *$28 billion* in acquisition debt, and the stock price dropped by 55 percent. It got so bad that, in November 2002, management considered splitting the AOL business back into a separate corporation. The ill-conceived combination ultimately cost AOL Chairman Stephen Case his job on January 13, 2003. He stated, "Given that some shareholders continue to focus their disappointment with the company's post merger performance on me personally, I have concluded that we should take steps to . . . focus fully on our business" (*New York Times*, January 13, 2003).

that a large environmental issue is discovered that was not disclosed on the target's balance sheet because it is "too early" to know if the target has exposure. The sequence of events for the due diligence team could go something like the following:

1. The issue is identified by the legal/environmental team.
2. Discussions are held with the target about the potential scope of and exposure to the issue.
3. An outside environmental consultant may be engaged to provide an independent review of the situation.
4. Discussions are held with the target's deal team about protecting the buyer from exposure related to this issue that happened preclosing.
5. Based on the result of these negotiations, one of the following normally occurs:
   a. The seller agrees to indemnify the buyer for all exposure related to the issue; that is, any exposure to this issue will be borne by the seller.
   b. The seller agrees to keep the account and manage the exposure itself; that is, the buyer does not purchase the exposure and related claim, and the seller works it out with no impact on the buyer.
   c. The seller does not think there is a material exposure and will not agree to any provision or adjustment to the purchase price. In this case, the buyer needs to perform its own assessment of the issue, its relative cost, and the buyer's willingness to take on the exposure.

Category c is where the financial representative needs to get involved. The purchase accounting model must reflect the buyer's view of the expected exposure if no provision is made in the target's accounts and a purchase price adjustment can't be negotiated. This will normally reduce the expected returns to the buyer, assuming that the buyer truly believes that exposure to this environmental issue exists. This is an example of how legal, environmental, finance, and the business development leader all have to interact and adapt as the deal evolves. The finance team must have frequent discussions with other deal team members to ensure that any issues are either negotiated away or reflected in the purchase accounting model and the expected returns to be achieved.

DISCOUNTED CASH FLOW APPROACH

Discounted cash flow is the purest method of determining the value of the target. It is based on the premise that the buyer is getting the right to an estimated level of cash flow streams each year that it owns the target. In other words, it is getting the cash left over after revenue from customers has been reduced by all expenses, liabilities, and other contractual payments.

GAAP income, or the income reported on the target's audited financial statements, is not relevant to this analysis. Rather, the company is viewed like a bond or any other financial instrument that produces a certain level of cash for the investor each year. In the case of a bond investment, the cash received is the interest coupon each year and the principal repayments. In the case of an acquisition, it is the amount of cash that the target will generate for the purchaser each year. An amount (i.e., the purchase price) must be paid up front to obtain the right to a stream of cash flows in the future. A proxy often used for these cash flows is the target's earnings before interest, taxes, depreciation, and amortization (EBITDA). The cash flows are then discounted by the investor's required rate of return to arrive at a net present value. In an acquisition context, the required rate of return is normally represented by the buyer's return on equity (if free cash flows to the equity are used) or the investor's weighted average cost of capital (blended cost of the buyer's debt and equity capital structure applied) if free cash flows to the firm are used.

1. *Forecast cash flows by year.* The financial projections provided by the seller are reviewed by the buyer and used as a basis for determining the future cash flows. In most situations, the seller will provide a presentation on a GAAP basis, requiring a restatement of these financial balances into cash flows as follows:
   - *Free Cash Flows to the Equity (FCFE).* This is free cash flow available to common equity holders. Common equity holders get paid after all other claims of the corporation have been paid out—debt payments, capital expenditures (CAPEX), preferred dividends, and expenses.

	Net Income
Add:	Depreciation on fixed assets (noncash expense)
Less:	CAPEX
Add/less:	Decrease/Increase in net working capital

Add: New debt
Less: Debt principal repayments
Less: Preferred dividends
Equals: Free cash flow to the equity
- *Free Cash Flows to the Firm (FCFF).* This is cash available
  to satisfy the claims of all investors—common stock-
  holders, preferred stockholders, and debt providers.

Free cash flow to the equity
Add: Interest expense × (1 − tax rate)
Add: Debt principal repayments
Less: New debt
Add: Preferred dividends
Equals: Free cash flow to the firm
- Another way to calculate FCFF uses EBITDA as a start-
  ing point:

EBITDA (1 − tax rate)
Less: Gross CAPEX − depreciation
Add/less: Decrease/Inecrease in net working capital
Equals: Free cash flows to the firm

2. *Determine the appropriate discount rate using the capital asset
   pricing model.* The buyer's board of directors will be looking for some minimal rate of return on the acquisition in
   order to approve the deal. Every company has a finite
   amount of capital to invest in its business. One of the
   roles of the board of directors is to determine where the
   company should invest its free cash flow. This can involve
   starting a new manufacturing facility, funding research
   and development, or making an acquisition. Projects
   with higher rates of return are chosen before those that
   do not hit the "hurdle," or required rate of return set by
   senior management. If FCFE is used to estimate the target's performance postacquisition, then the buyer's cost
   of equity is the appropriate discount rate to be applied.
   - *Cost of Equity.* The capital asset pricing model (CAPM) is
     used to calculate the buyer's cost of equity. CAPM is
     based on the theory that investors want more return as
     the risk of the transaction goes up. It breaks risk into two
     components, diversifiable (firm-specific) and nondiversi-
     fiable (common to all firms). This well-known formula
     determines this return as a function of the risk-free rate
     plus a risk premium based on the level of volatility that

the firm experiences relative to the market, or beta. Beta is calculated by regressing the changes in the firm's stock against changes in the overall market over time. Beta values higher than 1 (i.e., the stock is more volatile than the market) indicate more risk, and betas less than 1 (i.e., the stock is less volatile than the market) indicate less risk.

$$\text{Equity cost} = \text{risk-free rate} + \text{beta} \times (\text{market return} - \text{risk-free rate})$$

- *Weighted Average Cost of Capital.* The buyer's weighted average cost of capital (WACC) is the appropriate discount rate to apply if FCFF is used as a basis for predicting the target's performance. This rate represents a weighted average of the firm's after-tax debt cost and the firm's cost of equity. For example, assume that ABC Company has the following simple capital structure (in millions of dollars) and a corporate tax rate of 40 percent.

Component	Amount	Coupon/Cost
Debt	$50	7% fixed
Preferred stock	$30	10% fixed
Common stock	$20	18%

The firm's weighted average cost of capital is calculated as follows:

$$\text{WACC} = 0.5 \times (0.07 \times 0.6) + (0.3 \times 0.1) + (0.2 \times 0.18) = 8.7\%$$

Note that the debt rate is multiplied by 0.6 (assuming a 40 percent tax rate) to adjust for the tax savings on debt interest payments. The target's forecasted free cash flows to the firm would be discounted at this rate to derive an estimated purchase price for the acquisition.

3. *Estimate acquisition purchase price.* The final step is to take the cash flow estimates by year and discount them using the relevant discount factor, that is, the cost of equity if FCFE is used or WACC if FCFF is used. This net present value reflects an *estimate* of the amount that can be paid for the target and still achieve the required rate of return set by the buyer's board of directors. In practice, this net

present value is not cast in stone; it is used merely as a proxy for the amount that the buyer should be willing to pay. The calculations used to derive this value have numerous assumptions, starting with the volatility of the projected cash flows as noted earlier.

Business development professionals need to exercise judgment concerning the target's cash flow projections and the calculation of the buyer's discount rate. The DCFF method is normally used as one source of information to determine an appropriate amount to bid for the target. Factors such as how competitive the auction is, what others are bidding, the strategic value of the target, and so on, all come into play when fine-tuning a purchase price bid.

4. *Internal rate of return (IRR) versus net present value (NPV).* Another common method is to calculate the discount rate given a fixed purchase price and an estimated cash flow stream. The rate necessary to discount the cash flows back to a fixed purchase price is called an internal rate of return. The calculated IRR is then compared to the firm's required rate of return to determine if the acquisition meets that buyer's hurdle rate. Projects that exceed the hurdle rate should be pursued. If the project does not meet the hurdle rate, then the buyer should either (1) lower the purchase price or (2) walk away from the deal.

Pros and Cons of the Discounted Cash Flow Approach

Pros

1. It is an academically pure calculation. Cash flows rather than accounting-based income are used as a basis for the calculation. The cash flows coming from the acquisition are a better representative of the economic value that will be achieved than book accounting income.
2. It provides a single number, the present value, which can be used as a reference point to determine the amount to bid.
3. It relates level of risk to required level of return; that is, required return goes up as the perceived level of risk increases.

Cons

1. Small changes in the discount rate assumed can have a very big impact on the net present value calculated. Different bidders may have different discount rates, which can result in large differences in perceived value.
2. It is difficult to project the target's cash flows out into the future in an acquisition context. The ability to realize synergies, potential loss of personnel, disruption of the markets, and other such factors can all have a dramatic impact on the actual results achieved.
3. The measures used in DCF (discount rates, internal rates of return, and net present value) are financial, not GAAP accounting metrics. The stock market values public companies based on the dollars of net income that they produce. None of these financial metrics are included in the buyer's annual report.
4. Calculating a terminal value is difficult. Expected annual cash flows can be discounted out only so far. At some point, you have to derive a single value for the target from that point forward, i.e., the terminal value. The Gordon growth model is generally used to calculate this value as follows:

$$\text{Terminal value} = \frac{\text{cash flow at time } t}{\text{required return} - \text{growth rate}}$$

Small changes in the Gordon growth model assumptions can have a very large impact on the net present value calculation. See the following example for a calculation.

Discounted Cash Flow Example

	FCF Firm	FCF Equity
Year 1	100	80
Year 2	108	88
Year 3	117	102

Assumptions

Growth rate after year 3 = 5 percent
Weighted average cost of capital = 10 percent
Required return on equity = 12 percent

FCF Firm

$$\text{PV of cash flows} = 100/(1.1) + 108/(1.1)^2 + 117/(1.1)^3 = \quad 268.05$$
$$\text{Terminal Value} = (117 \times 1.05)/(0.1 - 0.05) = 2{,}457.00$$
$$\text{PV of terminal value} = 2{,}457/(1.1)^4 = \underline{1{,}678.28}$$
$$\text{Net FCFF} = 1{,}946.33$$

FCF Equity

$$\text{PV of cash flows} = 80/(1.12) + 88/(1.12)^2 + 102/(1.12)^3 = \quad 214.30$$
$$\text{Terminal value} = (102 \times 1.05)/(0.12 - 0.05) = 1{,}530.00$$
$$\text{PV of terminal value} = 1.530/(1.12)^4 = \quad \underline{972.05}$$
$$\text{Net FCFE} = 1{,}186.35$$

Internal Rate of Return Example

Using the same data, a slightly different method could be used to evaluate the project by applying an internal rate of return. Assume for a moment that the equity buyer had settled on a purchase price of $1,100 for the property. In theory, if the buyer's equity hurdle IRR was 12 percent or less, it would pursue this transaction because discounting the equity cash flow streams at 12 percent would result in a positive net present value. If the buyer's equity hurdle rate was higher than 12 percent, then discounting these cash flows would result in a negative number, indicating a dilutive deal.

Equity hurdle rate = 12%
Purchase price = $1,100

Net present value of the equity cash flows is determined as follows:

Year 0 = (1,100)
Year 1 = 80
Year 2 = 88
Year 3 = 102
Terminal value = 1,530

The net present value of this cash flow stream at the buyer's 12 percent hurdle rate equals $86.35. Theoretically, since the NPV is greater than zero, the buyer should proceed. Because of the limited amount of capital that companies have in practice, however, most firms will evaluate the NPVs of several projects and other more subjective factors in their purchasing decisions.

MARKET-BASED METHODS

Market-based methods apply some standard financial metric, such as price/earnings ratio, price-to-book-value ratio, or EBITDA multiple, of industry comparable companies or recent sales to value the target. These valuations are relatively easy to calculate and can provide a good benchmark for the projected value of the target. Assume as an example that you are evaluating the purchase of a hospital supply company with EBITDA of $130 million for the past 12 months. Industry data on companies similar to the target are as follows:

Company	EBITDA	Market Cap	Multiple
GFA Inc.	$100	$1,000	10×
Caroline Co.	$120	$1,050	8.75×
Perry, Inc.	$ 90	$ 950	10.56×
Average			9.77×

The relative value of your target could be estimated as $1,270 ($130 × 9.77). This would represent a benchmark value for the target firm.

Pros and Cons of Market-Based Methods

Pros

1. These ratios are relatively simple to calculate.
2. They compare the value of the target to the values of similar companies in the industry for reasonableness.
3. They provide a point estimate that can be used as a basis for more analysis or be compared to DCF values.

Cons

1. This method assumes that markets are efficient and that the current values of businesses reflect all information. The public value of a company may be higher or lower than the potential value to the buyer.
2. It is meaningful only for companies with stable earnings and cash flow. For example, during the "Internet bubble," companies were trading at multiples of revenue. These values had no relationship to the earnings or cash flow capabilities of the firm. The values of the majority of these firms plunged when positive cash flow or actual income never materialized.

3. A lot of judgment goes into determining "comparable" companies. Values can be changed by including or excluding certain companies. For example, in the previous calculation, the multiple would be 10.28 if Caroline Co. were excluded from the list of market comparables. This would result in a much higher purchase price of $1,336 (130 × 10.28) without any change in the target's fundamentals. Sellers will often argue that the "true comparables" for their firm are those with higher multiples in order to justify a higher purchase price.

ASSET-ORIENTED METHODS

Asset-oriented methods take some objective asset value represented on the target's financial statements to derive the value of the firm—total assets, net book value, and so on. The buyer can use a wide range of asset-oriented methods depending on the size and industry of the target.

Total Asset Value

This method values the target based on its total asset value, ignoring liabilities. It generally overstates the value of the firm when significant liabilities exist.

Tangible Book Value

This method attributes value only to the tangible assets of the firm. It is calculated as follows:

$$\text{Total assets} - \text{current liabilities} - \text{goodwill}$$

This method has a tendency to understate value because of GAAP's focus on historical cost. GAAP requires that assets be recorded at the *lower* of their cost or estimated market value at the date of the financial statements. In many cases, the current market value of these assets can be significantly higher than the recorded book value. Furthermore, certain intangible assets, such as trademarks and patents, can have significant value to the target, but have no value attributed to them on the financial statements. This can lead to a noncompetitive bid if the buyer uses this method exclusively.

Liquidation Value

This is a very conservative view of company value that is often used for targets in distress or bankruptcy. It represents the projected value of the assets if they were sold separately from the target's liabilities in a liquidation or bankruptcy of the firm. A 9- to 12-month period is normally assumed for an orderly liquidation of these assets.

Pros and Cons of Asset-Oriented Methods

Pros

1. This amount is very simple to calculate and understand.
2. It is based on the accounting values of the firm's assets and liabilities. This information should be readily available.
3. It can be used as a benchmark for reasonableness along with other valuation methods.

Cons

1. Such a simple approach can lead to incorrect conclusions and affect the firm's value.
2. It is a static estimate of firm value that does not consider the cash flow opportunities of the target.
3. It is not risk adjusted—the buyer's risk and the cost of capital are not reflected in the valuation.

GAAP INCOME APPROACH

Chapter 2 presented an example of the GAAP income approach for a first-round bid. The bid was based on the financial statements that the target had already prepared for internal/external accounting purposes. Final bids require a modification of this preliminary model based on the findings of each of the functional areas during the due diligence process. For example, the allowance for bad debt might be increased because of credit concerns. Overly aggressive revenue projections might be lowered in the final acquisition model based on discussions with the target's sales personnel. The business development professional needs to listen to the due diligence team's findings and, along with the financial modeling person, factor these issues into the purchase price calculation.

Creating the Model

The steps in the process are as follows:

1. Take the pro forma financial model from the first round of the due diligence process and update the historical results to reflect
   - A more detailed breakout of balance sheet and income statement accounts based on the information learned in due diligence. For example, the preliminary model may have had one line item for revenue. Second-round due diligence models should break revenue into its component products, markets, or geographic areas to arrive at a more precise picture.
   - An update for the latest financial information. Some number of months may have passed between the first-round model and due diligence. Historical financials need to be updated for subsequent results or the receipt of the most recent financial statements for the target.

2. Adjust the target's projected financial information to make it look as if the buyer owns the company going forward. The primary adjustments relate to changing the debt/equity ratio and weighted average cost of capital from those of the seller to those of the buyer.

3. Break out the financial statements in more detail and adjust the financial projections for elements or issues found in the detailed due diligence. As noted earlier, functional deal team members should have a view on the achievability of the target's forecasts based on their due diligence analysis. These findings need to be discussed with the business development leader and reflected in the model as deemed appropriate by the team. The business development leader needs to gain consensus that the forecasts placed in the model can actually be achieved by the buyer/target combination. These are the budgets (sales forecasts, expense budgets, write-offs, and so on) that the various functional areas will have to live with going forward.

4. Determine the expected project returns based on an assumed purchase price and the pro forma projections developed. Most firms will use a weighted average cost of capital or required return on equity to make this evaluation.

5. Run sensitivities and determine whether to proceed. This is another step in the process that normally generates much discussion on the due diligence team. Small changes in assumptions concerning expected growth rates, margins, expense levels, and other such factors can have a dramatic effect on the projected financial results, returns, and ultimately the decision on whether to proceed with the deal. An iterative process normally occurs, in which the seller or its representatives give a feel for where the bid needs to be if it is to be successful. The business development professional will then run this purchase price through the financial model to determine if the returns are acceptable at that given price level.

In other words, the calculation of bid price is not a scientific process. In many cases, the buyer starts with the purchase price required to win the deal and then determines whether it can achieve an adequate return at this price. The purchase price model is used to make this assessment. An example of a detailed GAAP purchase price model is given in Exhibit 6-2.

Pros and Cons to GAAP Method

Pros

1. An accounting-based approach is used, i.e., net income is used as a basis for calculating returns. Net income and return on equity are what show up in the financial statements used by investors to evaluate target performance. Relating the results of the acquisition to these metrics rather than to cash flow provides most investors with what they care about.
2. In most cases, the approach aligns well with how targets view themselves. In other words, the target does not have to recreate the historical financials. The GAAP financials as audited by an independent auditing firm can be used as the basis for the model without a special request to the seller.
3. The request for financial projections in income statement format is generally in line with how the target has budgeted its operations.
4. The return on equity calculation is a commonly used financial metric that can be readily compared to that for

the buyer's core business and other businesses comparable to the target.

Cons

1. There are inherent limitations in GAAP financial statements. For example, recognition of assets at lower of cost
   or market can undervalue a company whose assets have
   appreciated in value.
2. GAAP requires many estimates with respect to reserves,
   losses, depreciation lives for fixed assets, and so on, causing

EXHIBIT 6-2

Final Acquisition Model Example

	Holly Corporation					
	Income Statement (in millions of dollars)					
	Historical			Forecast		
	2003	*2004*	*2005*	*2006*	*2007*	*2008*
Product Line A	$11.2	$13.1	$17.5	$21.2	$22.2	$25.2
Product Line B	5.0	6.5	9.0	12.5	16.2	17.5
Product Line C	5.0	4.9	3.2	0.4	—	—
Revenue Synergies	—	—	—	5.5	8.5	10.0
Total Revenues	**$21.2**	**$24.5**	**$29.7**	**$39.6**	**$46.9**	**$52.7**
% Growth	*12%*	*16%*	*21%*	*33%*	*18%*	*12%*
CGS — A	$7.8	$9.2	$10.5	$14.6	$15.0	$16.5
CGS — B	4.2	4.5	5.5	8.8	10.5	11.7
CGS — C	3.8	3.5	3.2	0.1	—	—
Synergies	—	—	—	3.0	4.5	4.0
Cost of Goods Sold	**$15.8**	**$17.2**	**$19.2**	**$26.5**	**$30.0**	**$32.2**
% Revenues	*75%*	*70%*	*65%*	*67%*	*64%*	*61%*
Gross Profit — A	$3.4	$3.9	$7.0	$6.6	$7.2	$7.7
Gross Profit — B	0.8	2.0	3.5	3.7	5.7	5.8
Gross Profit — C	1.2	1.4	—	0.3	—	—
Synergies	—	—	—	2.5	4.0	7.0
Gross Profit	**$5.4**	**$7.3**	**$10.5**	**$13.1**	**$16.9**	**$20.5**
% Revenues	*25%*	*30%*	*35%*	*33%*	*36%*	*39%*

(*Continued*)

E X H I B I T   6-2

(Continued)

Income Statement (in millions of dollars), (continued)

	Historical			Forecast		
	2003	2004	2005	2006	2007	2008
SG&A	$2.2	$3.8	$6.7	$7.2	$8.1	$9.2 *(See Schedule 1)*
EBITDA	$3.2	$3.5	$3.8	$5.9	$8.8	$11.3
% Revenues	*15%*	*14%*	*13%*	*15%*	*19%*	*21%*
Depreciation/Amortization	$0.2	$0.2	$0.3	$0.6	$0.8	$0.9
Interest Expense	0.5	0.6	0.5	1.0	1.1	1.6
EBT	$2.5	$2.7	$3.0	$4.3	$6.9	$8.8
% Revenues	*12%*	*11%*	*10%*	*11%*	*15%*	*17%*
Taxes	$1.0	$1.0	$1.2	$1.7	$2.8	$3.5
Net Income	$1.5	$1.7	$1.8	$2.6	$4.1	$5.3
% Revenues	*7%*	*7%*	*6%*	*7%*	*9%*	*10%*

Schedule 1

	Historical			Forecast		
	2003	2004	2005	2006	2007	2008
Salaries/Wages	1,061	2,286	4,522	4,775	5,450	6,300
Benefits	600	650	700	925	1,000	1,100
Rent	112	183	444	500	550	575
Legal	175	388	592	625	650	700
Finance	180	196	240	200	200	210
Utilities	50	72	139	125	150	175
Permits/Licenses	22	25	63	50	100	140
	$2,200	$3,800	$6,700	$7,200	$8,100	$9,200

room for error in both historical and projected financial results. These areas of judgment can have a material impact on how much a bidder can afford to pay for the target.

3. Required rates of returns can vary significantly among bidders, making some bidders noncompetitive.

4. Valuation is based on accounting values rather than on the cash flows that the target is expected to generate (discounted cash flows). Academics would argue that future cash flows are more relevant than accounting net income in evaluating price.

EXHIBIT 6-2

(Continued)

	Holly Corporation Balance Sheet (in millions of dollars)					
	Historical			Forecast		
	2003	2004	2005	2006	2007	2008
Cash	$1.0	$1.0	$1.0	$1.0	$1.0	$1.0
Accounts Receivable	$1.5	1.7	2.0	2.1	2.2	2.4
Inventory	$2.5	2.6	2.6	2.6	2.6	2.3
Current Assets	$5.0	$5.3	$5.6	$5.7	$5.8	$5.7
Fixed Assets	13.5	13.7	13.9	14.0	14.5	14.3
Goodwill/Intangibles	0	0	0	5.0	4.9	4.7
Total Assets	**$18.5**	**$19.0**	**$19.5**	**$24.7**	**$25.2**	**$24.7**
Accounts Payable	$1.0	$1.1	$1.2	$1.3	$1.4	$1.5
Accrued Liabilities	0.6	0.8	0.8	0.9	1.0	1.0
Other Liabilities	0.4	0.4	0.5	0.5	0.4	0.2
Non Debt Liabilities	**$2.0**	**$2.3**	**$2.5**	**$2.7**	**$2.8**	**$2.7**
Net Investment	**$16.5**	**$16.7**	**$17.0**	**$22.0**	**$22.4**	**$22.0**
Net Income	**$1.5**	**$1.7**	**$1.8**	**$2.6**	**$4.1**	**$5.3**
Debt	8.3	8.4	8.5	12.1	12.3	12.0
Equity	8.2	8.3	8.5	9.9	10.1	10.0
Key Ratios						
Debt to Equity	50%	50%	50%	55%	55%	55%
Return on Investment	9%	10%	11%	12%	18%	24%
Return on Equity	18%	20%	21%	26%	41%	54%

CHAPTER 6 SUMMARY

1. The preliminary acquisition model needs to be adjusted for the things learned in due diligence.

2. A variety of methods can be used to assess the estimated value of a target company. In practice, no one technique is used 100 percent of the time. Rather, multiple sources of information are compared, along with a "gut feel" for where the bid needs to be to win the auction.

3. Target financial projections are used as a basis for these models. The team can start with the preliminary model

run before due diligence and expand it based on the information learned.

4. Synergies are net benefits that are planned in the acquisition. Revenue synergies reflect areas in which revenues can be enhanced by sharing customer lists, combining sales forces, and so on. Cost synergies represent savings in the combined entity by removing duplicate personnel, consolidating office locations, and so on. In general, cost synergies are easier to forecast and implement than revenue synergies.

5. The financial representative needs to work very closely with the due diligence team to ensure that exposure areas are factored into the purchase model.

6. The discounted cash flow (DCF) approach uses the net present value of the target's expected cash flows to estimate a purchase price. Although this is a pure form of analysis based on the true economics, it can be difficult to forecast the expected cash flows accurately.

7. The capital asset pricing model (CAPM) can be used in the DCF approach to determine the appropriate discount rate to apply to the cash flows. An internal rate of return can be used to rank projects and determine which ones deserve an allocation of capital.

8. Market-based methods use comparable companies to value the target. They are relatively simple to understand. However, the difficulty of finding proper comparables and room for management judgment can produce a misleading view of value.

9. The GAAP income approach uses the target's financial statement net income and projections to derive a value. This is generally in line with how most targets budget their own business. However, the inherent limitations in GAAP reporting (historical value, lower of cost or market, and so on) can distort the true value of the firm.

Pulling It All Together

The final purchase price is normally determined using some combination of the several valuation methods that we described in Chapter 6, along with consideration of where the bid "needs to be" in order to be competitive. None of the financial modeling approaches can be taken at face value because of the large number of assumptions and the degree of human judgment inherent in these calculations. The business development leader's job is to sort through all of this data and present a reasonable case to the buyer's senior management and/or board of directors for approval.

Effective business development professionals need to be in constant contact with the various function heads throughout the due diligence process. This allows the leader to stay on top of critical issues and deal with them on a real-time basis so as not to be surprised by "deal-breaking" issues at the end. Interim deadlines for preliminary feedback on major findings should be established for the deal team members. This normally happens throughout the due diligence process in informal meetings and discussions.

Each member of the due diligence team will write a report on the findings and critical issues from his or her area. These reports are circulated to all team members and the buyer's senior management to give a broad perspective on the issues. The interplay of ideas among the different functions often provides a valuable perspective on issues and a plan for handling them. For example, an issue regarding an exorbitant bonus plan that was brought to the surface by the HR team affects not only HR, but also finance (i.e., the cost to maintain the plan), legal (to analyze the terms and conditions of the plan), and integration (to determine how this plan can mesh with the buyer's existing policies).

POST-DUE DILIGENCE COORDINATION: SUMMARIZING RESULTS

The diligence reports prepared by each of the functional areas provide the basis for the deal approval presentation to senior management. However, there is far too much detail in these reports for the senior management team to digest. Business development professionals play a valuable role here, attempting to distill the relevant issues from the large amount of data amassed during due diligence while being careful to highlight all of those issues. A balanced presentation needs to be made so that the board of directors can make an informed decision.

This takes discipline on the part of the deal team. By this point, a huge amount of time and effort has gone into the deal. The business development leader normally has a vested interest (i.e., incentive compensation, prestige, career development, and so on) in getting the deal to happen. However, this must not cloud his or her judgment on the deal or how it is presented to the board of directors. All points of view must be considered for a balanced presentation. As recent history has shown, the consequences of pushing a bad deal too aggressively are much more severe than the upside to be gained from doing the deal.

SENIOR MANAGEMENT APPROVAL

The senior management approval process can be extremely difficult or very easy, depending on (1) your company's attitude toward acquisitions and (2) senior management's level of involvement in the process up until this point. Some firms have more of a "growth mindset" that makes them more willing to pursue acquisitions as a way to fuel business growth. They are used to looking at large, distinct projects and the risks and rewards associated with them. The approval process can be pretty efficient in this type of firm as long as the deal team is well prepared and has done its homework.

The approval process can be much more difficult at firms that are not used to making acquisitions. The unfamiliarity with the process can lead to a tedious process, with many questions and concerns being raised and a lack of focus on the most important issues. In either case, it is essential that the leader of the deal team be prepared to talk about any issues and concerns. By this point, the team should have achieved consensus concerning the deal from the various functional areas, so that a united front is shown to senior management. All of this is much easier if senior management has been involved in the process—the senior managers will better understand the people, issues, and opportunities presented by the deal, rather than being hit cold with these topics at the last minute.

The level of detail, formality of the process, and time allotted for deal discussion is different for each firm. On larger deals, a face-to-face meeting normally takes place to discuss the transaction. On smaller deals, approval can be a paper process, with the senior management team reviewing a written report or presentation on the deal. A meeting is usually preferable because it allows for an exchange of ideas, response to questions, and listing of follow-up items should the senior management decide to move forward with the transaction.

Exhibit 7-1 shows an example of a board of directors presentation for Cramer Industries' purchase of Wilson Boatworks. Most acquisition presentations to the board of directors will normally include the following:

PROVIDING FEEDBACK—FINAL BID LETTERS

The end of the due diligence process is a final written bid requested by the seller. Depending on how formalized the process is, the seller may include a list of requirements in addition to price, such as timing, financing requirements, and additional due diligence required. Final bid letters need to be crafted very carefully, particularly in competitive situations. This is the last impression that the bidders will leave with the seller, and it will obviously have a huge impact on who wins the deal. At the same time, bidders need to be careful about not overcommitting. Any remaining contingencies should be either cleared up before the bid letter is issued or clearly laid out as conditions to closing the transaction. Many of the problems that bidders and sellers get into are caused by not having a very clear understanding of what level of commitment is being given with this final letter. Both internal and external legal counsel need to be intimately involved in this process to ensure that deal professionals do not get ahead of themselves and overcommit their firm.

The final bid letter is a further refinement of the preliminary letter issued in the first round of the deal process. The purchase price range previously specified now needs to be narrowed down to

EXHIBIT 7-1

Board of Directors Presentation

Cramer Industries	Wilson Boatworks Acquisition

Executive Summary

- Opportunity to Purchase #4 U.S. Boat Manufacturer
- Family-run Company — 30-year history
- Solid reputation for high-quality, top-tier boat production
- Multiple synergies with Cramer's existing Boat Division — product line, customer base, manufacturing efficiencies
- Immediately accretive transaction — $6 million incremental net income expected in the first 12 months

Industry

- Main product lines include small outboard power boats, sailboats and one- to four- person kayaks.
- Market segments have shown 10 to 15% average annual growth rates.
- Demand should continue to rise as "baby boom" generation gets closer to retirement/leisure living.
- Good overlap with Cramer's existing product line, focused on higher-end luxury yacht market.
- Ability to cross-sell existing Cramer products to aging, wealth-accumulating, Wilson customer base should provide strong revenue growth.
- Wilson existing dealer network can be leveraged immediately to sell Cramer product line.

Company History

- Incorporated in 1964 by Noah Wilson, CEO
- Family-controlled/run limited liability corporation
- Headquarters in Madison, CT, product sold through 150 independent dealers throughout North America
- Aging owner seeks liquidity event and efficient tax planning
- Owner plans to stay on in consulting capacity. Senior management team to join Cramer

Management Team

- Noah Wilson, CEO. U.S. Coast Guard, age 58
- Josh Wilson, COO. Conn College, U.S. Navy Officer. 10 years industry experience, age 32
- Andy Rudof, CFO, CPA, age 42

Cramer Industries	Wilson Boatworks Acquisition

EBITDA Growth

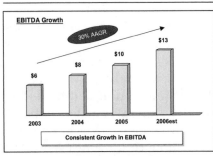

Consistent Growth in EBITDA

Historical Margins

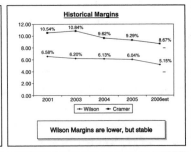

Wilson Margins are lower, but stable

U.S. Distribution Sites

Cramer Growth Opportunities

- Leverage existing Wilson centers to distribute Cramer products
- Immediate incremental benefit through lower shipping costs, faster customer response time
- Cross-sell existing Cramer products to Wilson customer base — ability to move customers "up market" to higher margin-products

Wilson's Solid EBITDA Growth, Margins and Location Overlap Provide a Great Opportunity

EXHIBIT 7-1

Continued

Cramer Industries / Wilson Boatworks Acquisition

Financials

Projections	2006	2007	2008	AAGR%
Revenue $	$140	$145	$160	7.5%
% Increase	7%	4%	10%	
EBITDA $	$13	$15	$18	20%
Net Income $/% Increase	$6/50%	$8/33%	$9/13%	25%
ROE%	15%	18%	20%	

Historical Detail	2005	2004	2003	
Historical Revenue	$131	$120	$118	5%
Historical Revenue AAGR%	9%	2%	5%	

Key Assumptions

* Senior management team joins Cramer. Noah Wilson as consultant for 3 years.
* Willingness/ability of Wilson customer base to move up market to Cramer luxury product lines.
* Ability to maintain product margins.
* Efficient delivery of Cramer products through Wilson distribution sites.
* Growing product demand as population ages.

Purchase Price

Cash Up Front:	$ 90 million
Contingent Payment:	$ 30 million
Total	**$120 million**

* 12× EBITDA in line with recent Regent, ANC sales
* Contingent payment based on future performance
* Aligns interests of Wilson with Cramer, more than efficient for Noah Wilson
* Growing product demand as population ages

Recent Transactions

Target	Buyer	Price	Multiple
Regent	Kelly	$200 million	8×
ANC	Nixon	$ 75 million	12×
Blank	Eisle Inc.	$130 million	10×
Norman	Lincoln Ind.	$ 55 million	14×
Reardon	Ennis Corp.	$100 million	10×
Average			*10.8×*

Cramer Industries / Wilson Boatworks Acquisition

Immediate Integration Needs

* Lock up senior management to employment agreements before close
* Cross-train sales forces on new product lines
* Immediate marketing—product visibility
* Transition services—payroll routines, cash availability, bank accounts, tax reporting, legal reviews established concurrent with closing
* Transfer Wilson employees to Cramer benefits

Midterm Goals

* Take cost out of Wilson manufacturing process—introduce Cramer streamlined approach
* Consider redundant employees on front end
* Expansion of Cramer products into Canada/Mexico via Wilson distribution network
* Consolidation of corporate office functions—tax, environmental, legal, and so on
* Off-site event to begin cultural integration

Risk and Opportunities

* Assimilation of Wilson "family" culture into Cramer
* Ability to maintain margins in increasingly competitive market
* Loss of key sales personnel postacquisition
* Integration challenges facing consolidation of production facilities
* Loss of focus on "lower-end" customers as Cramer pushes Wilson customers up market

Next Steps

* Formal board of directors approval by March 31
* Employment agreements negotiated with key employees by May 1
* Asset purchase agreement negotiated by May 15
* Contract signing, funded on May 31
* Press Release, PR Campaign begins on June 1
* "Kick-off meeting" with new employees on June 5 at Hyatt in Boston, MA

a specific number. The multiple areas of further due diligence should have been taken care of at this time, so that a firm commitment can be made, and any remaining contingencies need to be clearly laid out.

This bid will also normally include a listing of the major protections that a buyer will ask for from the seller. These guarantees, referred to as "representations and indemnities," give the buyer assurance that what is being purchased is really there. For example, a standard seller representation is that the seller has "clear and valid title" to the assets being purchased—that is, the seller owns the assets and has the right to sell them. Sellers want early identification of what will be required of them when they get to contract negotiation. In rare cases, the extent to which buyers want contract protections can sway a firm's decision on whom to sell to irrespective of the purchase price: All else being equal, the firm will choose the buyer that asks for the least number of seller guarantees.

An increasingly debated topic is the presence of "material adverse change" (MAC) clauses in purchase agreements. These clauses give the buyer the ability to walk away from the commitment if something "out of the ordinary" happens to the target between the time of commitment and the time of closing that has a material negative impact on the assets being purchased. Such events include acts of war, natural disasters, terrorism, or other events that do not occur in the normal course of business.

These clauses have historically been relatively standard, with not a lot of discussion about the specific terms and conditions. However, September 11, 2001, changed that. This attack had a material adverse impact on many companies and was particularly problematic for transactions that were in process on September 11. All of a sudden, the chance of a terrorist attack or other catastrophe became much more foreseeable. As a result, sellers have tried to tighten MAC clauses since then. In other words, the ability of buyers to back away from transactions has been more severely limited.

In fact, buyers that have insisted on more standard MAC clauses have lost transactions to those that are willing to be more aggressive. Once again, this is a very fine balance. Buyers need to be sure that they understand the properties being purchased and the significant risk imposed by entering into a deal without being protected by a comprehensive MAC clause. In many cases, it may not make sense for a buyer to proceed without these protections.

See Exhibit 7-2 for an example of a final bid letter, along with an explanation of major sections.

EXHIBIT 7-2

Sample Final Bid Letter

Dryden Robotics purchase of Sadie Industries

PLEASE NOTE THAT THIS IS AN EXAMPLE ONLY. ANY ACTUAL BID LETTER SHOULD BE REVIEWED AND APPROVED BY YOUR COMPANY'S LEGAL COUNSEL.

December 31, 2005

Ms. Cindy Wilson
Senior V.P. and CFO
Sadie Industries
130 Guilford St.
Columbus, OH   22122

Dear Ms. Wilson:

This letter replaces all previous correspondence regarding the acquisition of Sadie Industries and is prepared in accordance with instructions set forth in Arco Investment Bank's bid instructions dated December 1, 2005. This letter (1) includes a final purchase price for all of the current and ongoing operations of Sadie Industries ("Sadie"), (2) summarizes the primary assumptions on which the Dryden Robotics ("Dryden") bid is based, (3) provides a preliminary plan for the employees and organization of Sadie once the acquisition is completed, and (4) outlines the principal assumptions on which Dryden's bid is based and how these assumptions will be reflected in a final purchase agreement.

1. *Businesses to Be Acquired*
    Dryden's bid is for Sadie's complete Research and Development Group in Skanka, OH; its manufacturing facility in Trenton, NJ; and seven distribution centers located throughout North America.

    (Provides a description of the businesses to be acquired.)

2. *Purchase Price*
    The aggregate purchase price Dryden is prepared to pay is $175 million, plus assumption of all outstanding indebtedness on the date of close. In calculating this purchase price, Dryden has assumed that the net assets (defined as total assets less all liabilities, excluding all outstanding indebtedness) of Sadie as of September 30 are $152 million as represented by Sadie's 10-Q and audited by Hillman and Co. The total purchase price of $175 million comprises this net asset value of $152 million plus a premium of $23 million to Sadie's net asset value.

    At the time of closing of this transaction, contemplated to be March 1, 2006, Sadie will deliver a minimum of $150 million in net asset value. Should the value of net assets fall below $150 million ("asset floor"), as audited by a mutually agreed independent accounting firm, then the amount of the defined premium of $23 million will be reduced by 5 percent for each $1.0 million of value short of the $150 million asset floor.

(Continued)

EXHIBIT 7-2

Continued

(Describes the purchase price agreed to be paid and what this price is based on. Purchase price is based on the net assets of the target at the time of purchase plus a specified premium to book value.)

3. *Assumptions Underlying Purchase Price*

Dryden's bid is based on (1) materials provided in the Sadie data room visited on November 10 to 15, 2005, (2) the offering memorandum prepared by Arco Investment Bank dated September 15, 2005, (3) oral and written representations made by Sadie and its investment bankers during the due diligence process, and (4) financial projections prepared by Sadie and delivered to Dryden on October 1, 2005. Dryden will ask Sadie to make certain representations about the accuracy of these data, the ownership of the existing operations, compliance with laws, and the absence of material undisclosed liabilities in the definitive purchase agreement to be negotiated on signing of this letter.

(Requests that the seller represent that the data provided in the due diligence were accurate and fair. These representations will be made in the final asset purchase agreement between buyer and seller.)

4. *Noncompetition*

Upon closing, Dryden will request that Sadie not enter into any operations similar to the businesses being acquired by Dryden for a period of three years after the agreed-upon closing date. Businesses deemed to be similar to the purchased businesses would be defined in the definitive asset purchase agreement entered into between Sadie and Dryden. Such noncompete agreement will include a defined period in which Sadie will be prevented from hiring Dryden employees.

(Requests that the seller not reenter the business that it is selling. In other words, the buyer would not want the seller to establish identical operations to compete with the business being sold. This is normally a heavily negotiated part of the purchase/sale agreement, as the definition of the target's "business and industry" can be difficult to specify in writing.)

5. *Structure*

Dryden proposes to purchase 100 percent of the stock of Sadie Corporation and will assume liabilities of the company outstanding at the date of close.

(Discusses the form of the transaction as an asset or stock purchase.)

6. *Timing*

Dryden is prepared to proceed immediately to negotiation of a final purchase agreement upon signing of this document. We anticipate that such negotiations, along with the required regulatory approvals, will take 30 to 45 days from signing this agreement. This bid is contingent on Dryden's ability to access a minimum of $100 million in the public debt markets. Dryden will resolve and remove this contingency within 30 days upon signing of this proposal.

EXHIBIT 7-2

Continued

(Outlines a deal timeline and contingencies to closing, such as regulatory approval, buyer management approval, or the ability of the buyer to raise the necessary funds to close the deal. The buyer's bid becomes less competitive as more and more contingencies are added the deal. Sellers want as close to a "no outs" agreement as they can get.)

7. *Integration Plans*
Current employees and operations of Dryden will be evaluated immediately after closing of this transaction. Although specific plans have not been established, we view the operations and employees of Sadie as a critical part of our acquisition strategy, and Sadie will remain a stand-alone, independent entity within Dryden Robotics.

[Describes the buyer's preliminary plans with respect to target employees and locations. This could range from keeping everyone in place (normally preferred by the seller) to removal and replacement of all current employees at the target. This part of the letter is nonbinding and is subject to change as the buyer evaluates the target and its needs postacquisition.]

This letter is not meant to create a legally binding commitment. Such a commitment would be achieved only upon negotiation and execution of a definitive purchase agreement signed between the two parties. We have enjoyed getting to know the people and operations of Sadie Industries and look forward to progressing on this important transaction.

Dryden Robotics

By: Frances Smith, CFO
Dated: December 31, 2005

MANAGING THE PROCESS

It is not hard to see how critical the business development leader's role is, given the complexities of due diligence and bidding. A deal can die at any point in the process—often for the wrong reasons. The business development leader must be the advocate for the deal, while staying objective about the risks and rewards of the transaction. At the same time, the business development leader must manage the due diligence team so that it works well with the target and leaves a positive impression on the company's potential future partners. The interpersonal skills and ability to manage multiple priorities required and the need to negotiate with various internal and external constituencies make this an extremely demanding position. As we will see in Chapter 12, because of these unique demands and the frequent exposure to senior management, the business development role is a great training ground for future company leaders.

CHAPTER 7 SUMMARY

1. Business development professionals are responsible for summarizing the findings of the due diligence team and providing a balanced view of the transaction to senior management and/or the board of directors for approval. They also keep the deal team on track and try to facilitate a give and take of information.

2. Deal review presentations can be written or oral, depending on the size of the deal and the formality of the buyer's process. A meeting is a much better forum for an exchange of ideas and discussion and resolution of critical issues.

3. Written presentations should include an executive summary, planned purchase price, return analysis, risks, mitigants, deal timing, and integration plan.

4. Final bid letters need to be crafted very carefully. Business development leaders want to present their offer in the best light; however, they must take care not to overcommit the buyer until all the contingencies have been satisfied. See the example of a final bid letter in Exhibit 7-2.

5. Sellers provide buyers with representations and indemnities about their legal claim to the target being sold, the accuracy of historical financial statements, and other factors that the buyer relied upon in determining its bid.

6. The best business development professionals will present a balanced view of the transaction to senior management, highlighting both the positives and the risks of the transaction.

CHAPTER 7 CASE STUDIES

CASE STUDY 7-1

LOCKHEED MARTIN ACQUIRES TITAN CORP.[1]

It seemed to make great sense. Lockheed Martin Company, a major defense contractor, proposed a $2.4 billion purchase of Titan Corporation, a smaller firm with many synergies in the same industry. However, only a few months after the proposal was announced, Lockheed uncovered questions about possible improper overseas payments that Titan consultants may have made, leading the U.S. Department of Justice to open an investigation.

Then, a Titan employee became associated with the alleged U.S. abuse of prisoners during the invasion of Iraq in 2003–2004. While the employee's activities in Iraq did not stall the deal—Lockheed's CFO told an analyst conference that they "were not significant to our strategic decision" to acquire Titan—the foreign-payments situation certainly did. Upon discovery of these payments, Lockheed reduced its proposed purchase price by $200 million and made a settlement between Titan and the government a condition to closing the transaction.

However, why didn't the due diligence process uncover these issues? It was only during the planning process of the deal, after the price was initially agreed to, that these improper payments were uncovered and discussed. This required Lockheed to renegotiate a purchase price that had already been settled. Although such publicly sensitive issues in deals are rare, this case highlights the importance of a sound, balanced approach to due diligence. Buyers are in a much better position if they know about issues up front and deal with them head on, rather than having to revisit purchase price discussions later because an issue was missed.

CASE STUDY 7-2

BROOKTROUT TECHNOLOGY[2]

Brooktrout Technology, based in Needham, Massachusetts, uses three forms of due diligence to ensure a comprehensive analysis of target companies: business, legal, and financial due diligence. CFO Bob Leahy states, "As we get closer to actually doing the deal, we bring in our organizational heads. They ask different questions and help us uncover things that normal due diligence wouldn't uncover."

However, it hasn't always worked out. In the mid-1990s, for example, Brooktrout bought a small unit of a company. Leahy recalls, "We were given information in due diligence about how to build these products.

But lo and behold, when we tried to make the stuff, it didn't match what we had been told."

Leahy figures that the target company had not kept its documentation up-to-date, and had been relying on subcontractors to build the products. "It took us a good six to nine months to sort through it," he says.

To make matters worse, there was no recourse to the seller. A technical analysis of the project plans by an engineering team during the due diligence phase could have uncovered these relatively obvious issues so that either a) a price adjustment could have been proposed or b) requiring an update of the documentation as a condition of closing the deal. Potential buyers have some leverage over sellers up until contracts are signed and money has changed hands. However, once this happens, leverage shifts to the seller – they now have their money.

NOTES

1. Roy Harris, "Won't Get Fooled Again," *CFO Magazine*, July 1, 2004.
2. Ibid.

Final Bid Strategies/ Structuring the Deal

By this point in the process, due diligence has been completed, internal approval is in place, and all questions have been answered. The tendency of the deal team might be to relax at this point. However, if you are lucky enough to be selected for the next round, the real work involved in the deal is only beginning. In fact, business development professionals can often add the most value at this late stage of the project. In many cases, there still may be a gap between the seller's expectations or requirements and what the buyer is willing to provide. An experienced M&A team can be invaluable in finding creative structures to close this gap, satisfy the objectives of each party, and keep the deal on track. Many deals have been saved at the last minute by flexibility on the part of both buyer and seller, allowing them to meet their requirements in different ways. These "expectation gaps" generally fall into one of the following categories:

- Purchase price differences
- Timing requirements
- Deal structure
- Tax treatment
- Target employee protections
- Other unique circumstances

Deal teams can create a win-win environment for buyer and seller by considering such variables as the form of payment, the type of acquisition vehicle used, and the form of the acquisition.

The purpose of final-bid requests by the seller is often to squeeze out incremental purchase price increases or other considerations in exchange for the final award of the deal. During these times, it can be especially difficult for the deal team to maintain its composure and do the right thing for its company. Most of the individuals on the deal team have worked weeks, even months, on the transaction. In many cases, their incentive compensation is tied to getting the deal done. It takes a lot of discipline and appropriate senior management oversight to keep the team objective and focused.

CLOSING A PURCHASE PRICE GAP

More sophisticated buyers have found ways to close the gap between what the seller wants for the property and what the buyer is willing to pay. Through a flexible purchase price calculation, earnouts, royalties, fees, and other such elements, the gap can be bridged in a way that satisfies both sides.

Determining Purchase Price—Stock Method

In many larger public deals, the transaction proposed results in an exchange of the seller's shares for those of the buyer. In other words, each shareholder in the target will receive a certain number of the buyer's shares for each of her or his current shares. The ratio of the number of shares currently held to the number of shares to be received from the buyer is called the *exchange ratio*. For example, when Hewlett-Packard agreed to buy Compaq in September 2001, each Compaq shareholder was given 0.63 Hewlett-Packard share for each share of Compaq that he or she currently held. The value of a Hewlett-Packard share was determined to be higher than that of a Compaq share, so Compaq shareholders received only a fraction (63 percent) of a share of Hewlett-Packard for each Compaq share. The stock method is relatively straightforward and easy for investors to understand. The purchase price is tied to something they recognize—their own stock value. It is also easy to determine the relative values of each party to the transaction.

One potential issue arises in situations where there is a long time between announcing a deal and the ultimate closing of the deal. This delay can result from contract negotiations, remaining due diligence items, antitrust scrutiny, or a waiting period for regulatory approval. The problem arises when the relative value of the firms' shares changes between announcement and closing. If a fixed exchange ratio is agreed to up front and the relative values change, the deal could be unfair to one of the parties.

Most contracts will include an adjustment clause to account for changes in these relative values. If the trading values of the two companies stay within a specified band, the exchange ratio agreed to up front will remain in effect. If the values trade outside this band, an adjustment mechanism comes into play. This mechanism can be anything from a simple restatement of the exchange ratio to a full reopening of the negotiations around the deal.

Determining Purchase Price—Asset Method

Another type of purchase price calculation can be tied to the balance sheet value of the target company. Exhibit 8-1 provides data on the purchase of Jean Inc. by Grey Industries. The steps in determining purchase price under a balance sheet method include the following:

1. Obtain the target's balance sheet. The target needs to generate a balance sheet at the date of the due diligence or the announcement of the deal. This may be somewhat difficult for the target because M&A announcements and closings rarely coincide with the end of an accounting period. The target's finance staff must often estimate assets and liabilities as of this artificial interim period rather than at the normal closing at the end of a quarter or a year.

2. Calculate net investment. Calculate the total asset value of the target less its nondebt liabilities. This is referred to as the "net investment" of the target, or the real value being purchased. Note that it is assumed that the target's debt will be either assumed as is or paid off by the buyer at the closing, so that the seller has no remaining obligation. In the case of Jean Inc., the net investment equaled $2.1 billion on the date the agreement was announced.

3. Negotiate the premium. Most sellers will want a premium (i.e., a gain) if they are to sell the company. In this case, Jean and Grey negotiated a $600 million premium, or 29 percent over Jean's book value, to close the deal. Premiums will generally depend on the quality of the property being sold, the number of bidders interested, and the overall desirability of the target.

E X H I B I T   8-1

Grey Industries Buys Jean Inc.—Purchase Price Calculation (in millions)

Jean Balance Sheet	Nov. 15	Dec. 31
Cash	$100	$150
Accounts Receivable	1,100	700
Inventory	500	100
Fixed Assets	700	100
Other	100	120
Total Assets	$2,500	$1,170
Liabilities		
Accounts Payable	$300	$200
Accrued Liabilities	100	300
Net Investment	**$2,100**	**$670**

Purchase Price Calculation		
	Nov. 15	Dec. 31
Net Investment	$2,100	$670
Fixed Premium	600	600
Total Price	$2,700	$1,270
Premium %	29%	90%

4. Calculate the purchase price. The total purchase price equals the net investment of $2.1 billion plus a premium of $600 million, for a total price of $2.7 billion.

5. Adjust at time of closing. A contract provision is necessary to adjust for potential changes in value between when a deal is awarded and when it closes. For example, Jean's net value at November 15 was $2.1 billion. However, because of a reduction in accounts receivable, inventory, and fixed assets and higher liabilities, net investment had declined to $670 million by December 31. The balance sheet method automatically adjusts the purchase price for this change in value. The new purchase price at closing (December 31) is $670 million of net investment plus a $600 million premium, or $1,270 million, making it a fairer deal for the buyer than the original price of $2.2 billion given the change in asset balances.

As with the stock method, there is normally a band indicating how much the target value can change without a complete renegotiation of the purchase price being necessary. As noted previously, the purchase price for Jean was automatically adjusted to reflect the change in the value of the company from signing to closing. However, such a dramatic change in value can also change the *per-*

centage premium paid. At November 15, the buyer's premium was $600/$2,100, or 29 percent. Because of the decrease in Jean's value, this percentage had increased to 90 percent ($600/$670) by December 31. Therefore, although the formula technically works, the buyer's premium has gone up substantially on a percentage basis. This is why there is normally some range within which the price will not change; however, if there is a dramatic change in value between signing and closing, a renegotiation of the purchase price is allowed. In the case of Jean, Grey Industries would certainly ask for a premium reduction at the time of closing.

EARNOUTS, ROYALTIES, AND OTHER GAP CLOSERS

Earnouts

There may still be an expectation gap concerning price regardless of the calculation method deployed. An "earnout" clause is a form of incremental purchase price that can help to bridge the gap, particularly when

- The seller or the seller's management team will continue to influence the operations of the target postacquisition.
- The seller has very aggressive financial projections for the target, such as "hockey stick" projections (see Exhibit 3-3).
- A private or family-run business is being sold. The sellers may not want the entire purchase price up front for economic, tax, or estate planning reasons.
- All bids received are very close in price, and there is little other distinction among the bids submitted.

Under an earnout structure, some percentage (usually greater than 50 percent) is paid to the seller when the deal closes. Additional consideration will also be paid to the seller over time if certain performance hurdles are met. These hurdles are normally tied to the annual financial results of the target postclosing.

Exhibit 8-2 contains additional information on Grey Industries' purchase of Jean Inc. In this example, Grey lowered the initial premium paid from $600 million (Exhibit 8-1) to $300 million. The remaining premium of $300 million will be paid to Jean Inc. only if certain performance thresholds for EBIT (earnings before interest and taxes) are achieved. For example, if Jean's

E X H I B I T   8-2

Grey Industries Buys Jean Inc.–Earnout Formula

Jean Inc.	2004 act	2005 act	2006 est	2007 est	2008 est
Revenues	$100	$150	$165	$185	$200
EBIT	35	42	50	58	65
Net Income	8	10	12	15	20

Earnout Formula:

- Premium of $300 million paid at close
- Additional premium paid out as follows
  - $100 million if 2006 EBIT greater than $50 million
  - $100 million if 2007 EBIT greater than $58 million
  - $100 million if 2008 EBIT greater than $65 million
- Total "potential" premium equals $600 million

actual EBIT for 2006 is greater than $50 million, then Grey must pay another $100 million of purchase price. If actual EBIT is $50 million or less, no incremental payment is made. Similarly, incremental payments of $100 million might be owed in 2007 and 2008 if the minimum EBIT levels are achieved. Although earnouts generally protect buyers, since the incremental purchase price is contingent on the target's being successful after it has been bought, they can be used by a buyer to pay a little more for a deal, and pay it only if the seller achieves the projections it forecasts. The pro and cons of an earnout formula are summarized here.

Pros

- An earnout is a great way to bridge the purchase price gap between buyer and seller.
- It gives the buyer the ability to see whether a target's aggressive financial projections are achieved before making a final decision on how much to pay out.
- The interests of the buyer and the seller are more aligned postclosing. Each has an interest in maximizing the value of the target.
- The seller might be more realistic in its financial projections because it will have to deliver them in order to get paid any contingent value.
- Getting cash over time rather than up front can have a big tax advantage for some sellers.

Cons

- The seller may not view the structure as favorably because the entire purchase price is not paid up front, but is contingent on future performance.
- The calculation can be very complicated. Earnouts can be based on revenue, EBIT, net income, or many other financial variables. The calculation of these amounts should be agreed to in detail up front so that confusion does not arise later. It is very difficult to completely define in the contract how to calculate these values.
- Sellers will often blame buyers if the forecasts do not live up to expectations. They might argue that the buyer's policies, procedures, or management team caused the target to perform worse than expected. This can lead to litigation and a buyer's paying contingent consideration even when the seller's performance criteria have not been met.
- Either side (buyer or seller) can attempt to manage the results to achieve a desired outcome. For example, assume that the acquired company is way ahead of its targets in year 1. In order to maximize the earnout payment, the target company would have an incentive to slow down its growth so that it just hits the performance metric and apply the additional results to the next year's target. Alternately, assume that the acquired company misses its year one target and gets little/no earnout, but then far exceeds its year two target. Sellers will often ask for a "claw back" provision, meaning that they can claw back some of the earnout forfeited in year one because year two was so successful. The exact calculation methodology needs to be spelled out in detail in the earnout agreement.
- The earnout is normally calculated on an accounting rather than an economic basis. Contracts usually contain an audit clause, specifying that a third-party auditor will come in to audit the seller's books and records to determine whether the threshold targets have been met. The benefit of this is that each side can feel comfortable with the calculation and the incremental purchase price paid. However, cash flow, internal rates of return, and other such measures tend to be a better proxy for the actual economic performance of the target. Using accounting numbers, although convenient, can lead to perverse economic decisions on the earnout.

Royalties, Consulting Agreements, and Employment Agreements

An ongoing royalty payment from buyer to seller is another way to have a higher purchase price than is paid up front. For example, rather than paying for a brand name up front, the buyer may pay an annual royalty fee to the seller based on a percentage of actual revenues earned in each accounting year. The amount of this royalty could be tied to performance or could be a standard annual amount. This arrangement has the benefit of more closely tying the interests of the buyer with those of the seller, as each party has an incentive to maximize the revenue of the target postclose. However, care must be given to ensure that the royalty agreement has substance and is accounted for correctly under GAAP.

Consulting or employment contracts with the former owners are another method commonly used to defer purchase price and make it more contingent. Under this arrangement, a former owner or employee of the target agrees to consult/advise the company after the deal has closed. This can be very beneficial in small, family-owned companies where the buyer has not had time to learn the business and to get to know the people. The seller's employees also might feel more comfortable knowing that the person they trust, their former employer, is still around to help in the transition to a new parent.

Royalties, consulting agreements, and employment agreements also have the benefit of reducing the immediate payment that must be made by the buyer. Depending on the seller's tax situation, they could also defer a portion of the gain on sale of the property as payments are made over the term of the agreement. However, strict care must be taken to follow all applicable book and tax accounting regulations in all of these areas. The form of the agreement must reflect the true economic substance of the underlying agreement or it should not be done.

TIMING CONSTRAINTS

In certain circumstances, the time required to close a deal can be as important as the price agreed to. Take the U.S. savings and loan bailout by the U.S. government's Resolution Trust Company (RTC) in the late 1980s. The U.S. government ended up in possession of many thrifts and savings and loans that it needed to liquidate quickly and realize cash on. The RTC was brought in to *quickly* find buyers for these financial institutions before further damages were incurred. Buyers who could pay cash quickly had an advantage over those with funding contingencies or who did not have the financing available at close. Having a motivated seller is normally a good thing for the buying party because it can get a lower purchase price or other concessions from the seller if it is able to meet the tight time commitments.

FORM OF ACQUISITION VEHICLE— ASSET VERSUS STOCK DEAL

The legal structure of the agreement and the form in which the consideration is paid can have big implications for both buyer and seller. The first issue to be negotiated is whether the buyer is purchasing the assets or the stock of the business entity. An asset purchase can be 100 percent of the seller's assets or some portion of these assets. A stock purchase involves buying the seller's stock, either 100 percent or some other percentage of the outstanding shares. Although both methods can accomplish basically the same thing, a transfer of the business from buyer to seller, the tax and economic risks can be substantially different under each methods.

A main distinction between the two is that, with an asset purchase, the existing shell corporation of the target remains in existence. Some or all of the assets have been sold, but the existing legal entity remains. With a stock purchase however, the target company may no longer exist as a legal entity if 100% of the shares are purchased. The stock of the target may be cancelled, and new shares, those of the new parent (buyer) may be issued. As we will see, this simple difference can have a dramatic impact on the liability of the buyer postclose.

Asset Purchase

With asset purchases, either 100 percent or some portion of the target company can be purchased. As a result, there is much more flexibility to adapt the structure to deal with unique issues than there is with a stock transaction. If the seller is willing, the buyer can purchase only those assets that it wants and leave some assets behind. This can be a big advantage when unique assets are in place. For example, suppose Barkley Inc. was purchasing Hanna Industries and there were certain "environmentally sensitive" assets at Hanna. The buyer would probably not want to purchase those sensitive assets without a guarantee from

Hanna that Hanna would reimburse it for any subsequent losses on these assets. Hanna might argue that it will have "no control" over these assets once the company is sold and therefore no way to mitigate any liability. One way around this issue would be to have Hanna keep the assets—that is, to "carve them out" of the purchase. Hanna could then control the fate of these assets, and Barkley would be relieved of having to deal with them. Such a treatment works only when the assets in question are discrete, separable, and not a core part of the target's operations. If this is not the case, difficult discussions around allocation of risk on these assets need to be held during the contract negotiations.

From a seller's perspective, in an asset deal, it gets to maintain its corporate existence with whatever assets are left behind. It can continue to retain its name unless that is specifically prohibited in the asset purchase agreement. However, a negative side effect is that the seller retains responsibility for liabilities left behind in the seller corporation that have not been specifically assigned to the buyer. This retention of responsibility for liabilities may not be attractive to the seller. Many sellers will say, "I am selling this target to get out of the business; I don't want any more liability." They do not want to retain responsibility for many contingent or undisclosed liabilities after the deal has closed.

A large disadvantage of the asset purchase method is the inability to transfer licenses, patents, and in some cases customers to the new owner without significant effort. Customers may have "change in control" clauses written into their agreements that release them of their obligation if a controlling interest in the target is sold to another party. Licenses, patents, and other technologies do not automatically pass to the buyer; they must be specifically assigned. The time and risk associated with this can cause the target to lose access to valuable technology.

Take the sale of a U.S. commercial airline as an example. With a stock sale, title to its assets would normally pass as part of the stock purchase agreement. However, with an asset deal, each asset must be re-registered with the U.S. Federal Aviation Administration to the new buyer. This can be done only when the aircraft are on the ground—at substantial cost to the airline. The time and effort associated with retitling specific assets is one of the main drawbacks of an asset deal. There also may be state and local transfer taxes on the sale of assets that can add to the overall cost of the transaction and the time required to close.

EXHIBIT 8-3

Asset Purchase Pros and Cons

Buyer	Seller
Pros: • Get only the assets you want • Not responsible for all seller liabilities • "Step up" assets to fair market value • Tax depreciation benefits • Terminate benefit plans/liabilities • Terminate union agreements Cons: • Lose net operating losses and tax credits • Rights to licenses and patents can't be transferred • May need customer consent to change of control	Pros: • Can maintain corporate existence • Retains right to company name • Seller keeps net operating losses, however, what is left to apply them to? Cons: • Gain on sale of assets • Costs associated with the transfer taxes and retitling of assets • Rights to licenses and patents can't be transferred • Potential depreciation recapture when shell is liquidated — deferred taxes will reverse

The tax implications of an asset purchase can be significant, depending on the relative tax position of buyer and seller. The good news is that in an asset purchase, the buyer gets a "step-up" in asset basis. In other words, the buyer's tax basis equals the actual consideration paid to close the deal or the assets' "current market value." This allows the buyer to take more depreciation on these assets over time to offset taxable income generated by the company. However, any net operating losses generated by the target will go away and cannot be applied to offset taxable income in future years, as is possible in a stock deal. Finally, the seller probably faces a larger immediate tax liability when it sells assets for cash. The difference between the cash received and the seller's basis in the asset at the time of sale is considered a taxable gain. This can have a dramatic impact on the after-tax proceeds realized by the seller. See Exhibit 8-3 for a complete listing of the pros and cons of an asset purchase for both buyer and seller.

Stock Purchase

In a stock purchase, the buyer normally purchases up to 100 percent of the target's stock. This can be a much simpler and faster transaction than a purchase of specific assets. Most contracts will carry over to the buyer and will not need to be renegotiated. (Some contracts will contain specific change in control provisions that still require consent.) Assets do not have to be retitled in a new buyer's name, and they are not subject to transfer taxes. Finally, the seller is not hampered by any remaining assets or liability after the deal closes; it is completely out of the business sold.

All liabilities of the seller will be transferred to the buyer in a stock deal unless they are carved out contractually. While sellers normally prefer this type of arrangement for just this reason, a smart buyer will ask for protections against liabilities that exist, but are not known at the time of sale (see Chapter 9). Without these protections, the buyer is responsible for all postclosing liabilities, which could be very significant. Any employee benefit plans or union agreements will also be transferred unless they are specifically addressed in the purchase agreement.

The tax treatment for stock sales generally favors the seller, to the disadvantage of the buyer. In a stock-for-stock exchange (i.e., the seller trades its shares in the target for shares in the buyer), any taxable gains are deferred until the new shares are sold. In other words, there is no tax liability for the seller at the time of the acquisition. The new stock comes over at "carryover basis"; that is, the seller's tax basis in the new shares is the same as the tax basis in the shares being given up, and no current tax obligation is due. At the point when the shares are sold, the tax gain equals the cash ultimately received for these shares less the carryover basis. This can defer the payment of taxes for many years and greatly enhance the economic value of the transaction to the seller.

On the buyer's side, net operating losses of the target can be carried over and used by the new company if the transaction is structured properly. This can often be very helpful when a troubled company is bought by a performing entity. Net operating losses can be applied only to income, income that the target may never have had. However, when the target is combined with a profitable buyer, taxable income to which to apply the tax losses may be present, increasing the target's value to the buyer. Buyers also do not have to incur the time and expense of retitling all of the assets and renegotiating customer and supplier contracts. Once again, the finance team should be consulted to ensure that the structure has substance and is accounted for in compliance with GAAP and IRS regulations.

One of the larger issues for a stock deal buyer occurs when an asset-intensive industry is involved. Because the assets come

E X H I B I T   8-4

Stock Purchase Pros and Cons

Buyer	Seller
Pros: • Faster • Avoids transfer taxes • Net operating losses carry over • Continuity of contract/don't need to negotiate Cons: • Liable for all unknown, unrecorded, undisclosed contingent liabilities • No asset "step-up" — assets come over at historical basis unless 338 election is made • Employment/union agreements come over • Dissenting shareholders have the right to have shares appraised or stay in as minority • Normally can't pick and choose assets	Pros: • Defer taxes • Get stock for stock, taxes not paid until stock is sold — when sold, it is taxed at capital gains rate • All liabilities go to buyer — normally are indemnified for undisclosed liabilities • All assets are sold; none left to sell Cons: • Net operating losses and tax credits no longer available to seller • Have to sell all the assets • If 338 election made, do have a taxable gain

over at the seller's carryover basis, there is no step-up or revalu-ation of the assets to current market value. This causes two signif-icant issues for the buyer:

1. A lower tax basis in these assets and less value to take as a depreciation tax deduction going forward
2. A larger goodwill balance than in an asset deal because of the lower basis in the assets

A complete list of the pros and cons of a stock purchase for both the buyer and the seller is given in Exhibit 8-4.

338H10 Tax Elections

A 338H10 election can be used to mitigate the buyer's multiple tax issues in a stock deal. Buyers who purchase at least 80 percent of the stock of the target can treat the transaction as an asset deal for tax purposes. This allows the buyer to step up the basis of the assets at close and get a tax deduction through depreciation of these assets postclose, while still keeping the protection concern-ing assumption of liabilities inherent in a stock deal. Everything else being equal, a buyer should be willing to pay more to a seller when a 338 election is allowed, because the buyer's ultimate tax liability will be lower and its after-tax return higher. The negotiations for the deal will ultimately determine how these benefits are shared between buyer and seller.

Interplay of Acquisition Form and Purchase Price

The type of structure adopted for the deal can affect the price at which buyer and seller are willing to settle. Given a fixed purchase price, sellers will normally attempt to negotiate the most favorable treatment for themselves. For example, if the seller's tax basis in the assets was very low, it would push for a stock deal to avoid a large taxable gain on day one. If a seller has a large net operating loss that can be applied elsewhere, it might push for an asset deal so that the net operating losses would stay behind with the seller. In a tight auction situation where all the bidders are close on purchase price, a willingness to work with the seller on structure might win the deal. At times, sellers have been known to reject the highest-price bid for a lower price that has their preferred structure. In other words, sellers will look at their *after-tax* returns when evaluating offers.

TYPE OF BUSINESS ORGANIZATION—
TAX IMPLICATIONS

The type of business organization the buyer chooses for the target can have a significant impact on the legal and tax liabilities that the buyer faces postclosing. The requirements and eligibility for each form of agreement are generally governed by the state of incorporation of the buyer. A little time spent up front to form the most efficient legal structure can save buyers multiple headaches and tax liabilities down the road. Most acquirers will consult outside tax and legal counsel to help in this particularly complex part of the M&A process.

Corporations

Although this can vary by state, the most common form of ownership is the corporation, which includes "C corporations," "S Corporations," and limited liability corporations (LLCs). The C corporation is the standard form used by larger companies. These corporations are taxed on their profits at corporate tax rates, and their shareholders are taxed again when cash is paid out in the form of dividends. C corporations are subject to formal requirements such as annual reports, board of directors meetings, and so on.

The largest advantage of C corporations is the protection from personal liability that they provide to the shareholders. The corporation is a separate legal entity, and investors in it are liable only for the amount of equity they have invested in the corporation. In other words, their personal holdings—home, savings accounts, and so on—are not at risk because of the actions of the corporation. The largest disadvantage of C corporations is that the owners are subject to double taxation. As described previously, the profits of a corporation are taxed once at the corporate level and again when they are distributed to the equity owners via cash dividends.

S corporations have been used historically to mitigate this tax liability. S corporations are taxed only once, at the owners' individual rates in their private tax returns. However, S corporations have many restrictive provisions, including limits on the total number of shareholders allowed, the requirement that taxes be paid whether profits are distributed or not, and other IRS regulations. So although the S corporation may be easier for the company initially, problems can develop over time as the company grows and needs to raise additional capital.

Limited liability corporations help to avoid the double taxation without some of the restrictions and recording requirements of S corporations. As with C and S corporations, the owners' liability in an LLC is limited to the amount of their investment in the LLC. The corporate status of an LLC makes it easier for the firm to raise capital and facilitate changes in the equity structure for transfers or sales of equity interests.

Partnerships

Partnerships are a very easy way to establish a business operation. The partners are taxed as individuals on their personal returns, not at the business level, which avoids the double taxation problem that exists with corporations. However, a big issue is that each partner has unlimited liability. This might not seem like a major risk, but having one's personal assets at stake because of the actions of the partnership can have a harsh effect. Take the case of the U.S. public accounting firms, which were historically organized as partnerships. In the late 1980s, shareholders began seeking damages from auditing firms for their failure to detect issues in company clients whose financial performance subsequently deteriorated. The plaintiffs successfully argued that the accounting firms were at least partially responsible for the issuance of misleading financial statements to investors, subsequently resulting in investor losses. To make matters worse, since the firms were organized as partnerships, each partner's personal assets (home, car, savings, and so on) were at risk because of the actions of other partners in the group. This sequence of events caused a gradual transition to LLCs for many accounting, law, and other professional services firms.

Other, less dramatic issues involving partnerships include the following.

- Individual partnership units are not liquid. The partnership must be dissolved and reestablished when any partner leaves the firm.
- The resulting illiquidity of the partnership interests can make it difficult for the partnership to raise money or grow.

EMPLOYEE PROTECTIONS

A buyer's plans for target employees can have an effect on whether its bid is accepted, particularly in a smaller family-run business. Some sellers will feel a great sense of responsibility to their employees and want to know that they will be well cared for after the purchase. They might even insist that key employees be given long-term employment agreements before they are willing to close the deal. Negotiations on how to treat target employees can be long and complicated. On the one hand, most buyers will want to make their own mark on the target to ensure that planned synergies are achieved. However, too much change can scare away the seller before the purchase or result in turnover in target employees after the purchase.

Requests for bids will normally include a section on the buyer's plans for the target's employees after the deal closes. Although it is normally not binding, this language forces the buyer to think about its integration plans and gives the seller a feel for how its current employees will be treated. As we will see in Chapter 10, "The Importance of Integration," in a "consolidating" acquisition, there are usually many cutbacks and layoffs of staff. In these situations, the buyer walks a fine line between being honest about its plans for employees in its bid letter and trying to submit an attractive bid. Some sellers may prefer a "financial" buyer (a private equity group, hedge fund, or similar institution) to a "strategic" buyer (a current business in the same industry as the target or a related industry). Normally, a financial buyer is more dependent on the target's personnel to operate the business than a strategic buyer, which knows the business well and can find cost synergies by eliminating target personnel.

RISK ALLOCATION

We will discuss contract representations and indemnities in Chapter 9. However, an overriding principle is that the more protections a buyer wants, the less desirable its bid is to the seller. Most of the negotiation at the end of the transaction involves a discussion of risk allocation between the buyer and the seller. For example, who should be responsible for an environmental issue that was present at the time the deal closed but was not apparent until a regulatory agency discovered it one year after closing? Sellers will argue that they don't need to protect buyers from these types of issues because

- Buyers have already completed due diligence and should know the company and its risk well by this time.
- Sellers are selling because they want to be out of the business. Having contingent liabilities (i.e., guarantees that they have made to the buyer) hanging over their heads for years is not optimal.
- The buyer will operate the company postclosing and is in the best position to understand and mitigate issues that surface after close.

Buyers will argue that they should have complete protection for these types of issues because

- The buyer had a limited due diligence period, with access to data and employees restricted by the seller.
- Buyers should not be responsible for issues that arose while the seller owned the company. Postclosing issues should be borne by the buyer; however, those that arose while the seller owned the company, even if they were not apparent at the time of closing, should be the seller's obligation.

A seller's perception of its level of risk under various bid proposals can certainly have an impact on which buyer it selects.

Buyers must balance how much they want to close the deal against the amount of risk they are willing to live with going forward.

KEEPING THE DEAL ON TRACK

Each deal tends to have a life of its own, with unique issues arising throughout the process. In some cases, certain assets or categories of assets become problematic to the buyer during due diligence or thereafter. However, the seller might have an honest difference of opinion on these issues that could put an overall deal in jeopardy. For example, assume that Nicketuck Inc. was purchasing a $5.0 billion manufacturing division from NANA Finance. During due diligence, Nicketuck's environmental team discovered several underground oil tanks at a remote plant site. Nicketuck's deal team thought there was a real risk that these tanks had leaked and could pose environmental liability postclosing. NANA argued that the tanks were fine and that they had just passed an environmental study by the regulatory authorities. NANA could not help it if Nicketuck's diligence team felt differently. The deal was at a stalemate because of this issue.

One potential solution would be to structure the acquisition as an asset deal and to "carve out" the affected assets, that is, leave the remote plant with NANA. If NANA were confident of its position, it should not be worried about subsequent liability. Nicketuck could buy only the assets that it was comfortable with and leave the others behind. Although this takes a fair amount of structuring and negotiation, it can often be worth it to save a deal that would not otherwise get done.

LAST-MINUTE REQUESTS

Smart sellers, or their investment bankers, know that the bid finalists have made a substantial investment of time and money in the project by this point. They may try to take advantage of their leverage, particularly in a competitive bidding situation where multiple buyers have made it to the final round. It is somewhat like buying a house. You get that call from the selling broker that your price is "close," but it is not the highest bid. The broker asks you to raise your bid; however, the amount of the competing bid is not disclosed. Especially in larger M&A transactions, the tendency is to say, "What is another $1 million to own this $100 million asset?"

Deal teams need to guard against being "incrementalized" to an amount that does not make sense. All of the individual issues mentioned in this chapter—target employment, contract terms, closing purchase price, and so on—can be negotiated by the buyer at the closing table. It really comes down to which party has the leverage. In a robust auction with many potential buyers, sellers have the advantage. However, in the more unusual cases where there is a motivated seller and only one buyer, the buyer has significant leverage to manage these areas.

CHAPTER 8 SUMMARY

1. Experienced M&A teams can use various bidding strategies and deal structures to save a deal that otherwise might not get done.
2. Expectation gaps that arise between buyers and sellers include purchase price differences, deal structures, timing requirements, taxes, treatment of target employees, and other circumstances unique to each deal.
3. A stock purchase price is based on a simple exchange of the target's shares for shares in the buyer. The ratio of shares held to shares received from the buyer is called the exchange ratio and can adjust over time.
4. A balance sheet purchase approach uses the target's balance sheet plus a purchase premium to calculate the total purchase price. This method automatically adjusts for changes in the target's net asset value between signing and closing.
5. Earnouts can be used to close a gap between the seller's price expectation and what a buyer is willing to pay. It is a form of contingent consideration that is paid only if the target meets certain performance targets postacquisition.
6. Earnouts can more closely align the interests of the buyer with those of the seller, as both are motivated to grow the company postclosing. However, legal issues can arise if the acquisition does not turn out as planned.
7. Royalties, consulting agreements, and employment contracts are other methods for providing a contingent purchase price to the seller over time. Strict care should

    be taken to make sure that the accounting for these agreements is in accordance with GAAP.

8. Some sellers may be willing to accept a lower purchase price if buyers can satisfy their tight timing commitments.

9. Asset and stock purchases are different methods of transferring ownership of the target to the buyer. Each form of acquisition has certain advantages and disadvantages for the buyer and the seller.

10. Asset purchases generally provide more flexibility for buyer and seller to carve out assets that are a concern and still close the transaction.

11. Stock purchases can allow for a simpler transaction, without the need to retitle individual assets and the effects of a change in control on customer and supplier agreements. However, buyers may be more reluctant to enter into these deals because of the assumption of seller liabilities postclose.

12. A 338H10 election allows the buyer in a stock sale to treat it as an asset sale for tax purposes, providing significant tax benefits.

13. Buyers who show a willingness to work with sellers on deal structure may have an advantage in competitive auction situations.

14. Some sellers are very concerned about how their employees will be treated postclose. Sharing plans for integration and working to accommodate sellers' hot buttons can help soothe these concerns.

15. Final contract negotiations will often center around an allocation of risk between buyer and seller for known and unknown liabilities.

16. Carving sensitive assets out of the transaction can often solve differences of opinion between buyer and seller and put a deal back on track.

17. Deal teams for the buyers need to be careful about last-minute seller requests. They need to balance their strong desire to get a deal done with a healthy amount of skepticism about the deal.

Legal, Regulatory, and Other Issues

A business development professional's ability to manage the legal and regulatory functions can have a major impact on (1) getting a tough deal closed, rather than walking away, and (2) ensuring that the asset/stock purchase agreement contains adequate protections for the buyer against unexpected postclosing events. As in many other areas, the M&A professional walks a fine line, trying to ensure that insignificant issues don't derail the deal, while still maintaining a balanced perspective on items that justify attention. Efficient deal teams develop a sense of trust and perspective between the business development leader and both inside and external legal counsel to work through difficult issues. This chapter will discuss best practices in working with the legal function and also highlight particularly sensitive issues in the legal, regulatory, and accounting areas.

Entire textbooks have been written on legal issues as they relate to the M&A profession. For purposes of this text, we will outline the main objectives of the legal process in an M&A context and certain critical areas that have arisen in recent years.

I. LEGAL ISSUES

A. Inside versus Outside Counsel

The size, complexity, and timing of the deal normally dictate whether the team includes the buyer's in-house counsel, outside legal counsel, or both. Many firms prefer to "outsource" the legal work because

- Buyers may not have enough internal resources to work on the M&A project and handle their normal job responsibilities as well.
- Outside legal counsel may have expertise in particular industries or in the M&A process as a whole. M&A is a relatively specialized area of the law, so having the right representation is critical for protecting the buyer's rights.
- Having an outside counsel provides an independent negotiator. Discussions surrounding legal protections in the asset purchase agreement can often be the most difficult part of the process. Having a "third-party" legal team do the negotiating can help the buyer save face and mitigate bad feelings at the target after closing.
- Environmental, tax, Employee Retirement Income Security Act (ERISA), and other issues may arise for which the expertise of an outside firm is required. Outside legal firms will often provide opinions on how a court or a regulatory body would act on a particular issue or set of facts. This can be a very important addition to the legal due diligence, identifying potential issues that need to be handled in the purchase agreement.

The biggest detriment to using an outside firm is cost. Billing rates for senior partners at national firms can be $1,000 or more an hour. As the leader of the project team, the business development manager needs to set a budget and keep the legal team from spending excessive time on minor issues. However, proper perspective is again required. A few more dollars spent in the legal due diligence or contract negotiations can prevent massive dollar losses later.

B. Stock versus Asset Deals

As described in Chapter 8, there are two methods that can be used to transfer ownership in the company: stock purchase and asset purchase. With a stock purchase, the buyer purchases all or some percentage of the outstanding shares of the target corporation. This method is simpler to use and is normally most advantageous to the seller from a tax perspective. With an asset deal, a buyer can purchase all the assets of the target or only those assets that it wishes to own. It provides considerable flexibility to carve out undesired assets and handle particular issues involved in the deal. The main objective of transferring an interest in the target company from seller to buyer can be accomplished using either of these methods.

C. Elements of a Stock/Asset Purchase Agreement

Appendix C provides a complete example of an asset purchase agreement, and Appendix D provides an example of a stock purchase agreement. However, each contract will be different because of the following variables:

- *Type of industry involved*. In some industries, there may be sensitive areas that need to be addressed contractually. For example, the sale of an oil refinery may require substantial contractual coverage of environmental issues involving the target company that might be of concern.
- *Public versus private transaction*. Additional disclosures involving the public filing requirements, Sarbanes-Oxley, status of internal controls, treatment of public shareholders, and so on may make a sale of a public company more complicated than a sale of a small private company.
- *Amount of due diligence allowed*. In general, the less due diligence the buyer has been allowed to carry out, the more assurances it will want about what the seller has represented to it. These assurances can add considerable complexity to the asset/stock purchase agreement.
- *Issues discovered in due diligence*. The purchase agreement is a great place to cover issues uncovered during due diligence where the buyer has specific concerns about the target company.
- *Size of the deal*. In general, larger deals will justify longer purchase agreements. However, a small, private transaction with unique aspects can also be considerably challenging to document.
- *Contingent purchase price*. Earnouts, royalties, and noncompete agreements can be especially hard to document because of the very specific nature of the agreement. Careful and detailed documentation up front can prevent contract disputes down the road when earnouts or royalties are scheduled to be paid.

The following general areas are included in most purchase agreements.

1. Definitions

Each contract will normally start with definitions of the terms and conditions to be used in the document. A description of the specific legal parties to the agreement, the business being sold, the date of the sale, unique assets or liabilities, and other such information is normally included to clarify the transaction for the reader.

2. List of Exhibits

Detailed information such as explanations of all intellectual property owned by the target, a list of material contracts, specific assets and liabilities, contingent obligations, licenses, and other such data will normally be provided as schedules to the contract rather than in the body. An index of these exhibits is normally included up front.

3. Purchase Price

The number of shares (in a stock purchase) or the assets (in an asset purchase) to be sold and the price to be paid need to be defined clearly in the purchase agreement. Because of potential time lapses between the signing of the contracts and the ultimate funding of the deal, there needs to be an adjustment mechanism if the value of the target company changes between signing and closing. Chapter 8 described several ways to deal with this issue.

The purchase price calculation must be clearly defined in writing, allowing for little interpretation at the time of closing or thereafter. The timing of payments, the amount of the initial funding, and wiring instructions are normally specified in this section of the purchase agreement to ensure that there is no confusion about amounts or methods of payment. Business development professionals need to ensure that both buyer and seller have a clear understanding of the amounts and timing of payment and that these terms are accurately and precisely defined in the contract. Ambiguous or improperly defined contracts can result in significant problems later if parties interpret the contract differently.

4. Access to Information

The seller agrees to provide the buyer with access to employees, advisors, facilities, and personnel preparing information for the buyer prior to closing. Much of this has already been covered in the due diligence process.

5. Confidentiality

To prevent excessive press coverage, in some cases, buyer and seller will each agree to keep information about the deal and the target company confidential, both during negotiation and after the deal closes, unless disclosure is required by law. Sellers can be particularly sensitive to the potential negative impact that sale negotiations might have on the target company. Deals are never formally closed until contracts have been signed and money changes hands. Many deals have died at the closing table as a result of unforeseen circumstances. The worst case for a seller is to put a target through the uncertainty of a sale process with lots of publicity and have the deal never close.

Alternatively, buyers may not want to incur the potential adverse publicity resulting from paying a large premium for a company until they have funded and closed the deal. The stock market has been known to react negatively if it appears that the buyer is paying too much or is entering into a nonstrategic deal. Therefore, some contracts will bind the parties to keep the deal strictly confidential, both during contract negotiations and after the deal closes.

6. Representations and Warranties of the Seller

The seller has made basic representations to the buyer about the business being sold throughout the deal and due diligence process. These representations include things like

- Accuracy of financial statements and preparation of those statements in accordance with generally accepted accounting principles
- No legal or other liabilities beyond those disclosed in the financial statements
- Ownership of the assets/stock being sold
- General compliance with laws and regulations in areas where it does business
- Compliance with tax filing disclosures and deadlines
- Reasonableness of the financial projections provided
- That intellectual property and other rights don't infringe on others

The buyer has relied on this information when determining the amount and terms of the purchase price consideration. Sellers are normally required to "represent the accuracy" of this information as part of the purchase contract, allowing the buyer to seek relief from the seller if any of the representations turn out to be untrue. The tricky part is that, in most cases, errors in these data are not discovered until after closing—in some cases, not until years after closing.

7. Representations and Warranties of the Buyer

Although their information is not nearly as comprehensive, buyers are also asked to represent the accuracy of the information provided to the seller in certain areas, such as

- *Valid corporation.* The buyer is a valid corporation established in accordance with the laws of the state in which it resides.
- *Ability to enter into agreement.* The buyer has received all necessary internal approvals (board of directors) and government or regulatory approvals and has the ability to enter into the transaction contemplated by the purchase agreement.

8. Conditions Precedent to Closing

This section of the contract lists those provisions that must be in place before the purchaser is required to proceed with the purchase. In many cases, a contract will be signed weeks in advance of closing. This allows the buyer to get the necessary funds together and the seller to make the necessary preparations for sale before the deal actually closes and money changes hands. The conditions precedent list those issues that must be satisfied before the buyer can be forced to close on the deal.

- The seller's representations at the date of the closing were accurate.
- All terms and covenants were in compliance at the closing date.
- There was no litigation at the time of the closing that would prevent the seller from entering into the purchase/sale agreement.
- There has been no material adverse effect—nothing has happened between the signing of the agreement and the ultimate closing of the transaction that would have a material adverse effect on the assets and stock being sold.

- All legal matters required to consummate the agreement had been satisfied at the date of closing.

9. Limitations on the Target's Operations between Signing and Closing

This contract section is included to protect the buyer during the time between signing the agreement and the ultimate closing of the deal. It can be a tense part of the negotiation. The buyer wants to ensure that there are no major changes in the target's operations between signing and closing. Buyers will ask for the right to review and approve out of the ordinary events between signing and closing, such as the following:

- Changing the target's bylaws.
- Taking dividends out of the target.
- Issuing more shares in the target or altering the target's capital structure.
- Taking on more debt or other liabilities.
- Entering into purchase or sales contracts with third parties in excess of an agreed-upon dollar amount without the buyer's review and approval. This prevents the seller from entering into any unusual contracts outside of the ordinary course of business that the buyer would have to assume at closing.

Buyers will generally want fairly tight restrictions to ensure that what they buy does not change materially between contract signing and closing. Sellers will argue that there can't be too many restrictions on their ability to run the company without having to go to the potential buyer for permission on everything. Exhibit 9-1 gives an example of the type of issues involved.

10. Seller's Indemnity

The seller agrees to hold the purchaser harmless for any breach of the representations that it made in the contract, laws, regulations, investigations, and so on that may be present in the target company at the time of closing. In addition, seller "indemnifies" the buyers for certain postclosing issues that were present, but not necessarily disclosed, at the time of closing. For example, sellers normally indemnify buyers for any tax liabilities up to the date of closing that surface after closing. In the United States, the IRS is behind in auditing corporate tax returns. Therefore, an exposure for historical filings may not become evident until years after the tax returns are filed. In most

E X H I B I T   9-1

Molly Ltd. Purchases Kosh Inc.

Pre-Closing Events

June 1, 2006
Molly Ltd. and Soundview Equity signed contracts on June 1, 2006, for Molly Ltd. to purchase 100 percent of the assets of Kosh Inc. from Soundview for $365 million. The contract outlines a purchase price calculation based on net assets at closing of $300 million plus a premium of $65 million for a total purchase price of $365 million. To the extent that net assets on the day of closing are less than $290 million or greater than $310 million, the purchase price would be adjusted dollar for dollar on amounts in excess of or short of the asset target. Contract closing is scheduled to occur on June 30, 2006, after any remaining contract contingencies were cleared and Molly Inc. could arrange the necessary funding.

In the contract, Molly was allowed the opportunity to review and approve any events between June 1 and June 30 that were "out of the ordinary course" of business. In other words, Soundview needed to get Molly's consent for all larger transactions (in this case, over $10 million) that Soundview entered into on Kosh's behalf. Molly has successfully argued that it was "on the hook" to purchase Kosh Inc. once the contract was signed, and that Soundview was effectively running Molly's company for 30 days until the deal ultimately funded and closed. Soundview counterargued that it needed to be able to run the operations during this interim period to maximize the value of Kosh Inc. The compromise they struck was that Soundview could run Kosh, but Molly had the right to review "anything out of the ordinary" at Kosh during this period.

June 15, 2006
Kosh was approached by two customers, Hartford Industries and Ithaca Corp., to purchase a large piece of equipment with payment to be received over three years. Ithaca was a much stronger company than Hartford, and there would be less risk to receiving this cash payment over three years. Hartford, although a tougher credit, was willing to pay an incremental $25 to get this highly sought-after piece of equipment. The CFO for Kosh, Peggy Connors, wondered which way to go here. Her boss at Soundview was arguing that she should accept the higher bid from Ithaca. However, Peggy realized the implications of taking the Ithaca bid for the pending sale of Kosh:

- The Ithaca offer would increase accounts receivable by $25 million more than the Hartford bid.
- This would then roll through the purchase price calculation, driving Molly's purchase price up by $25 million.
- The longer-term risk of loss for collection of this account would be borne by Molly, not Soundview, as Kosh would be cashed out in 15 days.

Given this set of facts, Peggy Connors had the following questions:

- Was this an event that was "out of the ordinary course of business" and had to be discussed with Molly?
- Which offer should she take?

deals, the seller will agree to pay for any such judgments if they ultimately occur. However, this is a piece of the deal process with many gray areas, resulting in, at times, lengthy negotiations concerning certain issues and which party will ultimately bear the risk.

Business development professionals should rely heavily on both inside and outside legal counsel for what the standard representations are. In addition, areas highlighted in the due diligence process should be covered in the contract to protect the buyer's rights. For example, assume that the due diligence uncovered an environmental spillage at one of the target's main manufacturing sites. The EPA had not yet investigated, and no fines or remediation had been required as of the date of closing. This might be an area requiring a specific indemnity from the seller to cover any ultimate liability from the spill. Although this is difficult to quantify on the date of closing, it is likely that some fine will ultimately be assessed. Buyers will argue that the seller should retain liability incurred for events of this type that took place while the seller still owned the company.

In many cases, it may appear that a deal is going to break down over one of these disputed areas. To use our previous example, some sellers might take the position that they don't care about the spill; they are not going to retain any potential liability. The buyer had the chance to do due diligence and should have factored the expected liability into the purchase price. The position that the seller takes on issues of this kind depends on a variety of factors, including

- How committed it is to this particular buyer. Has the seller spent a lot of time negotiating a deal that must close by a certain time period?
- Whether the other buyers are still around. This is a common threat often used by sellers: "This is not a major issue. In fact, firm ABC will take the company with no indemnity for this issue; why should we give it to you?"
- Pressure to close. Starting up with a new buyer at this point in the process can be very time-consuming and costly, delaying the closing for months and introducing uncertainty about the deal's even happening.

Buyers must take each of these factors into consideration and determine how badly they want the target and how much liability they are willing to live with. Often, it simply comes down to negotiating leverage—which party has it and how that party is going to use it (see Exhibit 9-2).

Megan Inc. Purchases Someday Industries

Early Contract Negotiations

Setting: Assume that Megan Inc. recently signed a letter of intent to purchase Someday Industries, and the chief legal counsel of Megan, Vinny Kyle, is meeting with counsel for Someday Industries, Arthur Polk, for the first time for a broad discussion of the contract negotiations that are about to take place. Both sides thought it would make sense for the attorneys to get together for a brief meeting to set the ground rules surrounding the contract discussions. Megan Inc. had completed two weeks of due diligence at the Someday Industries corporate office prior to entering into the letter of intent.

The initial discussions surrounding such a contract normally take place very much like this:

Mr. Kyle: You know Arthur, we had very little time to review your books and records. Given the limited amount of information you made available and our restricted access to company personnel, we were not able to learn very much at all about the risks and issues surrounding Someday. Therefore, we will be requesting an extensive set of representations and warranties in the purchase agreement so that you stand behind what you represented to us during the process.

Mr. Polk: I am confused, Vinny. You and your team had two weeks at our corporate headquarters, where you turned this place upside down. Your auditors, legal counsel, and environmental, tax, and finance people crawled over every inch of this place. I would venture to say that you know more about Someday Industries than I do right now. You should not need many contract protections at all from us. If we haven't settled all of your issues by now, we never will.

Mr. Kyle: We are spending a lot of money to buy Someday, Arthur. I don't think it is at all unreasonable to ask you to stand behind the verbal and written representations that we relied on to derive our purchase price. After all, isn't what you said to us true?

Mr. Polk: We are selling Someday because we want to be out of the business. If I give you a 100 percent guarantee for everything, I will be living with any downside the business hits for years to come. In addition, you will be running the company. Why should we be responsible for issues that come up after you have closed and are running it?

Summary:
Discussions can continue along this vein for hours. Normally a give and take will ensue, where the seller ends up representing more than it originally wanted to, but less than the ideal level for the buyer. This is an area where deal negotiation skills, discussed in Chapter 12, can be of particular value.

11. Purchaser's Indemnity

Although this section is not normally as lengthy, the purchaser will be asked to hold the seller harmless for any violation of laws on its part or for a failure to meet the purchaser's representations in the purchase agreement.

12. Governing Law

This section identifies the state whose laws will apply to the governing and enforcement of the purchase agreement.

13. Asset Purchase—Unique Issues

Third-Party Consents   In an asset structure, assets are transferred from the old legal entity of the target company to the new structure of the acquirer. Therefore, consents must be obtained for the legal transfer of agreements covering suppliers, vendors, and customers from the existing target company to the new company; they do not transfer automatically, as they do in many stock deals. Agreements with major customers and suppliers can be an essential driver of value in the target. Asset deals will normally include a detailed schedule showing any consents that the seller was not able to get by the time of closing. The buyer will then negotiate with the seller over the course of action to be taken on the consents not obtained. If material consents are not obtained, this may hold up the closing. However, if there are only a few nonmaterial consents outstanding, the parties may agree to close the deal and use their "best efforts" to obtain these consents postclose.

Allocation of Purchase Price   In an asset deal, the total consideration paid must be allocated among the assets transferred. The buyer and seller must agree, usually in a supporting schedule to the contract, how the allocation will be recorded for both book (financial accounting) and tax purposes. These allocations can be very complicated, but are extremely important. The tax treatment of the buyer and seller postclose can be materially affected by the method of purchase price allocation.

D. Particularly Sensitive Areas for Buyers

Some liabilities, by their nature and timing, will be significantly more sensitive to a smart buyer. The common themes of these

areas are (1) the liabilities are potentially large, (2) they are difficult to determine at the time of closing, and (3) they may not surface for years after closing.

1. *Taxes.* As indicated earlier, there is generally a lag (multiple years) between the filing of a corporate tax return and
when the tax authorities review and validate the information. Therefore, any potential liability will not be known
at closing, making it impossible to adjust the purchase
price for this exposure.

2. *Environmental liabilities.* Environmental liabilities like
asbestos, oil in the ground, or contaminated drinking
water can take years to surface, and the potential liability
can be massive. Any educated buyer will want significant
protection in this area. The type of company and its industry also dictate the amount of pressure on this issue; heavy
industrial companies would have more potential environmental liability than a financial institution, for example.

3. *Employee obligations (ERISA).* Liabilities for unpaid benefits,
pensions, medical benefits, employee litigation, and so on
can be significant. The due diligence should include a
thorough review of the funding status of all employee benefit plans to make sure that enough has been set aside for
benefits at the time of closing. However, these are only best
estimates involving complex actuarial and other assumptions. There is always the chance for significant unexpected
liabilities in this area. The negotiation surrounding who
will cover these surprises can be especially challenging.

E. "Baskets," "Caps," and "Survival Periods"

At this point, the seller should be able to live with some level of
representations and indemnities. However, educated sellers will
generally argue three things:

1. *Materiality.* "I agreed to indemnify you for big issues, but
I don't want you coming to me every time you find a $50
item that I have to reimburse you for."

2. *Survival period.* "I am okay with indemnifying you for a certain amount of time, but I don't want my guarantees to be
infinite. At some point, this obligation needs to go away."

3. *Limit.* "I am willing to take some level of risk, but I can't have it be unlimited. We have to set some limit on the maximum amount that I will reimburse you under any circumstances."

Let's start with number three, limits, because it is usually the most contentious. Buyers will argue that there should be *no* limit. That is exactly what they are concerned about: huge liabilities that are undisclosed at the time of purchase and surface only after the buyers own the company. Smart sellers normally argue that, at a minimum, their liability should be capped at the amount of the purchase price. Why would the buyer ever demand more than the amount it paid as protection, and even then, shouldn't the buyer have some money at risk? This can be a very difficult area, with the lawyers for each side arguing their points for hours. For example, certain product safety issues may contain liability amounts in excess of the purchase price. In normal situations, a "cap," or maximum seller liability, is established at some percentage of the overall purchase price. The seller will reimburse the buyer for damages up to this cap amount; after that, the buyer assumes responsibility.

The second issue, survival period, is usually negotiated by splitting the potential liabilities into two categories. Potentially large latent liabilities like environmental liabilities and employee obligations will generally have a long or indefinite survival period to protect the buyer. Other, more routine liabilities like accuracy of financial statements may be limited to one year or until the next annual audit, the reasoning being that a good audit should uncover any inconsistencies in the financial statements that needs to be covered by the seller.

The first issue, materiality, is generally dealt with by having a "basket." The seller does not reimburse the buyer for individual claims until, in aggregate, they exceed some minimum floor amount. After this, the buyer is reimbursed dollar for dollar up to any negotiated cap. This reduces the record-keeping burden while still protecting the buyer for larger exposures. Buyers will keep a running total of liability and will notify the sellers when their floor has been met.

As indicated earlier, negotiations surrounding representations, indemnities, caps, baskets, survival periods, and other such issues can be complicated and detailed, adding hours or days to the negotiation. Business development professionals need to rely on the functional specialists on the due diligence team and their attorneys for guidance on how to handle these potential exposures.

F. Forms of Corporate Structure: Corporations, Limited Liability Corporations, Joint Ventures

The form in which a buyer decides to organize the target can have a big impact on the management, the assumption of liability, and the tax treatment of the company going forward. Most mergers and acquisitions are arranged as corporations, limited liability corporations, joint ventures, or partnerships. Close interaction with outside legal counsel, tax experts, and the internal financial organization is critical to making the right decision here. A host of issues that are generally beyond the capacity of the business development professional leading the deal need to be considered. Adequate discussion up front is essential because these are important decisions that are hard to reverse once they have been made.

G. Covenants Not to Compete

Another delicate, but critical, part of the legal discussion centers around covenants not to compete from the seller corporation and key management team members of the target. For example, take the case of a major U.S. corporation that is selling its engine manufacturing business to a private equity firm. The private equity firm is presumably paying a premium to get into the engine manufacturing business, and the seller is getting a premium because it is getting out of the business. Therefore, in most negotiations, it is considered "fair" that the seller provide the buyer with some assurance that it will not establish a new engine-building business for some period of time after the acquisition closes. The buyer certainly wouldn't want the seller to use its technical know-how, relationships with customers, and key employees to establish a business that competes with the target that was just sold.

Such protections are normally handled in a "covenant not to compete," in which the seller agrees to stay out of the buyer's business for some period of time. However, the details of these agreements are very hard to negotiate. One of the largest issues is how you define, in words in a contract, exactly what the business of the target is. To use the preceding example, should the seller be prohibited from manufacturing engines of any type going forward, or just engines for a certain type of vehicle? What about servicing of engines, sale of engine spare parts, or warranties on engines? Are these permissible actions of the seller postclose, or should they be included under the umbrella of the noncompete agreement? The discussion of these specific items by teams of attorneys for each side can result in some very late nights at the negotiating table. As you might imagine, buyers usually push for the broadest definition of the target's business as possible, while sellers want to narrow the definition to mitigate the limitations on them going forward. Other items that are heavily negotiated include the term of the noncompete agreement and the recourse available to the buyer should the seller violate the terms of the noncompete agreement: amount of damages, other recourse, and so on.

The other sensitive area is how to prohibit the key employees of the target from leaving and starting up a competing business. This may be even more difficult for the buyer to negotiate, because key employees are not obligated to sign any restrictions. Therefore, the clause is normally included in the employment agreement discussion with key employees, discussed in Chapter 8. The buyer will usually enter into negotiations with key target personnel and "lock them up" through a multiyear employment agreement with a guaranteed salary and bonus metric. A section of this agreement will specify that the key employee, by signing the employment agreement, agrees not to start a business competing with the target for a certain time period. An element of the compensation received is usually attributed to this limitation on the employee's ability to compete.

H. Who Is Your Indemnitor?

As described earlier in this chapter, a huge amount of effort is put into negotiating representations, warranties, and indemnities between buyer and seller. However, an area that is often overlooked is the financial strength and viability of the indemnitor itself. This can have severe ramifications for a buyer's ability to collect for breaches of contract by the seller. The most difficult situation is one in which a family-run or other small business is being sold and nothing really remains of the seller postclosing. In these situations, there is no strong party left to stand behind the seller representations in the contract. As discussed in Chapter 8, a variety of methods can be used to compensate for this, including deferred purchase price, earnouts, royalty agreements, and so on. The main focus of all of these techniques is to make part of the purchase price contingent so that the seller is motivated to stand behind the contract, at least until it has received the remainder of the purchase price. The focus is on having the seller continue to have a vested interest in the corporation and the representations it made at the time of sale, and using any of these techniques to hold back a piece of the purchase price can be particularly effective.

An easier situation is one in which a corporate parent is selling one of its divisions and a viable entity remains to stand behind the representations and warranties that were made. However, this is an often-overlooked situation in which business development professionals can get in trouble by losing their perspective in the detail. In too many cases, hours are spent negotiating representations, warranties, and indemnities, while too little time is spent analyzing which corporate entity of the seller will stand behind these assurances.

As a buyer, you should want the "top of the chain"—the parent company, with all of the remaining value, including the cash you gave it to buy the target. This helps to ensure that the parent indemnitor has enough net worth to cover potential claims of the buyers. In some cases, the seller will insist that some operating subsidiary other than the parent stand behind the contract rather than the ultimate parent company. If this is the case, extreme care must be taken in analyzing the financial viability of this subsidiary. It does little good for a buyer to get a great, well-protected contract if the indemnitor does not have the financial ability to stand behind potential claims. Buyers will also want some protection against the seller's transferring value out of the indemnifying entity postclose to lessen its value after the contracts are signed.

I. Material Adverse Change Clauses

Historically a very standard part of purchase agreements and bid letters, material adverse change (MAC) clauses generally allow a buyer to walk away from the deal if a material, unusual event occurs that changes the financial condition of the buyer or the seller. The general categories that were historically included in MAC clauses were severe acts of nature, war, terrorism, or other unusual threats to the transaction. However, after September 11, 2001, and with the recent advent of the volatile weather, sellers have begun to dramatically tighten the language in MAC clauses, making it more difficult for buyers to back away from deals.

The strong deal market of the early 2000s has also made sellers more aggressive in limiting buyers' options should an extreme event occur. This leaves buyers with a tough choice. How do you continue to act wisely in a market that is willing to take unusual risks to get deals done? Each case is situation-specific, but as the business development leader, your job is to weigh the risks here and not commit yourself or your company to unwise levels of exposure.

II. REGULATORY ISSUES

A. Sarbanes-Oxley

The Sarbanes-Oxley Act became law on July 24, 2002, to reform U.S. business practices and better protect public investors through tougher financial and accounting regulations. Some major provisions of the law for U.S. public companies that specifically relate to M&A include the following:

- Certification of financial reports by CEOs and CFOs
- More detailed disclosure requirements
- Potential criminal and civil penalties for violation of securities laws
- Significantly longer jail sentences and larger fines for corporate executives who knowingly and willfully misstate financial statements
- A requirement that publicly traded companies provide annual audit reports on the existence and reliability of internal controls

This last point on internal controls may have the most far-reaching impact on the M&A profession. For the first time, public company filings must attest not only to the accuracy of the financial statements, but also to the state of the company's internal controls. For purposes of Sarbanes-Oxley, this would include internal controls at the parent company and at any acquisitions made during the period. This puts more emphasis on an adequate assessment of the target's internal controls during the due diligence process. Deal teams can no longer just be concerned with the target's financial results; more scrutiny needs to be given to how these results were obtained, the controls surrounding reporting, and an assessment of the adequacy of those controls. The potential imposition of criminal and civil penalties and longer jail sentences under Sarbanes-Oxley further highlight the importance of this.

Sarbanes-Oxley has already had a big impact on the M&A profession. For example, certain deals have been postponed to allow time for an adequate review, assessment, and correction of the target's internal controls. Buyers are correctly demanding that an adequate internal control system be in place at the target *before* the deal closes. They are not willing to take the risk of an adverse opinion on their entire firm and the implications for earnings, stock price, and so on as a result of inadequate controls at a target company that was recently purchased.

We may also see a lengthening of due diligence periods to allow for a more complete assessment of the target's internal controls before buyers are willing to commit. Finally, integration periods may be accelerated to ensure that those systems that are weak at the acquisition date are corrected ASAP through integration into the parent company's control structure. As an M&A professional leading the deal team, you need to make Sarbanes-Oxley regulations a critical part of your due diligence plan. The potential ramifications for failing to pay attention can be significant for both your company and you personally.

The following should be considered "red flags" when evaluating the internal control structure of a target:

- Transactions in which a decentralized integration approach will be followed; that is, the target will be left as a stand-alone division, not fully integrated into the parent. In this case, the internal control procedures of the new parent will not be as much of a benefit to the target's stand-alone operations.
- Purchase of a nonpublic target that is not compliant with the Sarbanes-Oxley requirements for an adequate system of internal controls.
- Purchase of a division that has been "carved out" of an overall corporation. In such cases, the parent company's internal controls may have been adequate and properly covered the target. However, when the target is pulled away from its former parent, its control system may be inadequate on a stand-alone basis.
- Targets with many diverse operating locations. This puts more pressure on internal controls because of lack of direct oversight by parent-company personnel.
- Decentralized information systems at the target. This will normally create more risk of error than one centralized and controlled system.[1]

B. Hart-Scott-Rodino Antitrust Filing

The Hart-Scott-Rodino act of 1976 requires that U.S. mergers and acquisitions over a certain size (values are adjusted periodically) must be reported to the U.S. Federal Trade Commission (FTC) for approval at least 30 days before the transaction closes. This allows the regulators to review the proposed transaction for any anticompetitive effects it may have on the industry or on customers. The FTC is particularly concerned about transactions that combine major players in an individual market or industry into one company. The theory is that this new entity would have too much power to raise prices to customers or reduce prices paid to suppliers because it would own too high a percentage of a particular market.

The most common resolution to problems that are identified is either (1) to disallow the acquisition/merger or (2) to approve the deal contingent upon the buyer's disposing of assets/divisions in certain industries or geographic areas to prevent a consolidation of power into one entity. The buyer gets to move forward with the deal; however, certain assets must be disposed of within a certain time period.

International antitrust review is becoming increasingly important in large cross-border deals. In these transactions, deal teams need to ensure coordination with both U.S. regulatory agencies and the international regulatory agencies in countries where the parent/target will seek to do business. The conclusions reached by the regulatory bodies of different countries may differ, and the outlook for the new company can be very different in the various parts of the world. It is much better to identify any of these issues early in the process so that they can be factored into the purchase price and forecasts of the company's performance postclose.

III. ACCOUNTING/OTHER AREAS

A. FAS 141 and 142

In the late 1990s, investors developed some concerns about the accounting for merger and acquisition transactions. Under the rules that existed at that time, two identical business transactions could produce materially different accounting results depending on whether the "purchase" or "pooling of interests" method of accounting was selected. Key to both of these presentations was the concept of goodwill—the amount by which the purchase price exceeded the net book value of the assets purchased. Under purchase accounting, this value had to be recognized and amortized to expense over a selected time period, in some cases up to 40 years. However, if the target and the acquirer qualified for pooling of interests treatment, the organizations were combined at their carrying value on the date of acquisition and no goodwill was recorded. This normally resulted in a much better earnings profile for a pooling of interests transaction.

There were several severe consequences resulting from this diversity of treatment:

- Selection of the accounting method could produce materially different financial results.
- Management had considerable discretion in choosing the appropriate goodwill amortization period; periods from 1 to 40 years were acceptable under certain circumstances. Some management teams would justify as long a period as possible to improve the target's earnings profile in the early years.
- There could be different goodwill amortization periods for book and tax purposes. Buyers would try to write off goodwill as quickly as possible (up to 15 years) for tax purposes to take the maximum deduction from taxable income.
- Pooling of interests accounting had the potential to be abused to manage earnings.

After analyzing the situation, the Financial Accounting Standards Board issued *Statement of Financial Accounting Standards (FAS) 141*, "Business Combinations," and *FAS 142*, "Goodwill and Other Intangible Assets," in June 2001. These pronouncements effectively ended pooling of interests accounting and developed a compromise between the two previous forms of accounting. The statements focus on measuring the fair value of assets and liabilities on the balance sheet rather than on expense recognition through goodwill amortization.

Under the new rules, the buyer must record a goodwill balance equal to the purchase price less the net book accounting value of the assets being purchased. This goodwill balance is a permanent asset on the balance sheet as long as the target is owned. However, buyers must now complete a rigorous two-step process going forward to determine if goodwill has become impaired; if it has, a corresponding loss must be recorded. To determine if goodwill is impaired:

> *Step 1.* Look at the fair value of the "reporting unit" (i.e., the target company) that resulted in goodwill and compare it to the carrying value of the reported unit plus goodwill. If the fair value exceeds the carrying value (i.e., accounting book value), then no adjustment is needed.
>
> *Step 2.* If the fair market value is lower than the book value plus goodwill, the implied fair value of the target's goodwill should be compared to the book value and written down if appropriate. This writedown would be a charge against the current period earnings of the target.

This fair market value analysis must be completed any time there are events that might cause goodwill to be impaired (loss of a major customer, contract, employee, and so on), or at a minimum once per year.[2]

The general industry consensus is that the new rules have standardized the accounting for purchases and left management with less subjective judgment in purchase accounting. However, critics of the new rules point out the following:

- Management teams still have the difficult task of assessing the fair market value of a target, which is somewhat subjective. Also, the operations of the target will continue to change as it is integrated into the seller's operations, making such assessments even more difficult.
- As long as goodwill does not become impaired, the buyer's income statement never reflects the cost of the goodwill, since it is no longer amortized off the balance sheet into expense.
- The amount and timing of recognizing impaired goodwill is still subject to management discretion.

The accounting for M&A is another area in which the business development professional should seek the guidance of inside and outside finance professionals to ensure strict compliance with the new accounting rules. The overarching theme should be to disclose the financial results of the target and the parent company accurately in accordance with generally accepted accounting principles.

B. Accounting versus Economic Profit

Many of the concepts discussed throughout this book, including financial modeling, purchase price calculations, earnouts, adjustments of premiums, and other such topics, use the accounting-based results of the target. However, most academics would argue that concepts such as free cash flow, net present value, and internal rate of return are a much more accurate representation of a target's performance and return. The difficulty is that, for most companies, this pure financial information does not exist. For example, most purchase price calculations are based on the target's balance sheet because it is readily available and can be easily verified.

A more technically correct method would be to discount the expected future cash flows of the target by the buyer's required rate of return, generating what the buyer should be willing to pay for the acquisition. Most sellers struggle with even estimating the cash flows and timing of these flows into the future. Because of this, they struggle even more with representing the accuracy of these projections or tying a purchase price or earnout to these forecasts.

The balance sheet and income statement of the target may not be a perfect metric, but at least the information is

- Standardized under generally accepted accounting principles to allow for comparison of results among companies
- Readily available in most cases
- Normally audited under generally accepted standards by an independent third party
- Presented uniformly from period to period, allowing for an evaluation of the business performance between periods

Many stockholders analyze public companies based on the accounting results produced each quarter rather than on the net present value of the firm's expected future cash flow streams. GAAP financial statements therefore serve as a good basis from which to negotiate the transfer of ownership to the target.

However, the countervailing view would argue that GAAP financial statements are not a good representation of the value of the target because

- They are based on the historical cost of the assets and liabilities rather than their current market value.
- The need to make judgments in such areas as depreciation lives for assets, capitalization of expenses, revenue

recognition, and so on gives management too much discretion in recording results and limits the comparability of statements from one company to another.

- Financial statements use accrual accounting rather than reflecting the real value that comes in when cash is received.

Both sides of this argument have merit, and the business development professional should consult with his or her finance team about the appropriate way to model and negotiate the agreement. Investment banks working for buyers and sellers will often produce extremely complicated cash flow models giving the expected returns of the target along with the anticipated timing and resulting internal rate of returns. This can be extremely valuable in the early stages of the deal in evaluating returns and developing a purchase price bid. However, it is next to impossible to get any assurances about these forecasts at the time of closing, and, as a result, calculation of the purchase price, earnouts, and so on generally revert to an accounting-based metric. In practice, combinations of a financial cash flow metric and accounting-based earnings are used throughout the deal process to evaluate the target, determine an appropriate purchase price, and calculate expected returns.

CHAPTER 9 SUMMARY

1. The legal and regulatory aspects of the deal process are a critical part of the business development professional's responsibilities.
2. Business development professionals need to take extreme care to ensure that contracts have been documented in accordance with the agreement and that sellers are bound to stand behind the representations they have made, both verbally and in writing, about the target during the deal process.
3. Most transaction teams will include both inside and outside legal counsel to ensure that enough resources are available and that the necessary expertise in the complex law surrounding M&A is brought to bear.
4. Transfer of ownership in the target can occur through an asset or a stock deal structure. In a stock deal, the buyer purchases some or all of the stock of the seller. In

an asset deal, the buyer purchases 100 percent of the assets or only those assets that it wants from a seller corporation that remains in existence after the closing.

5. The complexity of the legal discussions are generally influenced by the amount of due diligence allowed to the buyer, any issues discovered, the size of the deal, and any contingent purchase price or other unique agreements.

6. All contracts are different, but most will generally include a definition of the terms used in the contract, a list of contract exhibits, purchase price mechanics, confidentiality provisions, and representations and warranties of the buyer and seller.

7. Sellers must generally represent the accuracy of such things as the target financial statements, absence of undisclosed liabilities, ownership of the assets sold, and general compliance with laws and regulations.

8. Buyers will normally request some protection to assure them that the target will be operated in the "normal course" between signing the contract and closing/funding. This can be a difficult area to negotiate and document in a contract.

9. Sellers will provide an indemnity to cover the buyer for any breaches in representations they made in the agreement, violations of laws, or other unique areas. Purchasers will in turn indemnify the seller for any breaches in their representations or violations of laws.

10. Negotiation of specific contract elements can come down to which side—buyer or seller—has more leverage to drive the deal that it wants.

11. Certain unique aspects of asset deals include the requirement to get third-party consents on the transfer of major customers/suppliers and allocation of the purchase price for tax and book purposes.

12. Taxes, environmental litigation, and employee obligations are usually very sensitive to the buyer because of the potentially large liability involved and the years that can pass before these liabilities surface.

13. Baskets, caps, and survival periods are all methods used to limit the seller's absolute exposure to liability for rep-

resentations it made in the contract. These areas are normally heavily negotiated between buyer and seller.

14. As discussed in Chapter 8, corporations, limited liability corporations, joint ventures, and partnerships can all be used to transfer ownership in the target from buyer to seller. Each method has its own liability and tax effects.

15. Covenants not to compete restrict the selling party or key employees of the target from competing with the company sold for a negotiated time period.

16. Care must be taken not only to negotiate solid contract representations, but also to analyze what entity is standing behind these representations. Buyers should demand a creditworthy party that can guarantee the promises made.

17. Material adverse change clauses allow the buyer to walk away from a transaction if certain unusual and unforeseen events occur. The hot deal market in the early 2000s has put pressure on buyers' ability to exercise these rights.

18. Sarbanes-Oxley, enacted into law in 2002, puts heavy emphasis on an adequate internal control system at targets purchased. The due diligence team must take extra care to ensure that adequate controls are in place at the target before the deal is closed. A material weakness in internal controls can have a dramatic effect on the target company and the buyer after the closing.

19. The Financial Accounting Standards Board in the United States tightened up the accounting surrounding M&A by issuing *FAS 141* and *FAS 142* in 2001. Under the new rules, goodwill is recorded as the difference between the amount paid and the carrying amount of the target at the time of purchase. Goodwill remains on the balance sheet but must be reviewed at least annually to determine that the fair market value of the target continues to exceed the carrying amount of the assets plus goodwill. If it does not, goodwill is impaired and a writedown must be taken.

20. In reality, a buyer is purchasing the rights to the cash flows that are expected to be produced by the seller postclose. However, because of difficulty in calculating

this data, most deals are based on the accounting book value of the property being purchased. The GAAP balance sheet provides an independent and standardized record of value that facilitates these negotiations.

NOTES

1. PricewaterhouseCoopers, *The Implication of Sarbanes Oxley on M&A*, Corporate Development Roundtable, Spring 2004.
2. Eddy Hsiao, "In with the New: Accounting for Goodwill and Other Intangible Assets under *FAS 142*," *SRC Insights*, second quarter 2002, pp. 2–12.

The Importance of Integration

In Chapter 4 we described due diligence as the most critical factor in *deciding whether to pursue* a transaction. Integration is the most vital, and often overlooked, step in *making a deal work once it has closed.* The common mistake that most acquirers make is considering integration as a separate, distinct part of the deal process. However, to be successful, the integration effort must start on the first day and continue throughout the deal process. The integration team can be successful only if it can get a complete understanding of the target's operations, knowing its management team well and having a feel for all issues that arose during the due diligence process. This chapter will outline the major elements of a successful integration and point out common pitfalls that acquirers fall into. See Exhibit 10-1 for a list of common reasons that acquisitions fail.

1. WHY IS INTEGRATION IMPORTANT?

Businesspeople rarely spoke of integration 25 years ago. Not until the many very public M&A failures in the mid-1980s did management start to realize that there were determinants of a deal's success other than simply paying the right price under the right terms. Many deals are predicated on the amount of revenue and cost synergies that can be generated when two businesses are put together. However, it is difficult, if not impossible, to achieve any of these synergies without a sound plan for addressing the integration process.

E X H I B I T   10-1

Why Acquisitions Fail

Pay Too Much
Overly Aggressive Forecast
Perceived Synergies Do Not Materialize
Poor Management
Insufficient Due Diligence
Losses Not Detected
Change in Strategy
Loss of Talent

The amount of integration needed depends on the type of deal and the type of buyer. "Financial buyers" are nonstrategic buyers such as private equity funds and hedge funds. In many cases, these firms buy companies to enter new markets or industries. The deals are not dependent on achieving synergies with existing businesses; as a result, integration periods can be shorter. Alternatively, "strategic buyers" are normally already in the target's industry. They are attracted to the target because it gives them new markets, areas, or products that can be combined with their existing portfolio. The integration period is normally longer in these transactions to ensure that the synergies that were forecast are actually achieved.

2. IMPACT OF CURRENT INDUSTRY TRENDS ON INTEGRATION

A confluence of forces have come together to make integration much more imperative for purchasers than it was even just a few years ago.

1. *More scrutiny of deals.* The proliferation of information over the Internet, more educated investors, and greater regulatory oversight are all directing more attention to deals and highlighting mistakes made by management.

2. *More conservative projections.* Buyers have learned from their past mistakes and are starting to take a more critical look at the often overly optimistic forecasts of sellers. They realize that the integration process can make the difference between achieving these forecasts and not achieving them. Too many deals have failed because a detailed plan to achieve results postclose was never developed.

3. *Fear of making mistakes.* High-visibility M&A failures such as AOL/Time Warner and those at Conseco and Tyco Corporation have cost CEOs and top management teams their jobs. This has started to make acquirers more conscious of the potential pitfalls for their companies and their own careers from pursuing bad deals.

4. *Difficulty in achieving synergies.* In most cases, the postmerger entity never achieves the revenue and cost synergies forecast in the purchase accounting model. Management teams have started to realize the importance of proper integration if they are to have any chance of getting the synergies forecast.

5. *Rating agency scrutiny.* Moody's, Standard & Poor's, and other rating agencies have started to analyze not just whether companies are growing, but where this growth is coming from. Companies that grow only through acquisitions rather than through internal "organic" growth are starting to be penalized. Rating agencies are analyzing the amount of goodwill on balance sheets to determine whether the actual results of the acquisitions justify the amount of premium paid.

6. *Change in accounting rules.* As discussed in Chapter 9, the Financial Accounting Standards Board changed the accounting for goodwill in 2001 and forward through *FAS 141*, "Business Combinations," and *FAS 142*, "Goodwill and Other Intangible Assets." Prior to the rule change, goodwill was gradually reduced or "amortized" over a period of up to 40 years. Subsequent to 2001, this goodwill stays unchanged as an intangible asset on the balance sheet.

7. This change in accounting helps the economics of acquisitions because a portion of the goodwill is no longer expensed to the income statement each year. However, a second requirement of the change is that the goodwill balance be reviewed periodically to ensure that the goodwill is still valuable, that is, that it has not been impaired. This puts a lot of pressure on the performance of companies postacquisition to continually "validate" the value of the acquisition, its results, and the amount of goodwill on the balance sheet.

8. *Sarbanes-Oxley accountability.* The far-reaching implications of the Sarbanes-Oxley legislation for public company

reporting has dramatic implications for the M&A industry, as addressed in Chapter 9. The need to maintain a system of internal controls at all entities, even those acquired, highlights the need for a prompt and detailed integration effort for all acquisitions. The implications for company management of not having these controls in place can be dramatic.

3. DEAL SYNERGIES

Deal synergies are those softer items that can be improved by the combined entity after the acquisition has been completed to make "1 + 1 = 3." The more easily identifiable and achievable synergies are cost synergies. The operating leverage of combining two separate companies can be seen in a variety of ways. For example, consolidation of facilities and workers can often be accomplished with little overall harm to the entity after an acquisition has closed. A great example is the consolidation of the U.S. banking sector in the 1990s. A typical city block had branches of many different banks located right next to each other. With such mergers as Fleet Bank and Bank of America, two branch offices in the same approximate location could be combined, with little impact on the customer. The savings from reduced rent, fewer overall employees, utility costs, and so on are generally referred to as cost synergies.

The integration team is often charged with delivering on the cost synergies that were factored into the purchase model to arrive at the purchase price. This is precisely why it is critical to get the integration team involved early—to assess the feasibility of the projected cuts and to start developing plans for executing these cuts before the deal closes. In too many cases, the acquisition team simply puts in an aggressive estimate of the amount of cost savings to make the deal look better and leaves it up to the integration team to worry about delivering on these promises. With a careful analysis and integration game plan, an acquirer can put itself in a much better position to deliver on the synergies promised to the board of directors and the shareholders.

A more complicated, but often more lucrative, form of synergies can be achieved on the revenue side. These types of benefits include the two companies sharing customer lists, marketing ideas, research and development, or other areas of common interest. For example, revenue synergies were advertised as a major advantage of the merger of AOL/Time Warner. The cross-selling of products to

AOL's Internet subscriber base and Time Warner's brick-and-mortar business was supposed to generate huge revenue synergies. However, in practice, the merger was a huge failure. The deal team did not factor in the very different cultures of AOL and Time Warner. The two businesses became competitive postacquisition and were reluctant to share access to critical customers. As a result, the forecasted revenue synergies were never achieved. Early involvement by the integration team in assessing revenue synergies could have helped to prevent the issues encountered here.

4. INTEGRATION STRATEGIES

A variety of methods have historically been applied to combine company interests. Two main methods are the "decentralized" and the "centralized" approaches. The type of deal and the culture of the parent are often the most important factors to consider when selecting an approach.

A. Decentralized Approach

As depicted in Exhibit 10-2, a decentralized approach to integration leaves acquisitions relatively independent and separated from the

EXHIBIT 10-2

Decentralized Approach to Integration

Decentralized Approach

- Leave targets stand-alone
- Autonomous units
- Separate legal, tax, finance, and other functions
- We bought them because they are unique — keep them that way
- Don't "contaminate" with corporate bureaucracy
- Little integration efforts
- Keep management interests aligned with budgets and results
- "We buy companies for a reason, because they are different. If we totally integrate them, we have lost what is unique and why we bought them to begin with"

acquirer/parent company. This approach often works when many disparate companies are combined under a parent company that may not be overly familiar with the target's type of business. The units remain relatively autonomous and continue to manage their business in much the same way as they did before they were purchased and consolidated under one parent company. This also has the benefit of keeping what is unique about the target in place after the deal is done. In too many instances, a target is initially approached because it is unique, only to be "standardized" by the parent company's policies and procedures. Keeping the target independent lets it continue to do what it does best without too much interference from the parent. As one M&A executive put it, "We buy companies for a reason, because they are different. If we totally integrate them, we have lost what is unique and why we bought them."

On the negative side, it is very hard to drive cost and revenue synergies with the decentralized integration approach. The separate functionality of the target—legal, tax, finance, marketing, and so on— makes it very difficult to consolidate these areas to take out cost. For example, you may end up with one accounting function at the target and a somewhat duplicate function at the parent company. Target management normally likes this approach because it can keep interacting with the people it is used to and it doesn't have to have difficult discussions about laying off loyal employees. However, from a strict cost perspective, this may not be the most efficient way to run the operation.

In addition, the decentralized approach makes it more difficult to leverage purchasing synergies, overall corporate knowledge, the value of the parent's brand, and other "global" areas of value that the parent/acquirer brings. On the revenue side, it is much more difficult to cross-sell products and realize revenue synergies when the subsidiaries remain as stand-alone, distinct units within the corporate structure. Finally, company culture is an issue with this approach. Since it remains a stand-alone unit, the target is not forced to adopt the practices, routines, and culture of the parent company. This does add value in terms of keeping the target unique, but it can make realizing on potential synergies difficult. For example, the AOL/Time Warner merger fell well short on its proposed synergies because neither unit was integrated into the other; each kept its own culture and was very reluctant to work with the other. Had these two businesses been completely integrated, such synergies would have been easier to achieve.

EXHIBIT 10-3

Centralized Approach to Integration

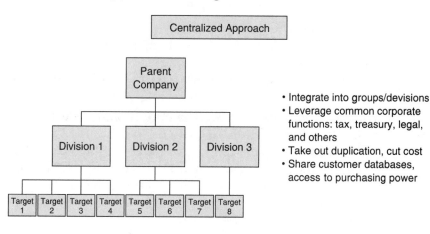

B. Centralized Approach

Exhibit 10-3 shows a centralized approach to acquisition integration. Each business is considered a division of the parent company rather than a stand-alone business unit. Here, the businesses are totally integrated to leverage common functions like tax, treasury, legal, and so on. Duplicate facilities are closed, cost is taken out, and synergies are maximized. For example, having a common purchasing function allows the combined entity to consolidate purchasing in one location and eliminate duplicate personnel. In addition, larger purchasing discounts can be obtained because one larger customer has much more power to negotiate discounts with vendors.

On the revenue side, synergies are much easier to obtain with a centralized approach. Sharing customer databases, sharing market intelligence, and cross-selling products are all easier when there is one consolidated sales force. The interactions needed to drive these synergies are forced by the structure. Finally, this structure facilitates the development of one common culture by driving more interaction as the two businesses are consolidated and work together.

A centralized structure does present a different set of integration challenges:

1. *Unique culture or practices.* The distinct culture and practices of the target company often do not survive the integration. Because the parent company is usually in charge, the

culture of the parent tends to overpower the target's culture, thereby eliminating some of the target's uniqueness
that made it attractive in the first place.

2. *Target employee morale.* Employees of the target can become
disgruntled when their culture changes and layoffs occur
during consolidation. Any change is always difficult for
people, but a centralized approach can have an even more
adverse impact on the overall morale of the target.

3. *Undesired employee turnover.* The impact on morale, uncertainty, and the difficulty of change can drive good people
in the target company to look for other employment. It is
normally the people you can least afford to lose (who are
the most marketable on the outside) that leave. Power
struggles can surface within the ranks as everyone jockeys
for position in the new enterprise.

4. *Impact on customer and supplier relationships.* Many customers
get very comfortable with a particular sales representative
or office. A centralized approach often involves consolidation and changes in sales force coverage that, if not handled
properly, can hurt customer satisfaction. Sometimes the best
thing to do from a cost perspective may not be the right
thing for the customer. Integration professionals need to be
careful to balance the adverse effects of consolidation
against the cost benefits from consolidation.

Supplier agreements can also be critical during this
phase. Many agreements include "change in control" provisions that allow a vendor to get out of a contract if the legal
entity it is doing business with changes. In the centralized
approach, targets are normally merged into the parent's legal
entity, creating potential problems with vendors who now
have a legal right to back out of unfavorable agreements.

Finally, the "brand value" or reputation of the target
may change in a centralized acquisition. Depending on
the public's perception of the parent company, customers
may be less willing to do business with the larger, parent
company organization. In many cases, customers like the
individual attention that the target has historically given
them. Although taking out cost is a good thing, consideration must be given to the overall customer experience once
consolidation is completed. A great example of capitalizing
on brand value without losing customer continuity can be

EXHIBIT 10-4

CVS Corporation Buys Eckerd

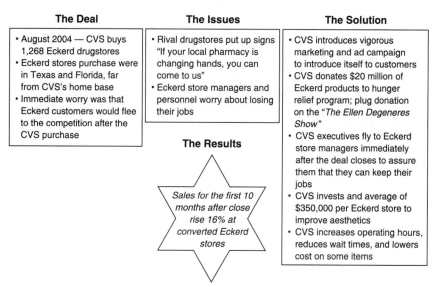

The Deal	The Issues	The Solution
• August 2004 — CVS buys 1,268 Eckerd drugstores • Eckerd stores purchase were in Texas and Florida, far from CVS's home base • Immediate worry was that Eckerd customers would flee to the competition after the CVS purchase	• Rival drugstores put up signs "If your local pharmacy is changing hands, you can come to us" • Eckerd store managers and personnel worry about losing their jobs **The Results** Sales for the first 10 months after close rise 16% at converted Eckerd stores	• CVS introduces vigorous marketing and ad campaign to introduce itself to customers • CVS donates $20 million of Eckerd products to hunger relief program; plug donation on the "*The Ellen Degeneres Show*" • CVS executives fly to Eckerd store managers immediately after the deal closes to assure them that they can keep their jobs • CVS invests and average of $350,000 per Eckerd store to improve aesthetics • CVS increases operating hours, reduces wait times, and lowers cost on some items

Source: Adapted from Gay Jervy, "Flight Risk", by *CFO Magazine*, October 2005.

seen in CVS's purchase of Eckerd Drug as outlined in Exhibit 10-4.

5. *Transparency of earnings.* In a complete consolidation, the identity of the target company normally goes away and results are reported only at the parent company level. This can make it hard to track the results of the target postacquisition and to evaluate the success of the acquisition. Many companies will compare the target's financials after six months, after a year, and annually thereafter to the projections included in the original board of directors approval pitch for the acquisition. This provides a level of discipline and accountability for the deal team and helps the overall M&A process be effective. However, in a centralized approach, the identity of the target may go away, making such accountability impossible.

C. Reverse Integration

In a typical acquisition, the target company is consolidated into the buyer using a centralized or decentralized integration approach.

However, in too many cases, the overconfidence of the buyer's integration team runs over the target's unique culture and operating rhythm. A target company may have an operating structure, competency, or expertise that the seller does not have and is seeking to acquire. In such a case, a "reverse integration" might be deployed. In a reverse integration, the parent company is merged into the target company, that is, the parent's organizational structure goes away and is consolidated into the target's organizational structure. The parent company learns from the target it has just acquired and adopts the target's practices and procedures. This can be an outstanding way to keep the morale at the target high and limit unwanted turnover. However, care also needs to be given to the seller's organization because it is now the one going through a difficult change.

5. STEPS IN THE INTEGRATION PROCESS

A. Representation on the Due Diligence Team

As stated earlier in this chapter, integration is not a discrete event that starts after the deal closes. Rather, it is a process that should start when the deal is identified and be maintained as long as the parent owns the target. Getting the integration team involved early helps firms react to problems in a real-time manner. The members of the integration team can provide a valuable service by helping to refine the price and the contract terms and by giving an opinion on the reasonableness of the synergies planned.

B. Assist in Contract Issues

Many of the early issues that need to be dealt with contractually actually relate primarily to the integration of the target. Issues surrounding the employment of critical target personnel, customer and supplier relationships, target health benefits, and so on should all involve the integration team as well as the legal team. The integration team has to live with whatever is negotiated by the business development team and should have input into the negotiations to make the transition easier.

Negotiating a transition services agreement is another critical task at this stage. This document generally arranges for the seller to continue to provide (for a fee) such common functions as payroll, benefits, and so on until the new owner has time to transfer these functions to the new parent. These contracts are normally three to six months in duration and allow for a more efficient transition of the target company to its new parent. Once the parent has had time to put employees on its payroll, combine operating systems, and so on, the transition services agreement is cancelled. A failure to have these services provided by the seller for some period of time can cause significant disruption at the target.

C. Postmerger Organization Development

The structure that the new entity takes (centralized, decentralized, or somewhere in between) needs to be planned well before the deal closes. While other members of the team are focused on closing the deal, the integration team needs to think about what happens the day after the deal closes. There may be many subintegration teams to handle the combination of certain computer systems or offices or to handle specific issues such as negotiation with the target's employee unions. Input from the target should be solicited wherever possible. This has the benefit of (1) leveraging the target's knowledge of local systems and procedures and (2) making the target feel part of and have ownership in the process.

D. Developing Communication Plans

A variety of constituencies have a keen interest in the events surrounding M&A. The integration team needs to develop a common message or theme for the deal that can be communicated to customers, suppliers, employees, and investors. For example, one of the main drivers of undesired turnover in the target's ranks is the absence of information about the acquisition plan and strategy. This is a very tense time for target employees, who are understandably concerned about how they will be taken care of postacquisition. A failure to communicate can result in unnecessary worry and, even worse, employees looking for alternative employment. A communication that there is "nothing to report at this time" is far better than no communication at all. The integration team needs to work very closely with human resources on internal communications and with the public relations department regarding external reporting. Public relations should focus its message on how the acquisition will help customers to ease any fears that the various constituencies might have.

Employees

Employee concerns can include job security, work location, specific responsibilities, and compensation and benefits under the new company. These items may well be resolved if the integration team is involved in the deal early. However, in many cases, it takes a number of weeks to decide how to handle these items postacquisition. Regular communication along the way can significantly reduce the tension and jumping to conclusions that can happen when there is an information void. The rumor mill tends to be extremely active, and usually incorrect, following a deal. Employees can tend to freeze up after the deal is announced because of this uncertainty. Employment recruiters will get a sense of this and be more aggressive in approaching your best people. Getting the true story out to the people is critical to prevent a panic situation.

Customers

Customer turnover of 10 to 30 percent should be expected in most acquisitions. You have to assume that your competition will invariably present the deal as an unfortunate event that is going to lower the quality of the buyer's service or products. There may be some customer overlap between buyer and seller that causes additional confusion. You must quickly create a positive customer experience and get your side of the story out to customers early. Benefits of the merger could include a broader range of products, more services, better coverage, or more expertise. Buyers also need to inform customers that there will be little change in product quality and that deliveries will stay on track. Once again, early involvement of the integration team so that it is ready on Day 1 gives the buyer a much better chance of delivering on these promises.

Suppliers

Early information on the merger will make key vendors feel more like partners than like adversaries and make them more willing to work with the buyer through the integration period. Change in control provisions can cause some turnover in supplier relationships. However, early identification of key vendor contracts and open communication with these suppliers can significantly smooth the transition.

Investors

Through close interaction with the public relations group, buyers can craft a theme around the deal that generates a positive message and forward momentum. The public's expected reaction to a deal is often a major consideration of the board of directors during the approval process. Completing some preclose due diligence with investors can help mitigate the risk of a negative reaction. Frequent updates during the integration period are helpful in keeping the support of key investors, the public, and other constituencies. A target would much rather have its story and its version of events in the public domain than a competitor's view or the public's developing its own uninformed view.

Communities

The target's local community may also be a key constituency that needs to be communicated with. The community will be particularly concerned about a loss of jobs or tax base as a result of plant consolidations under a centralized integration approach. Keeping the local authorities apprised can significantly help community relations postacquisition.

E. Functional Integration

Functional integration involves establishing routines and procedures for each of the functional areas of a company. There are different theories on how quickly such integration should take place. Some argue that the pace of change should be *gradual* to get people used to their new environment, rather than hitting them with too much too quickly. This also gives the acquirer time to understand the operations, examine employee talent, and build credibility before making any difficult decisions. Others argue that the change should be *immediate* to reduce the stress and uncertainty surrounding the target. This allows the new team to get through the transition phase quickly and focus on what needs to be done. Rather than worrying about whether they will have a job or not, the team is in place and driving toward a common goal immediately. The following areas should be covered in any functional integration:

Marketing. Develop a consistent and complete marketing campaign for the newly created entity.

Purchasing. Drive cost synergies through combined purchasing power discounts; select the best vendors postacquisition.

R&D. Share research information, eliminate duplicate projects, and maximize R&D dollars.

Human resources. The acquirer usually has the upper hand over the target in determining what the personnel policies and procedures will be. However, making the target employees feel that they have a say in the process can significantly ease the transition.

Finance. Review the internal controls and budget systems of the target, and prepare for financial reporting on a consolidated basis.

Operations. Review potential cost savings from facility consolidations and elimination of duplicate personnel.

Information technology. Consolidate target and parent company systems onto one common platform.

Legal. Review standard contracts, purchase orders, sales orders, and so on for applicable terms, protections, and conditions.

Buyers must remember that it is normal to find new issues or gaps in information during the integration phase. No matter how well due diligence is done, it is completed over a fixed time period in an artificial environment. Rather than being upset about "how did we miss this in the due diligence?" buyers should focus on (1) how to quickly remedy any issues that are uncovered and (2) how to improve the due diligence process for future deals so that the same mistakes are not made again.

6. INTEGRATION BEST PRACTICES

A. Institutionalize the Integration Process

Acquisitive companies have started to engage a full-time staff to manage the integration process for each new deal. These professionals get better with experience and can more easily build credibility with the internal constituencies whose support is required to make a deal successful. A full-time team ensures that adequate attention is paid to the target and its employees throughout the process.

B. Define Roles and Responsibilities

The integration manager can't be the only person responsible for the integration process. Multiple contact points between the buyer and the target need to be established to ensure a smooth flow of information. The roles and responsibilities of everyone involved in the integration need to be clearly defined and laid out. A timeline should be developed for critical tasks and when they need to be completed. The integration leader should be a project manager to ensure that things stay on track, not the only person responsible for getting the multitude of tasks accomplished.

C. Keep Business Development Accountable

It is essential that the people involved in pricing, negotiating, and gaining approval for the deal also be involved in the integration process. They have lived with the deal the longest and have the most credibility with target senior management, while also knowing the major players at the buyer. The business development team can be very helpful in driving the change necessary at both organizations for a successful integration effort.

In too many companies, the business development team moves quickly from acquisition to acquisition and is never held accountable for the projections made to get the deal approved. Business development professionals can learn a lot about what is realistic and what is not by staying around to see how well they forecast what could be done with the target. It also helps to keep them honest in future acquisitions.

Some companies insist that the business development professional who worked on a deal stay with it all the way through closing. Who can better effectuate the integration than the person who knows senior management and determined the areas where cost and revenue synergies are expected in the first place? Opponents of this structure argue that most business development people are best at finding, negotiating, and structuring deals. They argue that taking business development professionals out of this role and trying to get them to integrate is an inefficient use of company resources—that is, it is much more efficient for a dedicated integration team to become expert at postclose integration.

D. Hold Periodic "All Hands" Status Reviews

Communication and resolution of issues is critical, particularly at the start of an integration process. The integration manager should hold periodic, at least weekly, reviews with all of the functional areas to monitor progress and make sure that the necessary cross-functional communication is happening. Periodic meetings with timelines and accountability also help to keep team members focused on the tasks at hand. These meetings should include both parent and target company personnel, giving the target employees a forum where they can raise issues that they are encountering in the integration. In too many cases, a parent company imposes its ideas and routines on the target without listening to perhaps better ways to get the integration accomplished.

E. Stay Flexible

No matter how much prior planning goes into an acquisition, you can be sure that one if not more of the following will happen shortly after the deal is announced: people will leave, there will be surprises that were missed in the due diligence, markets will change, customers will react, and your competition will sell against you. It is very important to keep your perspective at these times and evaluate the overall implications of the change. Although the tendency is to overreact, this change can be beneficial to the long-term success of the new organization in many cases.

F. Don't Forget the Culture

Meetings between target and parent need to happen early and at the most senior levels of the corporation. A new culture can form only as the people get to know one another. The parent company needs to focus on the positive, pointing out the benefits of the combination to all constituencies. At the same time, it must be realistic about the time it will take to create a new culture and to realize the synergies, or it will lose credibility.

G. Communicate, but Do Not Overcommit

Communication is critical to keep people at ease during the tough transition period. A critical mistake that is often made is setting unrealistic deadlines. It usually takes much longer than expected to get even simple things accomplished postacquisition. This hurts the new management team's credibility with the target at the critical time when first impressions are being formed. Rather, a logical, conservative plan that can be achieved in an orderly manner starts to build a level of trust between parent and target.

H. Make Tough Decisions as Soon as Possible

There is a very fine line between making decisions too quickly and putting off difficult decisions for fear of retribution. Many of these decisions will involve termination of employees, plant consolidations, and other actions that directly affect people's lives. The natural tendency is to put these decisions off because they are uncomfortable. However, it is better to make a well-thought-out decision about the future organization and let employees know where they stand. Management teams do not help affected employees by holding back on information once the decision has been made. Having key people in limbo can also have a severe impact on the morale of the new organization. Rather, treat the employees fairly, let them know where they stand, and support them in finding alternative employment. This is the best thing for the new organization and for the employees affected.

I. Cooperate

As Donald DePamphilis points out in *Mergers, Acquisitions and Other Restructuring Activities*, creating a new culture is all about having a vision centered on shared goals, standards, services, and space. *Shared goals* provide a common goal at both the target and the parent to encourage cooperation. *Shared standards* refers to the adoption of the best practices of each organization, rather than simply having the parent company dictate how things will work. *Shared services* means the consolidation of legal, public relations, accounting, and so on under functional integration. *Shared space* involves a mixing of offices and people at the parent and the target in the same space so that they get to know each other.[1]

7. SPECIAL CHALLENGES WITH JOINT VENTURES, PARTNERSHIPS, OR OTHER STRATEGIC ALLIANCES

Strategic alliances are often created to combine the best talents of both organizations. The first question from an integration perspective is, how much integration should there really be in these situations? In Exhibit I-1 we looked at the Dow-Corning joint venture formed to develop materials based on silicon chemistry. Corning Inc. supplied the expertise in silicon technology, and Dow proved chemical processes and manufacturing processes. The integration challenge was how to realize the cost and revenue synergies without diluting

Corning's R&D capabilities in silicon or Dow's manufacturing expertise. The cultures required to provide these different elements of the
manufacturing process could be very different. Therefore, the challenge for a strategic alliance is to maintain the best of each organization, while still making the joint venture seem like one organization
with a common set of goals.

A second issue with a 50/50 joint venture is that neither party
has clear control over the other. This can make the decision-making
process especially difficult. It requires that each party have a certain level of trust in the other party and a willingness to work
together as a team. In many cases, a joint committee with representatives from each organization, with preset meeting times and
agendas, is established to resolve issues.

Finally, there is a tension in joint ventures between the allocation of resources to the joint venture and to the core business. Dow
and Corning teamed up via this joint venture in the silicon industry, but still remained competitors in many other markets. Again, a
certain level of trust is required to ensure that each party is allocat-
ing enough and *the right* resources to the venture and contributing
its fair share.

CHAPTER 10 SUMMARY

1. Integration is the most vital, but often overlooked, step in
   making a deal work once it has closed.
2. Many factors, such as more scrutiny of deals, rating agency
   scrutiny, changes in accounting rules, and Sarbanes-Oxley,
   have combined to make integration more important to successful deals.
3. Deal synergies, in the form of revenue and cost synergies,
   are softer areas that can be leveraged once two firms are
   combined.
4. Integration may take either a centralized or a decentralized
   form. In a decentralized approach, the acquisitions are left
   relatively autonomous, without much integration. This
   helps maintain what is unique about the target and mini-
   mizes the disruption to operations.
5. In a centralized approach, the firms are totally integrated,
   leveraging the best of both organizations. This can help to
   maximize the cost and revenue synergies, but often
   results in more disruption and turnover at the target.

6. In a reverse integration, the target's operating structure and management methods are adopted by the buyer. This is normally done in situations where the target has some unique skill set that the buyer is trying to maintain in the new organization.

7. Steps in the integration process include helping on the diligence team, assisting on contract issues, postmerger organization, developing communication plans, and functional integration.

8. Integration is a process that should start with due diligence, *before* the contracts are signed, to ensure early resolution of significant issues.

9. Communication plans are critical to employees, customers, and other constituencies during the transition period. Frequent and clear communication can significantly ease the burden during a difficult integration period.

10. Functional integration involves establishing procedures for marketing, R&D, finance, information technology, and other areas of the company. The type of deal and the culture of the organization can dictate whether the integration should be immediate or over time.

11. Successful acquirers tend to have a full-time integration team, hold business development teams accountable for their projections, and create a culture of trust, cooperation, and open communication at the target, even when difficult decisions need to be made.

12. Integration of joint ventures and other strategic alliances is even more difficult because no one party is in charge. Although decision making is more difficult, great synergies can be realized by leveraging the strengths of both organizations.

NOTES

1. Donald DePamphilis, *Mergers, Acquisitions and Other Restructuring Activities* (New York: Academic Press), July 2005.

Special Considerations for Sellers

This text has been written from the perspective of a business development person working for the buying party in an acquisition. Although many of the topics covered apply equally well to both buyers and sellers, sellers do have some unique issues that should be considered separately. This chapter highlights those parts of the M&A process that are particularly relevant to sellers.

1. REASONS FOR SELLING

There are many reasons why parties agree to sell a piece or all of their company. Although each deal is situation-specific, the motivations behind the sale generally fall into one of the following general categories:

- *The seller needs cash.* Selling an entire company, a division of a company, or specific assets can be a quick way to raise cash. Companies may need a cash infusion for investments in new products or technologies, developing new markets, international expansion, current tax liabilities, or a host of other reasons. The after-tax cash flows from the divestiture can be redirected to these more important growth areas.

    However, sellers need to analyze whether a major divestiture, rather than raising debt or equity capital to fund these other business purposes, is the most efficient way to generate cash. In some cases, the current tax liabilities generated by a sale can eat up much of the proceeds received. In addition, it is easy to underestimate the impact on the parent company of selling a division that is considered nonstrategic. The damage to employee morale, both at the target division and in what remains of the seller, can also have a negative impact on productivity. So, although a sale can be a quick fix for current liquidity problems, sellers need to look at the long-term implications of the transaction as well.

- *Estate planning.* Many small to midsize privately held companies started as family-run operations. As the senior member of the family ages, he or she may start to think about a sale of all or part of the company for estate planning purposes. There may not be a next generation of family members willing or qualified to assume control of the company. In these cases, estates can minimize their tax liability through a coordinated sales approach and plan an orderly flow of proceeds to their heirs.

  An increasing number of family-owned companies are turning to the private equity community to provide liquidity. In a typical transaction, the family-owned company sells a majority of its equity to the private equity fund today in return for current liquidity. However, the family keeps a minority interest in the firm, and family members remain as employees/advisors to help the company grow and maximize the value of their equity. This allows the family to continue to have a say in running the operation, while deferring a portion of the tax liability until the remaining economic interest is sold. Private equity firms like this arrangement because the owner/operator has an economic interest in continuing to grow the business going forward. The private equity firm can provide management expertise, access to low-cost capital, and operating efficiencies to the company. Many family-owned companies begin to struggle when they reach a certain size. The skill set needed to run a company with $5 million in revenue is much different from the skills needed to run a $50 million enterprise. In these cases, the management expertise of private equity firms can be of particular value.

  However, family owner/operators need to be very careful when deciding to partner with a private equity firm.

Each firm has a distinct personality and style of doing business. Although price should certainly be a major consideration when selling, small firms need to ensure that their business philosophy is aligned with that of their future owners. If it is not, significant conflict can occur postclose, significantly impairing the performance of the company.

- *Nonstrategic divisions.* Certain divisions of a parent company may fall out of favor because of poor performance, changing public perceptions of the industry, or a change in strategic direction by the parent's management or board of directors. In these cases, a business that is now undesirable to a seller may be extremely attractive to certain buyers.

  Take the case of Tyco's initial public offering of its commercial lending platform, CIT Group, in 2002. The deal, which was done partially to raise cash to pay off debt, also spun off a division, financial services, that was not intricately tied to the other Tyco product lines: health care, electronics, fire protection, security, and so on. Although selling assets is not always the right thing to do, Tyco argued that CIT was not part of the company's strategic focus going forward and that the cash was needed to pay down debt. It decided to focus on its other lines of business, which, in its opinion, had better growth prospects and could better utilize the cash capacity freed up by the sale of CIT.

- *Antitrust concerns.* In the United States, the U.S. Justice Department will review major transactions to determine whether they will have an anticompetitive impact on the industry or on customers. (See the discussion of Hart-Scott-Rodino in Chapter 9.) The regulators get concerned when any one company owns too much market share in a particular industry or geographic area. One solution that is frequently prescribed is to have the buyer sell off certain assets or divisions of the target company shortly after closing to limit the anticompetitive effect of the transaction.

  This was the course of action taken in SBC's $6.0 billion purchase of rival phone company AT&T in 2005. Regulators were concerned that in some markets, such as Chicago, Dallas, and New Haven, Connecticut, SBC and AT&T had the majority of the infrastructure to provide wireline phone service; that is, there was no other company that was capable of providing the service. With the two major players consolidated into one, regulators worried that the merged companies would have the ability to raise prices without consumers having any other choice for local wireline phone service. As a result, a condition of the regulators' approval was that SBC sell certain portions of its capacity in these cities to an independent third party that would provide adequate competition going forward. Situations like these often arise and provide buying opportunities for private equity firms or other strategic investors. There was nothing "wrong" with these assets; rather, the buyer was forced to divest them.

- *Poor-performing divisions.* Sellers will frequently divest poor-performing operations that are dragging down the overall value of the firm or its stock price. Potential buyers must tread carefully in these situations. In some cases, the core competencies, revenue synergies, or cost synergies of the buyer can help turn an underperforming division around. But in just as many cases, the target continues to underperform under the new buyer. These properties may be sold at a discount to their current book value, causing a current period loss. Buyers may be willing to take this short-term hit for the longer-term strategic viability of their firm.

- *Private equity "flips."* Chapter 12 will discuss the impact that private equity has had on M&A. One phenomenon is the increasing number of companies being sold by one private equity investor to another. These funds are arranged to provide a return of capital to investors over time as individual investments age and are liquidated. Private equity firms want to show a good track record of realizations, that is, sales of companies they bought at values in excess of their purchase price. Finally, the more quickly a private equity firm can realize a profit, the higher its internal rate of return—a key indicator of performance by investors in the firm. For all of these reasons, private equity firms may be motivated to sell a perfectly good company in order to realize the cash and return principal to the investors. Other private equity firms are frequently buyers of these properties because of their need to put investors' cash to work and their network within the private equity community.

2. HIRING AN INVESTMENT ADVISOR

Investment bankers can be especially helpful on the sell side of M&A transactions. In consultation with the company, bankers will assemble an offering memorandum ("book") to market the company. This book includes background on the company, the industry it is in, the management team, and financial projections for the expected future performance of the firm. In many instances, small to midsize companies do not have the time or expertise to put these materials together. Investment bankers are familiar with the format of these books and how the data are accumulated. They are also well positioned to provide recent market transactions that show what similar properties have sold for and, as a result, a range of values for the target company (see Exhibit 11-1).

Other advantages of hiring a banker include the following:

- *Access to the investment banking network.* Investment banks normally have contacts with many potential buyers who have been in the market previously. Engaging an investment bank as an advisor provides the seller with access to this network.
- *Due diligence assistance.* The due diligence process can be very disruptive to the seller if it is not managed properly. Investment banks have been through the process many times and know how to control prospective buyers, limit

E X H I B I T   11-1

Sparky Industries Market Comparables

Outlined here are recent sales of companies similar to Sparky Inc. along with the multiples of cash flow and net income they sold for. If Sparky's cash flow for trailing 12 months was $10 million, the value of Sparky Industries should be in the range of **$150 million** to **$250 million**.

Company	Date	Sale Price	Net Income Multiple	Cash Flow Multiple
Amy Inc.	9/05	$422 million	22×	15×
Iron Industries	5/05	$350 million	25×	16×
Kevin Corp.	1/05	$670 million	24×	16×
Snow Corp.	4/05	$150 million	30×	25×
Ginger Corp.	5/05	$225 million	20×	19×
Average		$363 million	24×	18×

access to data, and minimize the disruption to the seller's operations.

- *Independence.* Although it is engaged by the seller, a reputable investment bank can help provide a sense of objectivity and professionalism to the process.
- *Negotiations.* Investment banks have been through multiple sales processes and are adept at negotiating the best price and terms for the seller. The sales price, terms, and conditions can all be positively affected by a smart negotiator working for the seller.

Depending on the situation, investment bankers can be very expensive, however, often asking for a fixed fee plus a percentage of the sales price as a "success fee" if the property is sold. On larger deals, this success fee can be in the tens of millions of dollars. Each seller needs to analyze the cost/benefit of hiring a banker and make a disciplined decision. In addition, multiple bankers should be interviewed before a decision is made. Each firm has its own personality, style of operating, and associated cost. A firm that is right for a $10 million deal may not be right for a $100 million sale.

3. AUCTION VERSUS PRIVATELY NEGOTIATED SALE

As a general rule, setting up a competitive auction will provide a seller with the best price and most favorable terms for the property being sold. Buyers are likely to be more aggressive with their bids if they know that others are looking at, and bidding on, the property. They have to consider not only what the property is worth to them, but also how much they need to bid to be competitive with the other bidders. This generally sets up a nice dynamic for the seller: competition for the property it wants to sell.

Nonprice conditions would include things like the speed to closing, type of consideration (cash, stock, or other) received for the property, contractual guarantees required by the seller, noncompete requirements, and other such factors. Again, the more potential buyers there are, the better leverage the seller has to negotiate the ideal terms and conditions; that is, an auction situation would normally create a better environment for negotiating these terms and conditions.

However, it is not unheard of to have a private sale negotiated between a buyer and seller without going through a formal auction process. This happens most often in smaller deals or with family-owned companies that find a buyer that they are comfortable with. In these situations, prior familiarity with a buyer and a good working relationship can lead a seller not to show the property to other buyers. In such cases, the parties normally trust each other enough not to require a competitive auction to validate the terms and market price. The other common situation is a merger or acquisition involving two companies in the same industry sector. As competitors or suppliers, these companies have come to know each other, often spurring discussions of a "strategic combination" of the two companies. This can be a very efficient way to get a deal done if both seller and buyer work in good faith to arrive at a fair price, terms, and conditions.

4. WHAT IS MORE IMPORTANT: TERMS OR PRICE?

As with many other topics in this book, the choice between price and terms is dependent on the particular situation. Variables in the decision include the size of the deal, differences in bid terms and price, private or public sale, full or partial sale, and so on. In general, the bidder with the highest price will win the auction. However, the following factors can at times result in a lower bid being accepted:

- *Partial sale.* In a partial sale of a business, the seller may be more concerned about who the buyer is and its plans for the target postacquisition than about how much cash it is getting up front. A seller will be more concerned about the buyer's plans for the company postsale if it is maintaining a piece of the equity going forward. In these cases, sellers may want to evaluate bids based on price, but ultimately go with the buyer that is best positioned to maximize value going forward.
- *Public deal.* It is more difficult to go with a lower bid in a public deal because the seller's board of directors has a fiduciary obligation to maximize shareholder value. Accepting the second highest bid is more likely to happen in a stock-for-stock acquisition than in the purchase of a public company for cash. The seller's board may argue in a stock-for-stock deal that, although the initial value put on the company by the buyer is lower, the synergies, management team, product overlap, and so on of this particular buyer will help to maximize shareholder value going forward. Therefore, the

discount to purchase price up front is more than offset by the growth prospects of the new company going forward.

- *Private deal.* The most common situation in which lower bids are accepted is when a small to midsize family-run company is up for joint venture/sale. In many cases, the management team of such a company may want to go with a buyer it is more comfortable with despite receiving a lower price up front. One example that is frequently seen is a start-up company selling to a private equity firm or some other financial buyer. The start-up may have never had anyone else in control of it. Its managers might be concerned about how things are going to work in the new regime, how much latitude they will have to make decisions, and who will really be running the firm going forward. A private equity firm that takes the time to develop a relationship and sense of trust with the management team may be able to drive a deal at a lower price. Obviously, the magnitude of the difference between the highest and second highest bidders will influence all of these factors. It is very hard to turn down a bid that is significantly higher than the others, unless some very unusual circumstances exist.

5. FINANCIAL VERSUS STRATEGIC BUYERS

As we will discuss in Chapter 12, financial buyers include hedge funds, pension plans, and private equity firms that may make a complete or partial equity purchase of the target. Strategic buyers are companies, generally in the same industry as the target or a related industry, that are buying the company to integrate it with an existing platform company or with planned add-on acquisitions. The main drivers on which way to go here are whether the seller is cashing out 100 percent or only a portion of its position and how concerned the seller is about continuing employees and the franchise. In most cases, when cashing out 100 percent, the seller will take the highest buyer's bid—it has little reason not to. This can be a strategic or a financial buyer. Because it will have no remaining economic interest in the target, the seller is less concerned about the buyer's plans postclose. However, even though they have cashed out, some sellers will still be concerned with how their employees are treated (this occurs most often in small, family-run operations). They may use their leverage to ensure that certain individuals are offered roles with the surviving company, that broad-based benefit plans remain in place, and so on.

However, when the seller is to retain some equity, the choice between a strategic and a financial buyer can be important. The general wisdom is that a strategic buyer should bring more to the table than a financial buyer because of its knowledge of the industry, shared customers and suppliers, cost and revenue synergies, and ability to drive growth faster. However, many of the private equity firms have become very large, with their own in-house senior executive teams in multiple industries. The financial buyer may already have a complement of portfolio companies that fit well with the target. Again, the level of comfort with the personnel and operating philosophy of the buyer, whether strategic or financial, could have a major impact on the success of the company and the ultimate value of the equity that the seller has rolled into the new company.

6. DUE DILIGENCE PREPARATION: HOW TO MANAGE THE PROCESS

Due diligence on the target can be an especially trying time for the target's parent company and its employees. The parent company is never overly comfortable with having several strategic buyers, who are probably current competitors, come into the target company to learn its business philosophy, discover its operating secrets, review customer lists, and so on. Employees of the target are even more concerned about their jobs. How will they be integrated, what will happen to their position, whom will they report to? This is another area where an investment bank may help in managing the process, given its familiarity with due diligence procedures.

Some general operating parameters can be applied to minimize the disruption caused by multiple sellers wishing to analyze the target:

- *Create a data room.* One centralized place should be designated for the potential buyers to complete the due diligence analysis. Buyers should never have free access to the target's employees and facility. In many cases, sellers will establish a data room at a nearby hotel or other location rather than on site. This reduces the disruption of normal operations and can mitigate the distraction of target employees. Meetings with company personnel can then be scheduled for the off-site data room, allowing more controlled access. Here again, an investment banker can be particularly helpful in managing the process.

- *Information index.* A standard package of due diligence materials should be put together for all sellers, with an index of the contents. These materials should not leave the data room without the permission of the seller's representative controlling the room. Any copies of materials should also be requested through the data room leader.

- *Limit the time period.* Due diligence periods should never be open-ended. Specific dates should be decided in advance, with each potential buyer getting equal access to the company's records and personnel.

- *Limit interaction with target employees.* As indicated previously, access to target employees should be limited to prescheduled meetings with the approval of the seller. Representatives of the seller need to be present at these meetings to ensure that discussions stay on track and that only appropriate questions are asked.

- *Strong confidentiality agreements.* No bidder should be allowed into the data room until it has signed a strict confidentiality agreement covering the data it receives. This agreement should be reviewed by the seller's attorneys to ensure that there is proper protection against the data revealed being disclosed to outside third parties or used to the competitive advantage of the bidder. This second issue, competitive advantage, is much harder to control because of the difficulty of tracking whether or how the bidder uses any competitive information exchanged.

- *Nonsolicitation.* Depending on the type of sale—whether just assets are being sold or assets plus people—a nonsolicitation agreement may be prudent. This document prohibits bidders from hiring employees of the target company or the parent that they meet during the due diligence process. The fear is that potential bidders could use the due diligence period as a recruiting event to attract good employees.

Once again, a cost/benefit analysis is needed. As a seller, you want to give buyers adequate information to make an informed bid for the target. On the other hand, uncontrolled access to data and target employees, particularly by buyers who later drop out of the process, can be particularly harmful to the seller and its ability to compete going forward. In more than one case, buyers have entered into a due diligence process not to buy the target, but to learn as much as they can about a competitor and how it operates. Although they are normally bound to strict confidentiality agreements, bidders will at times use the information obtained during due diligence to better compete with the target and its new owner. As a result, sellers need to be careful with the amount and flow of information released during the sales process.

7. PREPARING PERFORMANCE FORECASTS

A part of almost every sale process is the seller's forecast of what the business can achieve going forward. Sellers need to take extreme care to provide thoughtful, realistic projections. These numbers should be based in part on historical performance, with an eye toward what can realistically be obtained going forward. Too many sellers, or their advisors, hype the projections, hoping to drive up the purchase price. However, this short-term strategy rarely works. Most sophisticated buyers will ask about the assumptions underlying the projections and perform their own sanity check on the numbers. If they sense exaggeration, buyers will discount the purchase price accordingly—in some cases, to a level lower than if the seller had just been conservative and honest in its approach. Therefore, overly aggressive management projections can hurt the credibility of the seller and lower the actual range of bids received.

8. MAINTAINING EMPLOYEE MORALE

Another critical factor in a successful sale is limiting turnover and maintaining morale at the target company. Although this is more important to sellers when they are selling only part of their interest, potential buyers will factor poor morale or high expected target turnover into their purchase price. Employees in any company that is going through a merger or acquisition will be uncomfortable with the uncertainty surrounding their jobs and their future. To add to this uncertainty, the treatment of target employees can vary widely depending on who wins the auction. A financial buyer who is not in the industry may view the company as a platform to drive new markets. In this case, the existing target employees may be critical to the new management team going forward. On the other hand, a strategic buyer may be viewing the purchase as a consolidating acquisition, with large cost and employee takeouts from the buyer's existing infrastructure. This can cause perverse behavior on the part of employees, who are "rooting" for one particular buyer over another because one buyer is likely to provide continuing employment for the target employees and another buyer is not.

The two best courses of action are to limit the different bidders' exposure to target employees and to keep an open and frequent dialogue with target employees. The worst situation is for there to be an information void, as target employees will usually assume the worst. The sales process inevitably takes longer than planned, causing further confusion for target employees. The rumor mill can exaggerate the potential consequences of the merger, ruining morale and productivity. The best practice is to communicate as much as possible, even if the communication is that there is nothing new to say. This prevents employees from jumping to conclusions and will often calm down the operation.

9. FORMS OF CONSIDERATION

As discussed in Chapter 8, there are a variety of pros and cons to each form of consideration that can be received—stock, cash, or asset exchanges. It really depends on the size and the financial and tax position of the seller. Sellers need to balance their desire for cash liquidity against the potentially negative tax implications that might be avoided in a stock-for-stock deal. There is often interplay among the various bidders concerning the actual price to be paid and the form in which this consideration will be received. Intelligent sellers look at their *after-tax* proceeds as the relevant measure when evaluating multiple offers.

10. FAIRNESS OPINIONS

The board of directors of a public or private seller may request that an investment bank, appraiser, or other independent third party provide a fairness opinion on the transaction being entered into. Sellers want to verify that the offer they accept represents a fair market value rate for the property. The opinion is normally based on other recent sales of similar properties deemed to be good comparables to the property being sold. Boards of directors and senior management teams receive these opinions as a sanity check for themselves on the fairness of the deal and as protection against potential shareholder arguments that they did not get the maximum value for the property sold.

CHAPTER 11 SUMMARY

1. There are several topics that are unique to the seller's role in the M&A process that can have a significant impact on the price, terms, and conditions received.

2. Sellers have a wide variety of motivations for selling, including a need for cash, estate planning considerations, a desire to divest nonstrategic divisions, a desire to get rid of poor performers, a desire to return capital to investors, or antitrust concerns. This can result in a win-win environment in which buyers are happy with what they received and sellers are happy to be out of the business.

3. Antitrust concerns are becoming increasingly relevant as industries in the United States consolidate and M&A activity continues to rise. Government agencies are concerned about deals that will limit the competitive landscape in a particular industry or location.

4. Sellers should carefully evaluate whether to engage an investment banker. Investment bankers can be extremely helpful in preparing the due diligence materials, helping to manage the due diligence process, providing independent oversight, and assisting in the negotiation of price, terms, and conditions. Investment bankers can be expensive, however, with fees on larger deals ranging into the tens of millions of dollars.

5. Another decision that sellers have to make is whether to negotiate a private deal or solicit a competitive auction among several bidders. The general rule is that the best conditions can be obtained through an auction because of the pressure to compete with other bidders. However, there are situations in which a privately run negotiation with one seller is most efficient.

6. A partial sale of a company can allow the current owners to stay involved and provide continuity for employees and key customers and suppliers. In a small, family-run company, this also allows the seller to defer a portion of the tax liability associated with the interest not sold. In general, sellers will be less concerned with who the buyer is in a 100 percent sale of their interest.

7. The specific terms of the deal, as well as its price, are important to most sellers. Nonprice factors include such

things as timing of closing, form of consideration, level of seller representations, and the quality of the buyer (for partial sales).

8. Financial and strategic buyers each bring unique qualities to an M&A situation. As a general rule, strategic buyers should be able to better enhance the value of the company postclose because of revenue and cost synergies. However, some private equity firms have become so large and diverse that their access to industry-leading companies and senior management talent is extraordinary.

9. The due diligence process can be particularly disruptive to the seller's operations. Suggestions for limiting this disruption include creating one centralized data room, controlling access to specific documents through an index, establishing a fixed time period for due diligence, limiting interaction with target employees, and strong confidentiality and nonsolicitation agreements with all bidders before access is granted.

10. Part of a seller's job is to prepare forecasts of what the company's financial performance might be going forward. Sellers need to be careful not to overstate these forecasts. They should be based on historical data along with a reasonable set of assumptions concerning business conditions and expected activity levels going forward.

11. Sellers need to be mindful of deteriorating employee morale once the sales process has been announced. The uncertainty about the company and individuals' own careers can really hurt productivity during this period.

12. Each seller's unique financial and tax position will drive it toward receiving consideration in the form of cash or stock. All else being equal, sellers may be willing to accept a slightly lower purchase price in exchange for the preferred method of consideration.

13. Fairness opinions are often prepared by investment banks for the seller's board of directors and shareholders. The investment bank gives an opinion concerning the reasonableness of the price received for the target company, given its current fair market value.

M&A Trends, Career Paths, and Other Topics

This final chapter will cover M&A topics that are not included elsewhere in the book, as well as a discussion of the relevance of M&A skills to a business career, regardless of what specific area you decide to pursue.

1. INDUSTRY STATUS—HEDGE FUNDS AND PRIVATE EQUITY FIRMS

The late 1990s and early 2000s have seen a very competitive landscape for M&A properties and a related rise in prices. This has been driven by an increasing desire by corporations to reposition their portfolios by divesting stale businesses or by using M&A to add new products, markets, and industries to their portfolios. In addition, the amount of money chasing acquisitions has dramatically increased through the introduction of more hedge funds and private equity firms.

Private equity firms are taking an increasing share of the M&A market away from strategic buyers such as corporations or industry management teams. The private equity industry has come a long way from its early beginnings and, at times, negative image in the leveraged buyout days of the 1980s. As depicted in movies such as *Wall Street* and books such as *Barbarians at the Gate: The Fall of RJR Nabisco*, leveraged buyout firms were viewed as corporate raiders that would take control of large companies by loading them with huge amounts of debt, then selling off divisions to pay down this debt.

Now private equity is viewed as a more legitimate source of patient capital that is willing to spend the time and effort to grow a company, either organically or through strategic add-on acquisitions. The purchasing power of private equity funds has exploded as the funds continue to grow; for example, Blackstone's latest buyout fund is $20 billion! This allows these funds to pursue not just small private companies, but even household names like Burger King, Polaroid, and Toys "R" Us.[1] Private equity firms have also beefed up their operations staff with seasoned executives who have retired from well-known major corporations to help their portfolio companies grow.

A more recent trend has been the "clubbing" of private equity deals to further enhance these buyers' purchasing power and diversify their risk. For example, in March 2005, seven large equity firms clubbed together to pay more than $11 billion for the data-processing company Sungard. Clubbing allows the firms to do even larger deals than their massive funds would support on a stand-alone basis because of the concentration limitations on any one investment. Clubbing can also reduce the level of competition in an auction situation, resulting in a lower price for the club than would have been achieved had each firm bid by itself.

However, a private equity club situation can have the following drawbacks:

- *Leadership issues.* Who is really in charge?
- *Inefficient due diligence process.* Multiple buyers may ask the same questions, even though they are part of the same team.
- *Conflict in operations.* Having multiple masters after the deal closes can cause confusion and put extra strain on the integration process.
- *Cultural differences.* Different private equity firms have different personalities. The cultural integration of a target is hard enough when one buyer is involved; these problems expand exponentially as the ownership structure becomes more complicated.

Despite these issues, corporate buyers are increasingly having difficulty competing with the size, financial strength, purchasing power, and deal savvy of these private equity concerns.

The proliferation of private hedge funds is also starting to have a material impact on the M&A market. Hedge funds have historically been formed by groups of wealthy individuals to earn high returns through aggressive trading of securities, swaps, and derivatives. They are limited by law to no more than 100 investors, and their activities are not as closely regulated as those of mutual funds. The overall hedge fund market is estimated to be $875 billion, growing at 20 percent a year, with 8,350 active funds today.[2] There has been a recent shift in focus by some hedge funds from short-term trading in securities to longer-term, strategic investments in private equity and M&A transactions. This has added to the liquidity of the M&A market, further driving up the demand and price for properties.

2. M&A AS A CAREER

The skills outlined in this book will be relevant at some point in your career, whether you pursue investment banking, corporate finance, consulting, private equity, or general management as a career path. A particularly important skill set is the ability to get teams of employees to work together toward a common goal. In an M&A context, this is the due diligence team. The components of this skill set include:

- *Interpersonal skills.* The ability to relate well to different people, with different skill sets, at varying levels of seniority will always be critical in business. M&A transactions are normally reviewed at the highest levels of the organization, ensuring that people who are involved in big deals will get the senior management visibility that is critical to a successful career.

- *Dealing with pressure.* Frequent deadlines are part of any deal. Whether it is first-round bids, final bids, due diligence time frames, or ultimate deadlines for closing the deal, people involved in M&A need to learn to deal effectively with pressure.

- *Financial acumen.* Many of the financial modeling and purchase price calculations required of a deal professional can be applied in other areas of business. Although not primarily responsible, the business development leader must work closely with the finance function to put together an acquisition model and projected financial returns. The business development team leader must learn a general understanding of a balance sheet, income statement, and due diligence findings. A healthy dynamic between the business development function and finance can produce a challenging, yet achievable forecast for the new business.

- *Assessing risk versus reward.* The longer a deal goes on, the more vested business development professionals become in the deal and the more pressure there is to close. The ability to step back from the detail and look at the big picture is critical for a successful M&A professional. By working with the risk and finance functions, M&A professionals can learn the softer skills involving interpersonal relationships and taking a balanced approach to problems that will serve them well throughout their career.

- *Negotiation skills.* As we will see in the next section, negotiation skills are a critical part of the M&A process from start to finish. The ability to get to the right answer without having either side walk away is a difficult, but critical skill. Seasoned M&A brokers have this skill set refined further and further with each deal they negotiate.

- *Presentation skills.* One of the most difficult tasks facing the business development professional is boiling down the weeks, in some cases months, of due diligence findings into a concise, yet comprehensive summary to enable senior management to make an investment decision. Senior management presentations need to include all of the relevant issues, yet not be so detailed that they can't be completed in one meeting or a series of meetings. Once again, the ability to summarize large complicated issues in a complete, yet concise presentation is a skill set that is especially valued in the business world.

As discussed at the outset of this book, there are a variety of career paths that include M&A as a critical element of their job responsibilities:

- *Investment banking.* The most traditional of all the M&A roles is that of M&A banker with a global investment bank. This experience could include working the "buy side," as an M&A buyer, or the "sell side," with an entity looking to sell its position in a company. This experience can be particularly fulfilling and intense, exposing the M&A banker to a wide variety of companies, industries, and deal types. The skills involved in structuring a deal, financial modeling of a transaction, and due diligence coordination can all be developed extremely well in these roles.

- *Corporations.* This experience could range from being in the middle of the M&A process as a business development professional to being part of the process as a functional expert from a particular corporate area to simply being a general manager. Almost every aspect of the corporation is involved during a big deal, from public relations and legal to finance and risk. Having a basic understanding of the concepts in this book is essential if you are to fulfill this very important aspect of your job responsibility.

- *Hedge funds/private equity.* Acting as principals in these transactions, partners, vice presidents, and associates all can gain valuable experience with the M&A process. Once again, having a basic understanding of financial modeling, due diligence, integration, legal issues, and the other concepts in this book will be essential to the effective performance of this role.

- *Consultant.* Some buyers or sellers hire outside consultants to help them evaluate an acquisition or disposition strategy or expansion into a particular industry or geographic area. Having a basic understanding of the terms of art and the steps in the M&A process is essential for becoming a valuable consultant.

- *Public accounting.* Buyers are increasingly turning to public accounting firms to "outsource" the due diligence effort rather than tying up their own organization with a complicated due diligence process. Public accounting firms may have more expertise in-house to evaluate a target more efficiently. If they routinely participate in due diligence exercises, they can better learn what to look for and how to organize the diligence effort.

- *General management/board of directors.* At some point in your career, you may be in a senior general manager role or be asked to sit on a board of directors. In such a role, you may very well be asked to approve a major acquisition or divestiture at some point during your tenure. Hopefully, the basic concepts described in this book will better prepare you for these complicated decisions, which must be made quickly and under a fair amount of pressure. You should have a better perspective on potential traps and issues, so that you can avoid the disasters that have overtaken some M&A efforts.

3. M&A NEGOTIATING STRATEGIES

Throughout this text, we make reference to the importance of interpersonal skills in the M&A process. There is no more critical area where these skills surface than the negotiations involving multiple aspects of the deal. Whether it is a first-round bid, length of the diligence period, or contract discussions, the way you negotiate a transaction can have a material impact on the ultimate outcome of the deal and your success as a buyer. Outlined here are some general rules to follow when involved in an M&A negotiation.

A. Keep Your Eye on the Ball

One of the hardest parts of a deal is trying to sort through the massive amount of detailed data and focus on what is really important. In too many cases, deal professionals and attorneys get bogged down in details that are not especially relevant to the ultimate outcome of the deal, while missing the big-picture issues. This can unnecessarily delay the closing and hurt the relationships between representatives from the buyer and the seller. As the business development leader, you need to add perspective to the process, not glossing over important factors, but also getting the team to move beyond issues that are not that important.

Knowing, and perhaps even keeping a list of, your key issues can help you stay focused. In some cases, you may be able to trade away something that is of little value to you but may have greater value for the seller. This exchange of items that have different values for the different parties is the heart of the negotiation process (see Exhibit 12-1).

B. Be Patient

Another difficult part of the process is realizing that the other party is probably as willing, if not more willing, to make a deal happen as you are. Deal professionals need to be patient and to use time as their ally. Too many deal teams feel the pressure to get a deal done and do not hold out for what is important to them. A level of balance and

EXHIBIT 12-1

Negotiation Case Study—Blank Industries Acquisition

Sandy Blank had been negotiating the sale of her Power Boat Division (PBD) to Ellie Industrial for 60 days. A purchase price and letter of intent had been agreed to, and the relations between Ellie and Blank had been fairly positive throughout the negotiation process. However, for the past week, Blank has kept bringing up her desire to make a satellite warehouse in San Diego part of the deal, even though it was not central to Blank's PBD operations. Ellie's lead negotiator, John Mia, did not have a big problem with taking the warehouse; it was just that Sandy's insistence on including a noncore asset in the deal had started to worry him. Perhaps there was something wrong with this warehouse that Mia did not know about and Blank was trying to jam Ellie with a problem.

Unbeknown to Mia, Sandy Blank had never told her parent company about the purchase of the San Diego property. Technically, corporate approval should have been obtained to open up this warehouse, but it had been done in a hurry without the proper approvals. To make matters worse, the corporate auditors were making a special audit of all Blank locations within the next 30 days. Sally saw the sale of PBD as an opportune time to get rid of the problem. The property would be gone by the time of the audit, if she could convince Ellie to make it part of the PBD sale.

Discussion Questions

1. How would you deal with this situation if you were Sandy Blank. What are the pros and cons of the way she is dealing with it. Would it do more harm or good to just be honest with Ellie and tell Mia the real reason that she wants to include the warehouse.

2. What would you do if you were Mia? Can this situation be used to cut a better deal for Ellie in any other areas?

3. Who has more negotiating leverage in this situation, Mia or Blank?

patience is difficult, but it can help you negotiate much better terms and conditions.

A related concept is your willingness to bluff. This is a double-edged sword, and you must be willing to accept the consequences if your bluff does not work. However, bluffing can be an effective way to get to the bottom line of your counterparty's position quickly. For example, presenting a "best and final" offer (i.e., "take it or leave it") on purchase price will certainly focus the seller on what its bottom-line sales price would be. Often this can be helpful in closing a gap in purchase price and bringing the negotiations to a quicker conclusion. However, you must also consider what your response will be if the seller tells you that your "best and final" offer is not enough. Deal teams can suffer from a lack of credibility if they continue to negotiate from a position that was supposedly best and final.

C. Develop Relationships and Trust

As stated many times in this book, your ability to develop a relationship with the counterparties can be critical to the ultimate success or failure of a deal. A healthy dynamic can help the parties get over minor issues quickly rather than getting sidetracked by the egos and personal agendas of each side. Similarly, it is much easier to get through major issues that surface if the deal teams have developed a level of trust and cooperation. The worst negotiations tend to be those in which neither party trusts the other, leading to petty arguments about irrelevant issues and a constant desire to beat the other side, rather than focusing on getting a good deal done. The best transactions are those in which both sides feel that they have ended up with a fair deal.

Deal professionals also must remember that the M&A community is relatively small. The reputation you build on the current deal will have a significant impact on your ability to get future deals done. Those deal professionals who are viewed as being fair and balanced are most successful in the long run. In too many cases, a professional will push a current deal too far, perhaps getting a better outcome on that particular deal, but damaging his or her (or the firm's) reputation in the market and ability to get deals done going forward.

Another technique to keep in mind is spending time with your counterparty outside of the negotiation process to build a relationship. Try to get to know the person on the other side of the table—his or her personality, interests, and tendencies. Time spent in developing a sense of trust and cooperation away from the negotiating table, whether it is over drinks after a session, dinner, or a simple chat, can pay huge benefits in increasing your productivity at the negotiating table.

D. Know When You Have Leverage

Knowing when you have leverage and being willing to use it can be a very effective negotiating technique if it is used in the right way, so that relationships are preserved. Having a feel for what is important to the seller can be critical to your ultimate success. A classic example is a seller that must sell a business by a certain date—for financial reasons, regulatory constraints, tax reasons, or some other reason. The longer the process goes and the fewer the potential buyers, the more the leverage passes to the buyer. Buyers should be aware of this and use it to their advantage as the deal progresses.

However, buyers need to be very careful not to take advantage of this leverage unfairly. In some cases, buyers have become unreasonable toward the end of a deal when they know that the seller is forced to sell. This can often backfire, with the seller coming up with a backup plan to foil an unreasonable buyer. Even more importantly, nothing hurts a deal professional's credibility more than retrading a deal at the closing table unfairly just because the buyer has the leverage to do it. Buyers have a moral responsibility to stick to the basic terms and conditions that they previously agreed to, regardless of how much negotiating leverage they have.

E. Be Sensitive to Culture

As we will discuss later in this chapter, deals in an international setting may require a different approach to negotiation. Even within different parts of the United States, cultures and personalities of the professionals may be different, justifying a different approach to the deal. For example, the hard-line, direct negotiating approach that is typical in New York City may not play well in a deal being negotiated in western Kentucky. You need to try to adapt your negotiating style as the situation justifies it.

Try to modify your negotiating style to that of the seller. For example, in some negotiations, both parties make concessions on smaller items to try to make the process more efficient. As long as this is a fair give and take—that is, each side is willing to make concessions—this works well. However, when you are dealing with a strong counterparty you may have to take a harder line. These smaller concessions can add up over time to a material difference in the deal. Unfortunately, you need to solidify your positions to prevent being taken advantage of by a hard-line negotiator on the other side. The last thing you want is a lack or respect from the other side; you need to draw the line somewhere. There is obviously a fine line between developing a relationship with the seller and being taken advantage of. Experienced deal professionals learn to spot these tendencies early and adjust their negotiating style accordingly.

F. Listen

Probably the single most important aspect of the M&A negotiation process is your *ability and willingness* to listen. You can often learn as much by watching the facial expressions and body language of the people on the other side of the table as from what they have to say. While you are at the negotiating table, you have to force yourself to stop talking and listen. You also need to pay attention to the timing and delivery of what you have to say, ensuring that your responses are well thought out and balanced. Once you have put an offer or concession on the table, it is very hard to retract it.

4. INTERNATIONAL ISSUES

All of the problems and complexities of a domestic deal are magnified in an international setting. Trying to learn about a target company is hard enough when the people at that company speak the same language as you; it is much more difficult in an international setting, with different languages, customs, and procedures. There may also be more hesitation on the part of target company personnel to open up to due diligence team members from another country. Getting adequate information to make an informed bid can be especially challenging in these settings. Finally, negotiating techniques can vary significantly from country to country. For example, U.S. executives are often criticized for being too aggressive and direct in their international negotiations.

Here are some areas that can raise particular problems:

- *Taxes*. Hiring a well-qualified tax advisor is particularly important in an international setting. A thorough understanding of the tax laws of the buyer's country and the country and local tax laws of the target company is required. Thoughtful tax planning can help you deal efficiently with the tax codes of both countries and keep a deal on track. You can also improve the economics of the deal by looking at the tax position of the proposed target along with the other holdings of the new parent company. In some cases, the taxes paid in one jurisdiction can be offset against taxes paid in another. The buyer's corporate tax people should be involved to take a global look at the effect of adding the target to the current international portfolio of companies owned by the buyer.

- *Legal.* Like taxes, legal principles and customs are unique to an individual country. For example, in some emerging economies, buyers may decide that the legal system has not evolved enough to transact business safely. Issues such as legal title to property and rights against creditors and customers should be carefully considered before investing abroad. In most cases, it will be very important to engage a local outside counsel who is familiar with the laws of the target's home country and jurisdiction in addition to a good international counsel. The potential negative consequences of not fully understanding local laws can't be underestimated.

- *Enforcement/courts.* Consideration should also be given to the credibility of the local court system, even when a buyer gets comfortable with the written laws and regulations. As a buyer, you need to be sure that you will get a fair hearing if you have to enforce your rights in the local courts. In some countries, the courts may be more sympathetic to the local company than to a large foreign corporation that is trying to buy it. Once again, you need both international and local legal counsel in order to get a good feel for this based on past history in the local courts.

- *Foreign ownership limits.* Many countries restrict the foreign ownership of local companies to 50 percent or less of the overall capital structure. These countries do not want foreign corporations to control companies, industries, or geographic areas in their home country. Expert international legal counsel with experience in the target's home country can help to navigate these complex situations.

- *Integration.* We discussed the added complexities of international integration in Chapter 10. It is much harder for a foreign investor to even get a feel for a target's culture and methods of doing business, never mind trying to influence it to move toward the culture of the new owner. Furthermore, the distance and time differences between the target and the parent company can lead to a sense of isolation and make it harder for the target to feel that it is part of the new parent. Frequent visits to the seller by the buyer's integration team are obviously important. However, it is equally important for the target personnel to spend time at the parent's headquarters to get a better perspective on how things operate and to build relationships with the constituencies that will be critical to the target's getting business done in its new world.

CHAPTER 12 SUMMARY

1. The proliferation of private equity and hedge funds has changed the dynamics of the M&A marketplace. The liquidity, management expertise, and deal savvy that these firms have are making it progressively harder for corporations and other strategic buyers to compete for deals.

2. The skills outlined in this book can be of value in any business career. The ability to deal with pressure; to assess the risks and rewards of situations; to understand a balance sheet, income statement, and financial modeling; and to interact well with subordinates, peers, and senior management are all critical to a successful business career. Being in and around M&A deals will help you sharpen these skill sets.

3. M&A is extremely relevant to a number of career paths, including investment banking, corporate business development, hedge and private equity funds, consulting, public accounting, and general management. In any of these specialties, it is likely that you will be faced with an M&A situation at some point in your career.

4. Solid negotiating skills can significantly enhance your ability to manage the deal process and close the transaction on the best terms and conditions possible. Being able to sort through massive amounts of detail, yet still arrive at the critical issues is a very valuable skill. The ability to be patient and to develop a relationship with the other side can also enhance your negotiating effectiveness. Finally, using leverage wisely when you have it and being sensitive to culture in international situations are critical to a successful deal process.

5. The difficulties of any domestic deal are multiplied exponentially in an international context. Legal, tax, and enforcement issues need to be carefully vetted with solid outside
   experts before any commitment is made. Restrictions on
   foreign ownership can add another level of complexity to
   the process. Finally, even the integration is harder when
   people from different parts of the world, in different time
   zones, are involved.

NOTES

1. Tapan Munroe, "Boom in Private Equity Funds," ContraCostaTimes.com,
   February 12, 2006.
2. Dion Friedland, "About Hedge Fund Strategies," Hedge Fund Association,
   February 2006.

Ten Steps for Better Acquisitions

More and more investors and third-party constituencies are taking a critical look at major deals to analyze the amount of premium paid, the underlying cash flows of the combined entities, and whether the acquisition will add value to the buyer's operations. This pressure will intensify in the twenty-first century as the proliferation of financial information to an informed investor base continues.

1. BE PROACTIVE

With the Target's Management

Before making a decision to bid, the due diligence team should demand access to all relevant accounting records and arrange meetings with key management personnel. Documentation should include minutes of board meetings, calculations of accrued liabilities, legal opinions on unrecorded liabilities, fixed asset analysis, inventory and receivables aging, and independent audit work papers. If the target has multiple locations across the globe, due diligence should include visits to all key operating locations and meetings with local management. As noted earlier, some sellers may restrict the buyer's access to local management until a deal is more committed. There is a frequent tension between a buyer's need for such access to do a comprehensive due diligence and a seller's willingness to provide it. However, if available, more detailed due diligence should ensure an adequate understanding of the target's operations and the risks involved in the purchase. With this understanding, management can better evaluate whether the premium needed to purchase the company is reasonable.

With the Seller's Investment Bankers

Investment bankers will be used as gatekeepers to the seller's operations. Don't let a seller's investment banker impede your ability to assess the target's management or its operations.

2. BEWARE OF "TROUBLED COMPANIES"

Many companies are put up for sale because their operating results have not met their parent's expectations. This raises questions about how achievable the company's projected financial results will be. A hedge that is commonly employed involves holding back a portion of the purchase price and putting it in escrow to reflect these risks (a "contingent payment" or "earn-out"). If the uncertainties at closing are ultimately resolved favorably, the seller can draw on the escrow for the incremental purchase price. If the risks do materialize and result in losses, the acquirer keeps the escrowed funds to cover these losses. This strategy is particularly helpful when target management is selling a portion of its equity interests, as it helps to align the interests of management with those of the buyer to grow the revenues and income to their mutual benefit postacquisition.

3. INVOLVE TOP MANAGEMENT *EARLY*

Senior management should be an integral part of the due diligence process to assess the target's management and determine whether the target's industry focus is truly synergistic with the buyer's existing operations. Particularly in industry-related acquisitions, senior management can bring its experience to bear to provide a higher-order assessment of the strength and quality of the target's management and its ability to execute in the new environment. Finally, the stress of working on due diligence teams may result in members losing their objectivity. The fresh and unbiased perspective of senior management ensures that the deal team doesn't get enamored, but remains objective.

4. INVOLVE THE INTEGRATION TEAM *EARLY*

Given the high premiums required to get deals done in today's market, it is critical that a sound business integration plan be in place before closing. Integration professionals should play a key role in the due diligence process. They can assist in evaluating the target's operating systems and procedures, get a head start on a plan to integrate the target into the buyer's existing operations, and also evaluate the reasonableness of the operating synergies and cost takeouts being factored into the pro forma projections. In some companies, no acquisition is approved until an integration plan has been developed and approved by senior management. This allows the new management team to hit the ground running the day after the acquisition is closed.

5. CRITICALLY EVALUATE DUE DILIGENCE REVIEWS

Due diligence findings and the resulting pro forma projections should be critically reviewed by management independent of the due diligence team. The assumptions underlying these forecasts need to be discussed thoroughly and reviewed for reasonableness. Downside scenarios should be developed that provide the results of the acquisition if key assumptions are not met as a result of macroeconomic changes beyond the acquirer's control. For instance, what would happen to the pro forma projections if interest rates moved up 50 basis points in the next 12 months, thereby increasing the target's cost of capital? In short, senior management needs to be comfortable with these sensitivity projections so that doing the deal makes sense across all probable scenarios.

6. CAREFULLY CULTIVATE INVESTMENT BANKING RELATIONSHIPS

Investment bankers play a critical role in providing buyers with "market intelligence" about the status of a blind auction and the premium that is likely to be needed to win the deal. For less sophisticated buyers, these bankers also run pro forma projections to project the target's operations under a variety of scenarios. However, because bankers are compensated for closing deals, listening to their counsel with a fair amount of discretion is imperative. By providing the opportunity for repeat business, acquirers can persuade investment bankers to represent their interests more aggressively.

7. DEVELOP A FORMAL POLICY
FOR POSTCLOSING AUDITS

Acquirers should implement a policy of requiring independent audits at the time of closing and each year thereafter. These audits need to be completed by someone outside of the immediate deal team, possibly the firm's internal audit function. The audit should encompass the following areas:

At the time of closing:

- Review of the goodwill amounts recorded
- Review of purchase accounting adjustments that are offset against goodwill
- Review of the integration plan, the team members assigned, and milestone dates for integration targets
- Establishment of operating targets for the acquired company that are consistent with the projections used for investment approval
- Annual audits thereafter
- Analysis of all accounting adjustments during the one-year purchase accounting window and afterwards
- Review of the status of the integration plan relative to its targets
- Detailed analysis of company performance relative to the goals that were established and approved by senior management. Explanations should be provided for all variances from plan, and corrective measures to improve performance should be established
- Review of unamortized goodwill balances for possible impairment

A formal policy for audits independent of the deal process helps to ensure the accountability of deal team members and more reasonable forecasts on future acquisitions. The results of these audits should be communicated directly to company senior management as well as to the deal team involved.

8. MAKE M&A PROFESSIONALS PART
OF THE INTEGRATION TEAM

Some companies assign members of the M&A team directly to the integration effect. This helps to ensure that the synergies planned are actually implemented within the company's operations. It also provides accountability for deal team members and provides a sense of accomplishment when forecast operating results are realized. Moreover, target companies generally appreciate the continuity of having personnel that they are accustomed to working with be part of the actual integration team. A contrary, but frequent, opinion is that the M&A team should move on to the next deal right after closing and not help in the integration. These professionals are best at closing deals and should be deployed there. The individual facts, circumstances, and personalities surrounding each deal generally dictate the best approach.

9. NEGOTIATE TIGHT PURCHASE AGREEMENTS

Many sellers will severely limit the amount of information that is provided to prospective buyers. Without the aid of extensive due diligence, buyers must rely on strong representations from the seller to protect themselves from hidden liabilities at the date of closing. Purchasers need to ensure proper representations and indemnities from the seller with respect to environmental, tax, employment, and other liabilities that may be present, but are not known at the time of closing. The underlying approach to the contract should be that all liabilities at the time of closing (whether known or not) remain with the seller. This is true even if these liabilities existed at closing but do not become apparent until some time after closing. However, liabilities that are in fact incurred post-closing should be the buyer's responsibility and need not be indemnified by the seller.

10. INCLUDE MATERIAL ADVERSE CHANGE (MAC) CLAUSES

M&A contracts can take months to negotiate. A MAC clause protects the buyers from major changes in the target's business between signing and closing the agreement. If a material adverse change occurs, the purchaser has the right to reduce the purchase price or in some cases to walk away from the transaction. Although MAC clauses are standard in the M&A world, the precise definition of a MAC is normally a heavily debated issue. To protect their interests, sellers generally want a MAC to be defined as narrowly as possible. However, buyers take the opposite approach so as to not be precluded from revisiting price or other discussions if the underlying business results change materially prior to closing. If you are a buyer, try to get as strong a MAC clause as possible to protect you from having to close on a deal that is not what you bargained for.

Sample Due Diligence Information Requests

As discussed in Chapter 3, a detailed information request should be prepared for each due diligence fundamental area. This list gives the target company some guidance as to what you will be looking for as a buyer in order to arrive at a value for the target. The various functional areas of the buyer generally prepare these lists. Although it is important to be as comprehensive as possible, it is extremely rare for all of this information to be available, because the seller will have confidentiality or other concerns. *Although the following lists can be used as guidelines, they are not comprehensive or complete. It is essential that the due diligence team requests be tailored to the specific industry and size of the company that you are examining.*

GENERAL COMPANY BACKGROUND

1. What is the history of the company, and how does it function?
2. Provide organization charts.
3. Describe how each department functions, what its objectives are, and how it interfaces with the overall business.
4. Provide officers' profiles—their functional responsibility and their direct reports.
5. Provide a general profile of the business—managers, staff, and functional reporting.
6. Provide a manual of job descriptions.

7. List the office locations and their staffing, and describe how field offices function in relation to headquarters.
8. Provide copies of the corporate charter and bylaws for all corporate entities being considered for purchase.
9. Identify all issued stock of the companies being considered for purchase, all holders of such stock, and all subscriptions, warrants, stockholders' agreements, or other agreements involving the stock of such companies.
10. Provide minutes of all meetings of stockholders, directors, finance committee, and so on for the last three years and the most recent interim period.

HUMAN RESOURCES

1. How many employees does the target have, broken down by exempt, nonexempt, hourly, full-time, and part-time?
2. Are employees organized? Identify these employees separately and indicate what unions represent them. Have there been any organizing attempts? If yes, please provide all relevant details.
3. What is the minority representation by geographic location? Break these down by location, indicating the number of employees in total, and the number for each minority age group.
4. Are there any outstanding equal employment opportunity (EEO) charges?
5. Is there a formal EEO policy? How is it communicated? Is it published?
6. What is the current cost of benefits? Provide actual costs of current coverages and overall cost as a percent of payroll.
7. What perquisites exist, and who is eligible for them? How are they taxed to eligible employees?
8. How is vacation accumulated? Describe eligibility. May it be carried over to future years? Are payments in lieu of vacation permitted?
9. How many holidays are provided? Are there any floating holidays?
10. How is the payroll handled—internally or by an outside service? When are employees paid, and with what

frequency? Are they paid currently or for a previous period? Provide contacts for information and payroll routines, federal and state filings for unemployment compensation, workers' compensation, taxes, state insurances, and so on. How are hours of work recorded?

11. What are sick pay benefits? Are employees compensated for unused days in any way?

12. What are the benefit policies (health, pension, and so on)?

13. Is anyone off the payroll protected?

14. Are there any retirees receiving benefits?

15. Describe HMOs and the associated cost.

16. Describe all welfare and pension plans, including the associated costs.

17. Describe the salary administrative program. Include bonus plan availability.

18. How and when are salaries reviewed? Is there a salary budget? How is it projected?

19. How are standards of performance set? Who reviews them? How often?

20. How are employees with below-standard performance handled?

21. What changes have been made to the benefit plan in the last year? Are the changes included in the benefit books? If not, how were employees advised of the changes?

22. Is there a service anniversary recognition program? If so, describe it.

23. Are benefits provided to part-time employees? Identify which are and which are not.

24. Describe pay for time not worked practices. What is the average number of absence days taken, paid or unpaid, in a year?

25. What is the percentage of turnover in the past two years?

26. Are there any employee morale issues? Are attitude surveys conducted? What have the results showed?

27. What has workers' compensation experience been over the last year?

28. Analyze the status of all company defined-benefit and defined-contribution pension plans.

29. Have there been any OSHA inspections, violations, or citations? If yes, provide the details. How is OSHA compliance handled? Are there regular inspections? How are records on accidents maintained?
30. How is the hiring process handled?
31. Whom do employees contact for benefit information?
32. Do new employees receive physical exams? Is there any ongoing physical exam program?
33. Are the salaries paid deemed competitive?
34. Are benefits reviewed periodically? By whom and when? What are employees' attitudes toward the current benefits?
35. Are there any employment contracts in place?
36. Make an assessment of the critical employees/management team that will be needed from the target postacquisition. Ensure that all of these critical players are locked in by employment contracts *prior to* the acquisition's closing.
37. Consider "stay packages" for all other important employees during the acquisition transition period and beyond.

RISK

1. Provide copies of the target's credit policy, including the approval of customers and vendors.
2. List the target's credit authorities.
3. Provide copies of collection policies, including past due reporting, problem account reporting, and extension and restructuring policies.
4. Provide the target's writeoff policies.
5. Provide the target's allowance for doubtful accounts and writeoff policies.
6. Provide a list of what services are provided to employees, which are included in standard rates, and which are billed as separate fees.
7. Discuss procedures for contract preparation, negotiation, and control.
8. Provide copies of any buyback agreements with vendors.
9. Identify all contracts that require customer approval to sign off or are nonassignable.

10. Provide a list of the top X customers and vendors, showing customer name, outstanding balance, new business generated, and number of accounts over the past three years.
11. Provide an aging of accounts receivable by business segment for the last three years, with the total over 30, 60, and 90 days past due listed by account.
12. Provide the gross and net (net of bad debt allowance) receivables for the past three years.
13. Indicate the status of problem accounts, watch lists, and other such data for the past three years.
14. Provide a summary of all currently active accounts that have been extended or modified within the past three years.
15. Provide a history of losses by account and by customer/supplier for the last three years, including gross writeoff, recovery, provision, and reversal of provision.
16. Provide a history (past three years) of reserves as a percentage of gross and net financing receivables.
17. List the 10 largest losses for the last three years.
18. Describe any significant customer backlog.

FINANCE

1. Provide the target's financial statements for the last three years and the most recent interim period. Note any unusual matters. Include the independent public accountants' opinion on the financial statements, noting any qualifications, exceptions, or disclaimers.
2. Provide a list of nonrecurring items.
3. Provide details of capital expenditures.
4. List fixed assets by location: original cost, net book value, and book life.
5. Provide a five-year revenue history, with details of acquisition expenditures and acquisition revenues by year.
6. Provide independent audit work papers for the last three years.
7. Provide internal audit work papers, reports, and correspondence for the last three years.

8. List audit adjustments for the last three years.

9. Provide the Accounting Policy and Procedures Manual.

10. Indicate any changes in accounting principles or estimates in the last three years, including those not deemed significant enough for inclusion in the annual report.

11. Inquire as to whether the target company is using alternative accounting methods in any of the following areas:

    a. Costing of inventories (LIFO, FIFO, or average).

    b. Depreciation methods (straight-line, machine hours, units produced, sum of the years' digits, double-declining-balance, sinking fund) and lives.

    c. Provision for pension costs.

    d. Income recognition:

        i. Sale of products, services, or real property (at time of sale, upon collection of sales price, upon completion of product, or on some other basis).

        ii. Sales to joint ventures or other affiliated companies.

        iii. Cash discounts taken by customers on sales and effect on income (at time of sale or at time of collection).

    e. Unamortized discount and expenses on debt or refunded debt.

    f. Capitalization of self-constructed assets.

    g. Interest during construction and start-up costs.

    h. Method of recording spare parts, supplies, and standby equipment.

    i. Accounting for repair and renewal costs.

    j. Accounting for retirement of plant, property, and equipment.

    k. Consolidation policies.

    l. Bases of valuation for long-term investments.

    m. Accounting for material leases of property items.

12. For each item in this list, indicate the impact on earnings that alternative approaches would have.

13. Provide copies of any other internal financial reports prepared on a monthly or quarterly basis.

14. Provide an accounts receivable aging, both the latest listing and one from a year earlier; a list of bad debt writeoffs and recoveries for each of the last three years, and a description of billing and collection policies and procedures.

15. Describe any related-party transactions.

16. Indicate whether a material part of the target is dependent on a single customer or a few major customers, such that a loss of one or more of these customers would have a material adverse effect on the company.

17. Provide an explanation for any significant "miscellaneous income" or "miscellaneous expense" for the last three years.

18. Provide a comparison of originally forecasted earnings to actual earnings by product line by quarter for the last three years.

19. List any personnel, facilities, systems, or other items shared with other businesses; a description of cost allocation procedures, if any; and plans for these items after breakup.

20. Provide quarterly income statements and balance sheets for the last eight quarters, with an explanation for significant variances.

21. List any contingent liabilities.

22. Provide copies of any purchase contracts, a description of any commitments or significant ongoing vendor relationships, and accounts payable aging.

23. Describe accrual procedures.

24. List the names, location, and type of all bank accounts, along with reconciliations, for the past two years.

25. Analyze operating expenses by department, function, and geographic area.

TAX

1. Provide copies of the target's tax policies.

2. Provide details on any tax-sharing agreements entered into by the company.

3. Provide federal audit information—what years are open, what years are currently under audit, and any outstanding issues.

4. Outline the tax department: number of people, location, responsibilities, and so on.

5. Indicate the company's legal/tax structure by operating division.

6. Provide copies of all federal, state, and local tax returns filed by the company during the last five years.

7. Provide any correspondence with federal or state tax authorities during the past three years.

8. Analyze the composition and calculation of the deferred tax balance.

9. Provide a schedule of any ongoing tax disputes.

10. Provide a list of state audits: income, franchise, sales, and so on.

11. Provide the amount of contingencies for taxes.

12. Describe the procedures used to file state and property tax returns.

13. Provide a list of current asset locations.

LEGAL/ENVIRONMENTAL

Provide all of the following items:

1. Company statutes as amended to date, share registers, and copies of all documents indicating that the shareholders are legal and beneficial owners of all issued and out-standing capital stock of the company.

2. A copy of the articles of incorporation, as amended to date.

3. A list of all authorized, issued, and outstanding shares of the capital stock of the company. Attempt to identify all shareholders and their respective holdings.

4. A list of any outstanding commitments to purchase warrants, calls, commitments, or other obligations with respect to the capital or other securities of the company, including stock option plans.

5. Copies of minutes of all shareholder meetings, directors' meetings, and meetings of any significant committee.

6. Copies of any private placement or public securities registrations over the past five years.

7. Copies of all agreements related to the redemption or repurchase of securities by the company.

8. A summary of all business acquisitions, mergers, or consolidations by the company in the last five years and those currently proposed.

9. A summary of all business dispositions by the company in the last five years and those currently proposed.

10. A discussion of all compliance programs related to environmental, business ethics, or any other matters.

11. Copies of all documents related to operating and capital lease obligations, summarizing these obligations by year and identifying those leases that can't be transferred and those for which consent is required.

12. A listing and copies of all third-party and intercompany loan agreements.

13. Copies of all leases and titles for company-owned property.

14. Copies of any environmental audits conducted in the last five years.

15. A listing of any hazardous materials (as defined by local statute) that have been on any premises where the company or a subsidiary has operated.

16. Copies of all documents related to pending or threatened civil or criminal actions or notices of violations of pollution control regulations or actions that might threaten the health and safety of workers or the public.

17. Copies of all notices from environmental regulatory authorities, including notices of violations.

18. A list of any underground storage tanks by location, with a description of the contents, and any underground storage tanks that have been removed or sold.

19. A description of any asbestos at property locations being sold as a part of this acquisition.

20. Details of planning applications, approvals, rejections, and restrictions.

21. Copies of any security agreements, mortgages, debentures, and similar agreements given by the company.

22. Copies of any guarantees, comfort letters, letters of credit, reimbursement agreements, or other documents relating to contingent liabilities of the company.

23. Access to all third-party service or supply agreements, including
    a. Vendors
    b. National accounts

  c. Dealers

  d. Delivery agreements

  e. Any other significant service or supply agreements

24. Copies of shareholder agreements.

25. Copies of documents showing that the company has an interest in any other corporation, joint venture, or other enterprise.

26. Copies of life insurance policies, with basic coverage, carrier limits, deductible, and renewal date. Summarize any major claims made over the last three years.

27. Copies of all documents relating to any special liabilities, including environmental, litigation, and tax matters.

28. A list of all product warranties and potential liabilities arising from them.

29. Details of significant discussions with prospects, customers, suppliers, or other third parties that have not yet been concluded that are material to this transaction.

30. Copies of letters from lawyers to public accountants during the last five years involving any litigation in which the company is a party.

SALES AND MARKETING

1. How is new business originated?

2. Describe the target's differentiation strategy:

  a. The company's competitive advantages

  b. Products or services offered

  c. Pricing policies

  d. Customer satisfaction surveys

3. Discuss the competition/the market.

  a. Are there other players similar to this company (size, geography, approach)?

  b. Who are key competitors, and what is their strategy?

  c. Describe market segmentation.

4. List any customers lost over the last three years and indicate why they were lost.

5. List customers lost over the past three years and those that are currently at risk for any reason.

6. Provide a marketing organization chart and the number of sales representatives, including the following information:
   a. Average tenure
   b. Experience before coming to the company
7. Describe incentive compensation programs.
8. Discuss business sourcing—seller reviews and authorities.
9. Provide marketing performance by product and by sales representative for the last three years.
10. List the top 25 delinquent customers by dollar amounts and industry.
11. List new customers in the last three years.
12. List all accounts extended or rewritten in the last 12 months.
13. Discuss new product development: frequency, cycle time, and process.

OPERATIONS

1. Provide a copy of company policies, procedures, and authorizations.
2. Summarize the accounting system and all major subsystems and their input to the general ledger.
3. Provide an overview of the general systems operating environment, including local and remote locations.
4. Provide a process flowchart for each major system.
5. For each database, provide the information stored, maps, fields, and data dictionary.
6. List all internal reports, computer generated or manual.
7. Provide copies of systems audits for the last three years.
8. Provide a list and copies of all reports sent to customers.
9. List all software or intellectual property owned by the company.
10. List all software or intellectual property used by the company under licenses, and a review of the licenses.

Sample Asset Purchase Agreement

The accompanying Sample Asset Purchase Agreement is intended to provide you with some of the issues that need to be addressed in any asset sale. The sample has been drafted using the assumptions that:

- The stock of the target company is held entirely by a single shareholder; and
- The assets being acquired constitute all or substantially all of the assets of the target company.

Specific representations applicable to the industry in which the target company does business will also need to be crafted.

This sample has been provided as a courtesy by (and the author thanks) **King & Spalding LLP.**

Any actual agreement should be prepared by your company's legal, tax and employee benefit counsels.

ASSET PURCHASE AGREEMENT

THIS ASSET PURCHASE AGREEMENT (this "Agreement"), dated as of [DATE], is made and entered into by and among [PURCHASER], a [STATE] [corporation] (the "Purchaser"), [TARGET], a [STATE] [corporation] (the "Company"), and [SHAREHOLDER], a [[STATE] [corporation]] [an individual resident of the State of [STATE]] (the "Shareholder"). The Purchaser, the Company and the Shareholder are sometimes individually referred to herein as a "Party" and collectively as the "Parties."

WITNESSETH:

WHEREAS, the Company, [directly and through its various subsidiaries,] is engaged in the business of [DESCRIBE BUSINESS] ("Business") at various locations in the United States of America [and other countries]; and

WHEREAS, the Parties desire to enter into this Agreement pursuant to which the Company proposes to sell to the Purchaser, and the Purchaser proposes to purchase from the Company (the "Acquisition"), certain of the assets used or held for use by the Company in the conduct of its business as a going concern, and the Purchaser proposes to assume certain of the liabilities and obligations of the Company; and

WHEREAS, the Parties desire to make certain representations, warranties and agreements in connection with the Acquisition;

NOW, THEREFORE, in consideration of the foregoing and the respective representations, warranties, covenants, agreements and conditions hereinafter set forth, and intending to be legally bound hereby, each Party hereby agrees as follows:

ARTICLE I
CONSTRUCTION; DEFINITIONS

Section 1.1 Construction. Unless the context of this Agreement otherwise clearly requires, (a) references to the plural include the singular, and references to the singular include the plural, (b) references to any gender include the other genders, (c) the words "include," "includes" and "including" do not limit the preceding terms or words and shall be deemed to be followed by the words "without limitation," (d) the term "or" has the inclusive meaning represented by the phrase "and/or," (e) the terms "hereof," "herein," "hereunder," "hereto," and similar terms in this Agreement refer to this Agreement as a whole and not to any particular provision of this Agreement, (f) the terms "day" and "days" mean and refer to calendar day(s) and (g) the terms "year" and "years" mean and refer to calendar year(s). Unless otherwise set forth herein, references in this Agreement to (i) any document, instrument or agreement (including this Agreement) (A) includes and incorporates all exhibits, schedules and other attachments thereto, (B) includes all documents, instruments or agreements issued or executed in replacement thereof and (C) means such document, instrument or agreement, or replacement or predecessor thereto, as amended, modified or supplemented from time to time in accordance with its terms and in effect at any given time, and (ii) a particular Law (as hereinafter defined) means such Law as amended, modified, supplemented or succeeded, from time to time and in effect at any given time. All Article, Section, Exhibit and Schedule references herein are to Articles, Sections, Exhibits and Schedules of this Agreement, unless otherwise specified. This Agreement shall not be construed as if prepared by one of the Parties, but rather according to its fair meaning as a whole, as if all Parties had prepared it.

Section 1.2 Definitions. The following terms, as used herein, have the following meanings:

"ADA" means the United States Americans with Disabilities Act and the rules and regulations promulgated thereunder.

"ADEA" means the United States Age Discrimination in Employment Act and the rules and regulations promulgated thereunder.

"Affiliate" of any specified Person means any other Person directly or indirectly Controlling or Controlled by or under direct or indirect common Control with such specified Person.

"Applicable Benefit Laws" means all Laws or other legislative, administrative or judicial promulgations, other than ERISA and the Code, including those of a jurisdiction outside the United States of America, applicable to any Company Benefit Plan.

"Assumed Contracts" means those contracts listed on Schedule 4.12 (unless indicated to the contrary thereon) and those contracts that relate to the Business and are not required to be listed on Schedule 4.12.

"Business Day" means any day except Saturday, Sunday, or any day on which banks are generally not open for business in the City of [_____].

"CERCLA" means the United States Comprehensive Environmental Response, Compensation and Liability Act and the rules and regulations promulgated thereunder.

"Claims Period" means the period during which a claim for indemnification may be asserted hereunder by an Indemnified Party.

"Closing" means the consummation of the transactions contemplated by Article II.

"Closing Date" means the date on which the Closing occurs.

"COBRA Coverage" means continuation coverage required under Section 4980B of the Code and Part 6 of Title I of ERISA.

"Code" means the United States Internal Revenue Code of 1986.

"Company Ancillary Documents" means any certificate, agreement, document or other instrument, other than this Agreement, to be executed and delivered by the Company or an Affiliate thereof other than the Shareholder in connection with the transactions contemplated hereby.

"Company Benefit Plan" means each Employee Benefit Plan sponsored or maintained or required to be sponsored or maintained at any time by the Company or to which the Company makes or has made, or has or has had an obligation to make, contributions at any time.

"Company Indemnified Parties" means the Company, the Shareholder and their respective officers, directors, employees, agents and representatives and the heirs, executors, successors and assigns of any of the foregoing.

"Company Intellectual Property" means any Intellectual Property that is owned by or licensed to the Company and used in connection with the Business, including the Company Software.

"Company Licensed Software" means all software (other than Company Proprietary Software) used in connection with the Business.

"Company Proprietary Software" means all software owned by the Company.

"Company Registered Intellectual Property" means all of the Registered Intellectual Property owned by, filed in the name of, or licensed to the Company and used in the Business.

"Company Software" means the Company Licensed Software and the Company Proprietary Software.

"Confidential Information" means any data or information of the Company (including trade secrets) that is valuable to the operation of the Business and not generally known to the public or competitors.

"Control" means, when used with respect to any specified Person, the power to direct the management and policies of such Person, directly or indirectly, whether through the ownership of voting securities, by contract or otherwise.

"Customers" means each customer that paid the Company more than $_____ during the 12-month period ended _____, 200__.

"Employee Benefit Plan" means, with respect to any Person, (a) each plan, fund, program, agreement, arrangement or scheme, including each plan, fund, program, agreement, arrangement or scheme maintained or required to be maintained under the Laws of a jurisdiction outside the United States of America, in each case, that is at any time sponsored or maintained or required to be sponsored or maintained by such Person or to which such Person makes or has made, or has or has had an obligation to make, contributions providing for employee benefits or for the remuneration, direct or indirect, of the employees, former employees, directors, managers, officers, consultants, independent contractors, contingent workers or leased employees of such Person or the dependents of any of them (whether written or oral), including each deferred compensation, bonus, incentive compensation, pension, retirement, stock purchase, stock option and other equity compensation plan, "welfare" plan (within the meaning of Section 3(1) of ERISA, determined without regard to whether such plan is subject to ERISA), (b) each "pension" plan (within the meaning of Section 3(2) of ERISA, determined without regard to whether such plan is subject to ERISA), (c) each severance plan or agreement, health, vacation, summer hours, supplemental unemployment benefit, hospitalization insurance, medical, dental, legal and (d) each other employee benefit plan, fund, program, agreement or arrangement.

"Employment Agreement" means any employment contract, consulting agreement, termination or severance agreement, change of control agreement or any other agreement respecting the terms and conditions of employment or payment of compensation, or of a consulting or independent contractor relationship in respect to any current or former officer, employee, consultant or independent contractor.

"Environmental Laws" means all local, state and federal Laws relating to protection of surface or ground water, drinking water supply, soil, surface or subsurface strata or medium, or ambient air, pollution control, product registration and Hazardous Materials.

"ERISA" means the United States Employee Retirement Income Security Act of 1974 and the rules and regulations promulgated thereunder.

"ERISA Affiliate" means any Person (whether incorporated or unincorporated) that together with the Company would be deemed a "single employer" within the meaning of Section 414 of the Code.

"ERISA Affiliate Plan" means each Employee Benefit Plan sponsored or maintained or required to be sponsored or maintained at any time by any ERISA Affiliate, or to which such ERISA Affiliate makes or has made, or has or has had an obligation to make, contributions at any time.

"Final Working Capital Schedule" means the Preliminary Working Capital Schedule as finally determined pursuant to Section 3.3.

"Financial Statements" means (a) the [audited] balance sheet of the Company at [DATES] and the [audited] statements of income and cash flows of the Company for the periods then ended and (b) the [unaudited] balance sheet of the Company for the ____-month period ending at [DATE] and the [unaudited] statements of income and cash flows of the Company for the period then ended.

"FLSA" means the United States Fair Labor Standards Act and the rules and regulations promulgated thereunder.

"FMLA" means the United States Family and Medical Leave Act and the rules and regulations promulgated thereunder.

"GAAP" means generally accepted accounting principles as applied in the United States.

"Governmental Entity" means any federal, state or local or foreign government, any political subdivision thereof or any court, administrative or regulatory agency, department, instrumentality, body or commission or other governmental authority or agency, domestic or foreign.

"Hazardous Materials" means any waste, pollutant, contaminant, hazardous substance, toxic, ignitable, reactive or corrosive substance, hazardous waste, special waste, industrial substance, by-product, process-intermediate product or waste, petroleum or petroleum-derived substance or waste, chemical liquids or solids, liquid or gaseous products, or any constituent of any such substance or waste, the use, handling or disposal of which by the Company is in any way governed by or subject to any applicable Law.

"Holdback Note" means the $_____ promissory note to be delivered by the Purchaser to the Company at the Closing substantially in the form attached hereto as Exhibit 1.2(a).

"HSR Act" means the United States Hart-Scott-Rodino Antitrust Improvements Act of 1976 and the rules and regulations promulgated thereunder.

"Indemnified Party" means a Purchaser Indemnified Party or a Company Indemnified Party.

"Intellectual Property" means any or all of the following and all rights, arising out of or associated therewith: (i) all United States, international and foreign patents and applications therefore and all reissues, divisions, renewals, extensions, provisionals, continuations and continuations-in-part thereof; (ii) all inventions (whether patentable or not), invention disclosures, improvements, trade secrets, proprietary information, know-how, technology, technical data and customer lists, and all documentation relating to any of the foregoing throughout the world; (iii) all copyrights, copyright registrations and applications therefore, and all other rights corresponding thereto throughout the world; (iv) all industrial designs and any registrations and applications therefore throughout the world; (v) all internet uniform resource locators, domain names, trade names, logos, slogans, designs, common law trademarks and service marks, trademark and service mark registrations and applications therefore throughout the world; (vi) all databases and data collections and all rights therein throughout the world; (vii) all moral and economic rights of authors and inventors, however denominated, throughout the world; and (viii) any similar or equivalent rights to any of the foregoing anywhere in the world.

"Knowledge" with respect to the Company means all facts [actually] known by any officer or director of the Company or the Shareholder or those additional individuals listed on Exhibit 1.2(b) on the date hereof [following due inquiry and diligence with respect to the matters at hand].

"Labor Laws" means all Laws and all contracts or collective bargaining agreements governing or concerning labor relations, unions and collective bargaining, conditions of employment, employment discrimination and harassment, wages, hours or occupational safety and health, including ERISA, the United States Immigration Reform and Control Act of 1986, the United States National Labor Relations Act, the United States Civil Rights Acts of 1866 and 1964, the United States Equal Pay Act, ADEA, ADA, FMLA, WARN, the United States Occupational Safety and Health Act, the United States Davis Bacon Act, the United States Walsh-Healy Act, the United States Service Contract Act, United States Executive Order 11246, FLSA and the United States Rehabilitation Act of 1973 and all rules and regulations promulgated under such acts.

"Laws" means all statutes, rules, codes, regulations, restrictions, ordinances, orders, decrees, approvals, directives, judgments, injunctions, writs, awards and decrees of, or issued by, all Governmental Entities.

"Leased Real Property" means the parcels of real property used in connection with the Business of which the Company is the lessee (together with all fixtures and improvements thereon).

"Legal Dispute" means any action, suit or proceeding between or among the Parties and their respective Affiliates arising in connection with any disagreement, dispute, controversy or claim arising out of or relating to this Agreement or any related document.

"Licenses" means all notifications, licenses, permits (including environmental, construction and operation permits), franchises, certificates, approvals, exemptions, classifications, registrations and other similar documents and authorizations issued by any Governmental Entity, and applications therefore.

"Liens" mean all mortgages, liens, pledges, security interests, charges, claims, restrictions and encumbrances of any nature whatsoever.

"Material Adverse Effect" means any state of facts, change, event, effect or occurrence (when taken together with all other states of fact, changes, events, effects or occurrences) that is or may be reasonably likely to be materially adverse to the financial condition, results of operations, properties, assets or liabilities (including contingent liabilities) of the Company, the Business or the Assets taken as a whole.

"Net Working Capital" means the current assets included in the Assets less the current liabilities included in the Assumed Liabilities, as reflected on the Final Working Capital Schedule.

"NLRB" means the United States National Labor Relations Board.

"Non-Assignable Contracts" means Assumed Contracts that require third-party consents for assignment that have not been obtained by the Company as of the Closing.

"Noncompete Period" means the period beginning on the Closing Date and continuing for a period of [____] years from the Closing Date.

"Owned Real Property" means the parcels of real property used in connection with the Business of which the Company is owner (together with all fixtures and improvements thereon).

"OSHA" means the United States Occupational Safety and Health Administration.

"Permitted Liens" means (i) Liens for taxes not yet due and payable, (ii) statutory Liens of landlords, (iii) Liens of carriers, warehousemen, mechanics, materialmen and repairmen incurred in the ordinary course of business consistent with past practice and not yet delinquent and (iv) zoning, building, or other restrictions, variances, covenants, rights of way, encumbrances, easements and other minor irregularities in title, none of which, individually or in the aggregate, (1) interfere in any material respect with the present use of or occupancy of the affected parcel by the Company, (2) have more than an immaterial effect on the value thereof or its use or (3) would impair the ability of such parcel to be sold for its present use.

"Person" means any individual, corporation, partnership, joint venture, limited liability company, trust, unincorporated organization or Governmental Entity.

"Preliminary Working Capital Schedule" means a statement of the current assets included in the Assets and the current liabilities included in the Assumed Liabilities as of the close of business on the Closing Date in accordance with GAAP applied on a basis consistent with the [audited/unaudited] balance sheet of the Company at [DATE].

"Purchaser Ancillary Documents" means any certificate, agreement, document or other instrument, other than this Agreement, to be executed and delivered by the Purchaser in connection with the transactions contemplated hereby.

"Purchaser Indemnified Parties" means the Purchaser and its Affiliates, their respective officers, directors, employees, agents and representatives and the heirs, executors, successors and assigns of any of the foregoing.

"Real Property" means the Owned Real Property and the Leased Real Property.

"Receivables" means the Company's accounts receivable as of [DATE].

"Registered Intellectual Property" means all United States, international and foreign: (i) patents and patent applications (including provisional applications); (ii) registered trademarks and service marks, applications to register trademarks and service marks, intent-to-use applications, or other registrations or applications related to trademarks and service marks; (iii) registered copyrights and applications for copyright registration; (iv) domain name registrations; and (v) any other Intellectual Property that is the subject of an application, certificate, filing, registration or other document issued, filed with, or recorded with any federal, state, local or foreign Governmental Entity or other public body.

"Release" means, with respect to any Hazardous Material, any spilling, leaking, pumping, pouring, emitting, emptying, discharging, injecting, escaping, leaching, dumping or disposing into any surface or ground water, drinking water supply, soil, surface or subsurface strata or medium, or the ambient air.

"Shareholder Ancillary Documents" means any certificate, agreement, document or other instrument, other than this Agreement, to be executed and delivered by the Shareholder in connection with the transactions contemplated hereby.

"Target Working Capital" means an amount equal to $_____.

"Taxes" means all taxes, assessments, charges, duties, fees, levies and other governmental charges, including income, franchise, capital stock, real property, personal property, tangible, intangible, withholding, employment, payroll, social security, social contribution, unemployment compensation, disability, transfer, sales, use, excise, license, occupation, registration, stamp, premium, environmental, customs duties, alternative or add-on minimum, estimated, gross receipts, value-added and all other taxes of any kind for which the Company may have any liability imposed by any Governmental Entity, whether disputed or not, and any charges, interest or penalties imposed by any Governmental Entity.

"Tax Return" means any report, return, declaration or other information required to be supplied to a Governmental Entity in connection with Taxes, including estimated returns and reports of every kind with respect to Taxes.

"Termination Date" means the date prior to the Closing when this Agreement is terminated in accordance with Article IX.

"Territory" means [DEFINE] [Should include, at a minimum, the area where any customer or actively sought prospective customer of the Company is located].

"Treasury Regulations" means the Income Tax Regulations, including Temporary Regulations, promulgated under the Code.

"WARN" means the United States Worker Adjustment and Retraining Notification Act and the rules and regulations promulgated thereunder.

"Working Capital Deficit" means the amount by which the Net Working Capital calculated in accordance with Section 3.3 is less than the Target Working Capital.

"Working Capital Surplus" means the amount by which the Net Working Capital calculated in accordance with Section 3.3 exceeds the Target Working Capital.

Section 1.3 Other Definitions. Each of the following terms is defined in the Section set forth opposite such term:

Term	Section

[List additional terms defined in the various agreement sections]

Section 1.4 Accounting Terms. All accounting terms not specifically defined herein shall be construed in accordance with GAAP.

ARTICLE II
PURCHASE AND SALE

Section 2.1 Agreement to Purchase and Sell. Subject to the terms and conditions hereof, at the Closing and except as otherwise specifically provided in this Article II, the Company, in consideration for the payment of the Purchase Price in accordance with Section 3.2, shall grant, sell, assign, transfer, convey and deliver to the Purchaser, and the Purchaser shall purchase and acquire from the Company, all right, title and interest of the Company in and to (a) the Business and (b) except for the Excluded Assets, all of the assets, properties and rights of the Company of every kind and description, real, personal and mixed, tangible and intangible, wherever situated (which assets, properties and rights are collectively referred to herein as the "Assets"), free and clear of all Liens, other than Permitted Liens, and the Purchaser shall assume the Assumed Liabilities.

Section 2.2 Assets. Except as otherwise expressly set forth in Section 2.3, the Assets shall include the following assets, properties and rights of the Company as of the close of business on the Closing Date:

(a) all inventory, including office and other supplies, spare, replacement and component parts, and other inventory property located at, stored on behalf of or in transit to the Company;

(b) all deposits, advances, prepaid expenses and credits (collectively, the "Deposits");

(c) all fixed assets, equipment, furnishings, computer hardware, vehicles, fixtures and other tangible personal property;

(d) all rights of the Company under the Assumed Contracts;

(e) all Real Property and all licenses, permits, approvals, qualifications, easements and other rights relating thereto;

(f) all goodwill, patents, patent applications, copyrights, copyright applications, methods, know-how, software, technical documentation, processes, procedures, inventions, trade secrets, trademarks, trade names, service marks, service names, registered user names, technology, research records, data, designs, plans, drawings, manufacturing know-how and formulas, whether patentable or unpatentable, and other intellectual or proprietary rights or property of the Company (and all rights thereto and applications therefore), including all Company Intellectual Property;

(g) all accounts receivable, notes receivable and other receivables and any security therefore;

(h) all rights to causes of action, lawsuits, judgments, claims and demands of any nature available to or being pursued by the Company, whether arising by way of counterclaim or otherwise;

(i) all rights in and under all express or implied guarantees, warranties, representations, covenants, indemnities and similar rights in favor of the Company;

(j) all Licenses to the extent that they are assignable, including those set forth on Schedule 4.25 (unless otherwise indicated thereon);

(k) all information, files, correspondence, records, data, plans, reports, contracts and recorded knowledge in whatever media retained or stored; and

(l) all other tangible and intangible assets of any kind or description, wherever located, that are (i) carried on the books of the Company or (ii) owned by the Company.

Section 2.3 Excluded Assets. Notwithstanding anything to the contrary set forth herein, the Assets shall not include the following assets, properties and rights of the Company (collectively, the "Excluded Assets"):

(a) all ownership and other rights with respect to the Company Benefit Plans;

(b) any permit, approval, license, qualification, registration, certification, authorization or similar right that by its terms is not transferable to the Purchaser, including those indicated on Schedule 4.25 as not being transferable;

(c) any accounts receivable from an Affiliate of the Company;

(d) the charter documents of the Company, minute books, stock ledgers, tax identification numbers, books of account and other constituent records relating to the corporate organization of the Company;

(e) the rights that accrue to the Company hereunder;

(f) [except as relating to the Deposits, any cash, cash equivalents or marketable securities and all rights to any bank accounts of the Company;] and

(g) all of the properties and assets that shall have been transferred or disposed of by the Company or any Affiliate of the Company prior to Closing in the ordinary course of business without violation of this Agreement.

[DESCRIBE ANY OTHER EXCLUDED ASSETS]

Section 2.4 Assumption of Assumed Liabilities.

(a) Except as provided in Section 2.4(b), the Purchaser shall not assume, in connection with the transactions contemplated hereby, any liability or obligation of the Company whatsoever, and the Company shall retain responsibility for all liabilities and obligations accrued as of or on the Closing Date and all liabilities and obligations arising from the Company's operations prior to or on the Closing Date, whether or not accrued and whether or not disclosed.

(b) As the sole exception to the provisions in Section 2.4(a), effective as of the close of business on the Closing Date, the Purchaser shall assume the following liabilities and obligations of the Company existing as of such time and arising out of the conduct of the Business prior to or on the Closing Date (collectively, the "Assumed Liabilities"):

(i) the obligations of the Company under each Assumed Contract to the extent such obligations are not required to be performed on or prior to the Closing Date, are disclosed on the face of such Assumed Contract and accrue and relate to the operations of the Business subsequent to the Closing Date; and

(ii) those current liabilities of the Company of the types listed on Schedule 2.4(b)(ii) to the extent and in the amount each such type is reflected as a current liability on the Final Working Capital Schedule.

(iii) [DESCRIBE ANY OTHER ASSUMED LIABILITIES]

Section 2.5 Excluded Liabilities. Specifically, and without in any way limiting the generality of Section 2.4(a), the Assumed Liabilities shall not include, and in no event shall the Purchaser assume, agree to pay, discharge or satisfy any liability or obligation hereunder or otherwise have any responsibility for any liability or obligation (together with all other liabilities that are not Assumed Liabilities, the "Excluded Liabilities"):

(a) relating to any liability or obligation (including accounts payable) owed to the Shareholder or any Affiliate of the Company;

(b) for (i) Taxes with respect to any period or (ii) any liability of the Company for unpaid Taxes of any Person (other than the Company) under Treasury Regulations Section 1.1502-6 (or any similar provisions of state, local or foreign law), as a transferee or successor, by contract or otherwise;

(c) for any indebtedness with respect to borrowed money, including any interest or penalties accrued thereon;

(d) relating to, resulting from, or arising out of, (i) claims made in pending or future suits, actions, investigations or other legal, governmental or administrative proceedings or (ii) claims based on violations of law, breach of contract, employment practices or environmental, health and safety matters or any other actual or alleged failure of the Company to perform any obligation, in each case arising out of, or relating to, (x) events that shall have occurred, (y) services performed, or (z) the operation of the Business, prior to the Closing;

(e) pertaining to any Excluded Asset;

(f) relating to, resulting from, or arising out of, any non-Business operation of the Company any former operation of the Company that has been discontinued or disposed of prior to the Closing;

(g) under or relating to any Company Benefit Plan, whether or not such liability or obligation arises prior to, on or following the Closing Date; or

(h) of the Company and the Shareholder arising or incurred in connection with the negotiation, preparation and execution hereof and the transactions contemplated hereby and any fees and expenses of counsel, accountants, brokers, financial advisors or other experts of the Company or the Shareholder.

Such Excluded Liabilities shall include all claims, actions, litigation and proceedings relating to any or all of the foregoing and all costs and expenses in connection therewith.

ARTICLE III
PURCHASE PRICE; ADJUSTMENTS; ALLOCATIONS

Section 3.1 Purchase Price. Subject to adjustment pursuant to Section 3.3 and to the indemnification obligations under Section 10.1, the aggregate amount to be paid for the Assets (the "Purchase Price") shall be $_____. In addition to the foregoing payment, as consideration for the grant, sale, assignment, transfer and delivery of the Assets, the Purchaser shall assume and discharge the Assumed Liabilities.

Section 3.2 Payment of Purchase Price.

(a) Not less than two Business Days prior to the Closing Date, the Company and the Purchaser shall agree upon the estimated amount of the Working Capital Deficit or the Working Capital Surplus, as the case may be.

(b) On the Closing Date, the Purchaser shall:

(i) deliver to the Company the Holdback Note; and

(ii) pay or cause to be paid to the Company or to such third parties as the Company may designate in accordance with Section 3.2(d) an amount equal to the Purchase Price minus the sum of (1) the estimated Working Capital Deficit, if any, determined in accordance with Section 3.2(a), (2) the aggregate principal amount of the Holdback Note and plus the estimated Working Capital Surplus, if any, determined in accordance with Section 3.2(a).

(c) Within five Business Days following the determination of the Final Working Capital Schedule in accordance with Section 3.3:

(i) [Add Working Capital Deficit Adjustment Procedure]

(ii) [Add Working Capital Surplus Adjustment Procedure]

(iii) Any payment made pursuant to this Section 3.2(c) shall include simple interest at the rate of [INTEREST RATE] per annum from the Closing Date through the date of such payment.

(d) All payments required under this Section 3.2 or any other provision hereof shall be made in cash by wire transfer of immediately available funds to such bank account(s) as shall be designated in writing by the recipient(s) at least three Business Days prior to the applicable payment date.

Section 3.3 Adjustment of Purchase Price.

(a) As promptly as practicable following the Closing Date (but in any event within 90 days), the Purchaser shall prepare and deliver to the Company the Preliminary Working Capital Schedule.

(b) The Company shall have 30 days following receipt of the Preliminary Working Capital Schedule during which to notify the Purchaser of any dispute of any item contained in the Preliminary Working Capital Schedule, which notice shall set forth in reasonable detail the basis for such dispute. In the event the Company does not notify the Purchaser of any such dispute within such 30-day period, the Preliminary Working Capital Schedule shall be deemed to be the Final Working Capital Schedule. The Purchaser and the Company shall cooperate in good faith to resolve any such dispute as promptly as possible, and upon such resolution, the Final Working Capital Schedule shall be prepared in accordance with the agreement of the Purchaser and the Company.

(c) [**Add Dispute Resolution Procedure**]

Section 3.4 Allocation of Purchase Price. Attached as Schedule 3.4 is an allocation of the Purchase Price, the Assumed Liabilities and other capitalizable costs to the Assets and the covenant not to compete contained in Section 6.13. The Purchaser and the Company shall file all Tax Returns on the basis of such allocation.

Section 3.5 Allocation of Certain Items. With respect to certain expenses incurred with respect to the Assets in the operation of the Business, the following allocations shall be made between the Company and the Purchaser: [**Consider Taxes, Utilities, Workers' Compensation, others**]

Appropriate cash payments by the Purchaser or the Company, as the case may require, shall be made hereunder from time to time as soon as practicable after the facts giving rise to the obligation for such payments are known in the amounts necessary to give effect to the allocations provided for in this Section 3.5; provided, however, that such payments shall not be required to the extent an accrued expense or prepaid expense is adequately reflected with respect to such item on the Final Working Capital Schedule.

ARTICLE IV
REPRESENTATIONS AND WARRANTIES OF COMPANY
AND SHAREHOLDER

The Company and the Shareholder hereby, jointly and severally, represent and warrant to the Purchaser as follows as of the date hereof and the Closing Date:

Section 4.1 Organization. [Each of] [T]he Company [and the Shareholder] is a corporation duly formed and validly existing under the Laws of the jurisdiction set forth in the introductory paragraph hereof and has all requisite power and authority to own, lease and operate its properties and to carry on its business as now being conducted. The Company is duly qualified or registered as a foreign corporation to transact business under the Laws of each jurisdiction where the character of its activities or the location of the properties owned or leased by it requires such qualification or registration. The Company has heretofore made available to the Purchaser true, correct and complete copies of its charter documents as currently in effect and its corporate record books with respect to actions taken by its shareholders and board of directors. Schedule 4.1 contains a true and correct list of the jurisdictions in which the Company is qualified or registered to do business as a foreign corporation.

Section 4.2 Authorization.

(a) The Shareholder has the right, power and capacity to execute and deliver this Agreement and the Shareholder Ancillary Documents and to perform its obligations hereunder and thereunder and to consummate the transactions contemplated hereby and thereby. The execution and delivery of this Agreement and the Shareholder Ancillary Documents by the Shareholder and the performance by the Shareholder of its obligations hereunder and thereunder and the consummation of the transactions provided for herein and therein have been duly and validly authorized by the Shareholder acting in a fiduciary, representative or corporate capacity (if applicable). This Agreement has been, and the Shareholder Ancillary Documents shall be as of the Closing Date, duly executed and delivered by the Shareholder and do or shall, as the case may be, constitute the valid and binding agreements of the Shareholder, enforceable against the Shareholder in accordance with their respective terms, subject to applicable bankruptcy, insolvency and other similar Laws affecting the enforceability of creditors' rights generally, general equitable principles and the discretion of courts in granting equitable remedies. Prior to the Shareholder's execution hereof, in the event the Shareholder is acting in a fiduciary, representative or corporate capacity, the Shareholder has furnished to the Purchaser a true and correct copy of each and every will, trust, agreement or other document that establishes or relates to the right, power, capacity or authority of the Shareholder to execute, deliver and perform this Agreement and the Shareholder Ancillary Documents and to consummate the transactions contemplated hereby and thereby.

(b) The Company has full power and authority to execute and deliver this Agreement and the Company Ancillary Documents and to perform its obligations hereunder and thereunder and to consummate the transactions contemplated hereby and thereby. The execution and delivery of this Agreement and the Company Ancillary Documents by the Company and the performance by the Company of its obligations hereunder and thereunder and the consummation of the transactions provided for herein and therein have been duly and validly authorized by all necessary board and shareholder action on the part of the Company. The Shareholder and the board of directors of the Company have approved the execution, delivery and performance of this Agreement and the Company Ancillary Documents and the consummation of the transactions contemplated hereby and thereby. This Agreement has been, and the Company Ancillary Documents shall be as of the Closing Date, duly executed and delivered by the Company and do or shall, as the case may be, constitute the valid and binding agreements of the Company, enforceable against the Company in accordance with their respective terms, subject to applicable bankruptcy, insolvency and other similar Laws affecting the enforceability of creditors' rights generally, general equitable principles and the discretion of courts in granting equitable remedies.

Section 4.3 Absence of Restrictions and Conflicts. The execution, delivery and performance of this Agreement, the Shareholder Ancillary Documents and the Company Ancillary Documents, the consummation of the transactions contemplated hereby and thereby and the fulfillment of and compliance with the terms and conditions hereof and thereof do not or shall not (as the case may be), with the passing of time or the giving of notice or both, violate or conflict with, constitute a breach of or default under, result in the loss of any benefit under, permit the acceleration of any obligation under or create in any party the right to terminate, modify or cancel, (a) any term or provision of the charter documents of the Company [**or the Shareholder**], (b) except as indicated on Schedule 4.12, any Assumed Contract or any other contract, will, agreement, permit, franchise, license or other instrument applicable to the Shareholder, the Company or the Business, (c) any judgment, decree or order of any Governmental Entity to which the Company or the Shareholder is a party or by which the Company or the Shareholder or any of their respective properties are bound or (d) any Law or arbitration award applicable to the Company, the Shareholder or the Business. No consent, approval, order or authorization of, or registration, declaration or filing with, any Governmental Entity is required with respect to the Company or the Shareholder in connection with the execution, delivery or performance of this Agreement, the Shareholder Ancillary Documents or the Company Ancillary Documents or the consummation of the transactions contemplated hereby or thereby except as required by the HSR Act.

Section 4.4 Real Property.

(a) Schedule 4.4(a) sets forth a true and correct legal description of the Owned Real Property. The Company has (and shall convey to the Purchaser at the Closing) good and marketable title to each parcel of the Owned Real Property, free and clear of all Liens other than Permitted Liens.

(b) Schedule 4.4(b) sets forth a true and correct legal description of the Leased Real Property.

(c) The Company has a valid leasehold interest in the Leased Real Property, and the leases granting the Company such interests are in full force and effect.

(d) No portion of the Real Property, or any building or improvement located thereon, violates any Law, including those Laws relating to zoning, building, land use, environmental, health and safety, fire, air, sanitation and noise control. Except for the Permitted Liens, no Real Property is subject to (i) any governmental decree or order (or, to the Knowledge of the Company, threatened or proposed order) or (ii) any rights of way, building use restrictions, exceptions, variances, reservations or limitations of any nature whatsoever.

(e) The improvements and fixtures on the Real Property are in good operating condition and in a state of good maintenance and repair, ordinary wear and tear excepted, are adequate and suitable for the purposes for which they are presently being used. None of the buildings and improvements owned or utilized by the Company are constructed of, or contains as a component part thereof, any material that, either in its present form or as such material could reasonably be expected to change through aging and normal use and service, releases any substance, whether gaseous, liquid or solid, that is or may be, either in a single dose or through repeated and prolonged exposure, injurious or hazardous to the health of any individual who may from time to time be in or about such buildings or improvements. There is no condemnation, expropriation or similar proceeding pending or, to the Knowledge of the Company, threatened against any of the Real Property or any improvement thereon. The Real Property constitutes all of the real property utilized by the Company in the operation of the Business in accordance with the Company's part practices.

Section 4.5 Title to Assets; Related Matters. The Assets constitute all of the assets necessary and sufficient to conduct the operations of the Business in accordance with the Company's past practices. Except as set forth on Schedule 4.5, the Company has (and shall convey to the Purchaser at the Closing) good and marketable title to the Assets (other than the Owned Real Property), free and clear of all Liens. All equipment and other items of tangible personal property and assets included in the Assets (a) are in good operating condition and in a state of good maintenance and repair, ordinary wear and tear excepted, (b) are usable in the regular and ordinary course of business and (c) conform to all applicable Laws. The Company has no Knowledge of any defect or problem with any Asset. No Person other than the Company owns any equipment or other tangible personal property or assets situated on the premises of the Company that are necessary to the operation of the Business, except for the leased items that are subject to personal property leases. Since [DATE], the Company has not sold, transferred or disposed of any assets, other than sales of inventory in the ordinary course of business. Schedule 4.5 sets forth a true, correct and complete list and general description of each item of tangible personal property of the Company having a book value of more than $_____.

Section 4.6 Inventory. The Company's inventory (a) is sufficient for the operation of the Business in the ordinary course consistent with past practice, (b) consists of items that are good and merchantable within normal trade tolerances, (c) is of a quality and quantity presently usable or saleable in the ordinary course of business of the Company (subject to applicable reserves), (d) is valued on the books and records of the Company at the lower of cost or market with the cost determined under the [first-in-first-out] inventory valuation method consistent with past practice and (e) is subject to reserves determined in accordance with GAAP consistently applied. No previously sold inventory is subject to returns in excess of those historically experienced by the Company.

Section 4.7 Financial Statements. The Company has delivered to the Purchaser the Financial Statements. The Financial Statements have been prepared from, and are in accordance with, the books and records of the Company, which books and records are maintained in accordance with GAAP (except as expressly noted on Schedule 4.7) consistently applied throughout the periods indicated, and such books and records have been maintained on a basis consistent with the past practice of the Company. Each balance sheet included in the Financial Statements (including the related notes and schedules) fairly presents the financial position of the Company as of the date of such balance sheet, and each statement of income and cash flows included in the Financial Statements (including the related notes and schedules) fairly presents the results of operations and changes in cash flows, as the case may be, of the Company for the periods set forth therein, in each case in accordance with GAAP (except as expressly noted therein or on Schedule 4.7) consistently applied during the periods involved. Since [DATE], there has been no change in any accounting (or tax accounting) policy, practice or procedure of the Company.

Section 4.8 No Undisclosed Liabilities. Except as disclosed on Schedule 4.8, the Company does not have any liabilities or obligations (whether absolute, accrued, contingent or otherwise) that are not adequately reflected or provided for in the [audited/unaudited] balance sheet of the Company at [DATE], except liabilities and obligations that have been incurred since the date of such balance sheet in the ordinary course of business, consistent with the past practice of the Company, and are not (singly or in the aggregate) material to the Business and in the aggregate are not in excess of $_____.

Section 4.9 Absence of Certain Changes. Since [DATE] and except as set forth on Schedule 4.9, there has not been (i) any Material Adverse Effect, (ii) any damage, destruction, loss or casualty to property or assets of the Company (including the Assets) with a value in excess of $_____, whether or not covered by insurance, or (iii) any action taken of the type described in Section 6.1, that, had such action occurred following the date hereof without the Purchaser's prior approval, would be in violation of such Section 6.1.

Section 4.10 Legal Proceedings. Except as set forth on Schedule 4.10, there is no suit, action, claim, arbitration, proceeding or investigation pending or, to the Knowledge of the Company, threatened against, relating to or involving the Company, the Business or the Assets before any Governmental Entity. No suit, action, claim, proceeding or investigation pending or threatened against, relating to or involving the Company, the Business or the Assets before any Governmental Entity (including any of those set forth on Schedule 4.10), if finally determined adversely, are reasonably likely, individually or in the aggregate, to have a Material Adverse Effect. The Company is not subject to any judgment, decree, injunction, rule or order of any court or arbitration panel.

Section 4.11 Compliance with Law. The Company is (and has been at all times during the past five years) in compliance with all applicable Laws (including applicable Laws relating to zoning, environmental matters and the safety and health of employees). Except as set forth on Schedule 4.11, (i) the Company has not been charged with, and has received no written notice that it is under investigation with respect to, and, to the Knowledge of the Company, is not otherwise now under investigation with respect to, a violation of any applicable Law, (ii) the Company is not a party to, or bound by, any order, judgment, decree, injunction, rule or award of any Governmental Entity and (iii) the Company has filed all reports and has all licenses and permits required to be filed with any Governmental Entity on or prior to the date hereof.

Section 4.12 Assumed Contracts. Schedule 4.12 sets forth a true, correct and complete list of the following contracts related to the Business (other than the Employment Agreements set forth on Schedule 4.14 and the Company Benefit Plans set forth on Schedule 4.15(a)): [List as applicable to transaction]

True, correct and complete copies of all Assumed Contracts have been made available to the Purchaser. The Assumed Contracts are legal, valid, binding and enforceable in accordance with their respective terms with respect to the Company and each other party to such Assumed Contracts. There is no existing default or breach of the Company under any Assumed Contract (or event or condition that, with notice or lapse of time or both could constitute a default or breach) and there is no such default (or event or condition that, with notice or lapse of time or both, could constitute a default or breach) with respect to any third party to any Assumed Contract. The Company is not participating in any discussions or negotiations regarding modification of or amendment to any Assumed Contract or entry in any new material contract applicable to the Business or the Assets. Schedule 4.12 identifies with an asterisk each Assumed Contract set forth therein that requires the consent of or notice to the other party thereto to avoid any breach, default or violation of such contract, agreement or other instrument in connection with the transactions contemplated hereby, including the assignment of such Assumed Contract to the Purchaser.

Section 4.13 Tax Returns; Taxes.

(a) Except as otherwise disclosed on Schedule 4.13(a): (i) all Tax Returns due to have been filed by the Company through the date hereof in accordance with all applicable Laws have been duly filed and are correct and complete in all respects; (ii) all Taxes, deposits and other payments for which the Company may have liability (whether or not shown on any Tax Return) have been paid in full or are accrued as liabilities for Taxes on the books and records of the Company; (iii) the amounts so paid, together with all amounts accrued as liabilities for Taxes (including Taxes accrued as currently payable) on the books of the Company, shall be adequate, based on the tax rates and applicable Laws in effect, to satisfy all liabilities for Taxes of the Company in any jurisdiction through the Closing Date, including Taxes accruable upon income earned through the Closing Date; (iv) there are not now any extensions of time in effect with respect to the dates on which any Tax Returns were or are due to be filed by the Company; (v) all deficiencies asserted as a result of any examination of a Tax Return of the Company have been paid in full, accrued on the books of the Company or finally settled, and no issue has been raised in any such examination that, by application of the same or similar principles, reasonably could be expected to result in a proposed deficiency for any other period not so examined; (vi) no claims have been asserted and no proposals or deficiencies for any Taxes of the Company are being asserted, proposed or threatened, and no audit or investigation of any Tax Return of the Company is currently underway, pending or threatened; (vii) no claim has ever been made against the Company by any Governmental Entity in a jurisdiction where the Company does not file Tax Returns and where it is or may be subject to taxation; (viii) the Company has withheld and paid all Taxes required to have been paid by it in connection with amounts paid or owing to any employee, independent contractor, creditor or stockholder thereof or other third party; (ix) there are no outstanding waivers or agreements by the Company or the Shareholder for the extension of time for the assessment of any Taxes or deficiency thereof, nor are there any requests for rulings, outstanding subpoenas or requests for information, notice of proposed reassessment of any property owned or leased by the Company or any other matter pending between the Company and any taxing authority; (x) there are no Liens for Taxes with respect to the Company or the Assets other than Liens for Taxes that are not yet due and payable, and no such Liens are pending or threatened; (xi) the Company has not been a member of an affiliated group filing a consolidated federal income Tax Return; and (xii) the Company does not have any liability for the Taxes of any Person (other than for itself) under Treasury Regulation Section 1.1502-6 (or any similar provision of state, local or foreign Law), as a transferee or successor, by contract or otherwise.

(b) Except as set forth on Schedule 4.13(b), the Company has delivered to the Purchaser true and complete copies of all open income Tax Returns (together with any agent's reports and any accountants' work papers) relating to its operations for the years for which Tax Returns are due to have been filed.

Section 4.14 Officers and Employees. Schedule 4.14 contains a true and complete list of (a) all of the officers of the Company, specifying their position, annual rate of compensation, date of birth, date of hire, social security number, home address, work location, length of service, hours of service, tax withholding history and the allocation of amounts paid and other benefits provided to each of them, respectively, and any other information reasonably requested by the Purchaser and (b) all of the employees (whether full-time, part-time or otherwise) and independent contractors of the Company as of the date hereof, specifying their position, status, annual salary, hourly wages, date of birth, date of hire, social security number, home address, work location, length of service, hours of service, tax withholding history and the allocation of amounts paid and other benefits provided to each of them, respectively, consulting or other independent contractor fees, together with an appropriate notation next to the name of any officer or other employee on such list who is subject to any written Employment Agreement or any other written term sheet or other document describing the terms or conditions of employment of such employee or of the rendering of services by such independent contractor and any other information reasonably requested by the Purchaser. Except as set forth on Schedule

4.14, the Company is not a party to or bound by any Employment Agreement. The Company has provided to the Purchaser true, correct and complete copies of each such Employment Agreement. Neither the Company nor the Shareholder has received a claim from any Governmental Entity to the effect that the Company has improperly classified as an independent contractor any Person named on Schedule 4.14. Neither the Company nor the Shareholder has made any verbal commitments to any officer, employee, former employee, consultant or independent contractor of the Company with respect to compensation, promotion, retention, termination, severance or similar matters in connection with the transactions contemplated hereby or otherwise. Except as indicated on Schedule 4.14, all officers and employees of the Company are active on the date hereof.

Section 4.15 **Company Benefit Plans.** [**Note: This representation and warranty is based on the assumption that the Purchaser is not assuming any of the Company's benefit plans. A longer form representation and warranty typical in a stock purchase agreement should be used if any benefit plans are to be assumed.**]

(a) Schedule 4.15(a) contains a true and complete list of each Company Benefit Plan currently sponsored, maintained or contributed to by the Company. [**Note: Identification of plans other than the most current plans is negotiable. In an asset deal, however, if no plans are assumed, current plans are identified merely to give buyer an idea of what benefits are available.**] Any special tax status enjoyed by such plan is noted on such schedule.

(b) Except as set forth on Schedule 4.15(b):

(i) With respect to each Company Benefit Plan identified on Schedule 4.15(a), the Company has heretofore delivered or made available to the Purchaser true and complete copies of the plan documents and any amendments thereto (or, in the event the plan is not written, a written description thereof), as is reasonably requested by the Purchaser.

(ii) The Company's records accurately reflect its employees' employment histories, including their hours of service and all such data is maintained in a usable form.

(iii) No Company Benefit Plan or ERISA Affiliate Plan is or was subject to Title IV of ERISA or Section 412 of the Code, nor is any Company Benefit Plan or ERISA Affiliate Plan a "multiemployer pension plan" (as defined in Section 3(37) of ERISA) or subject to Section 302 of ERISA. The Company has not terminated or withdrawn from or sought a funding waiver with respect to, and no fact exists that could reasonably be expected to result in a termination or withdrawal from or seeking a funding waiver with respect to, any Company Benefit Plan that is subject to Title IV of ERISA. The

Company has not incurred, and no fact exists that reasonably could be expected to result in, liability to the Company as a result of a termination, withdrawal or funding waiver with respect to an ERISA Affiliate Plan.

(iv) Each Company Benefit Plan has been established, registered, qualified, invested, operated and administered in all respects in accordance with its terms and in compliance with ERISA, the Code and all Applicable Benefit Laws. The Company has not incurred, and no fact exists that reasonably could be expected to result in any liability to the Company with respect to any Company Benefit Plan or any ERISA Affiliate Plan, including any liability, tax, penalty or fee under ERISA, the Code or any Applicable Benefit Law (other than to pay premiums, contributions or benefits in the ordinary course).

(v) No fact or circumstance exists that could adversely affect the tax-exempt status of a Company Benefit Plan that is intended to be tax-exempt. Further, each Company Benefit Plan intended to be "qualified" within the meaning of Section 401(a) of the Code and the trusts maintained thereunder that are intended to be exempt from taxation under Section 501(a) of the Code has received a favorable determination or other letter indicating that it is so qualified.

(vi) There is no pending or threatened complaint, claim (other than a routine claim for benefits), proceeding, examination, audit, investigation or other proceeding or action of any kind in or before any Governmental Entity with respect to any Company Benefit Plan and there exists no state of facts that after notice or lapse of time or both reasonably could be expected to give rise to any such claim, investigation, examination, audit or other proceeding or to affect the registration of any Company Benefit Plan required to be registered.

Section 4.16 Labor Relations. Except as set forth on Schedule 4.16:

(a) the Company's employees have not been, and currently are not, represented by a labor organization or group that was either certified or voluntarily recognized by any labor relations board (including the NLRB) or certified or voluntarily recognized by any other Governmental Entity;

(b) the Company has not been and the Company is not a signatory to a collective bargaining agreement with any trade union, labor organization or group;

(c) no representation election petition or application for certification has been filed by employees of the Company or is pending with the NLRB or any other Governmental Entity and no union organizing campaign or other attempt to organize or establish a labor union, employee organization or labor organization or group involving employees of the Company has occurred, is in progress or is threatened;

(d) the Company has not engaged in any unfair labor practice and the Company is not aware of any pending or threatened labor board proceeding of any kind, including any such proceeding against the Company or any trade union, labor union, employee organization or labor organization representing the Company's employees;

(e) no grievance or arbitration demand or proceeding, whether or not filed pursuant to a collective bargaining agreement, has been threatened, filed or is pending against the Company;

(f) no labor dispute, walk out, strike, slowdown, hand billing, picketing, work stoppage (sympathetic or otherwise), or other "concerted action" involving the employees of the Company has occurred, is in progress or has been threatened;

(g) no breach of contract or denial of fair representation claim has been filed or is pending or threatened against the Company or any trade union, labor union, employee organization or labor organization representing the Company's employees;

(h) no claim, complaint, charge or investigation for unpaid wages, bonuses, commissions, employment withholding taxes, penalties, overtime, or other compensation, benefits, child labor or record keeping violations has been filed or is pending or threatened under the Fair Labor Standards Act, Davis-Bacon Act, Walsh-Healey Act, or Service Contract Act or any other federal, state, local or foreign Law;

(i) no discrimination or retaliation claim, complaint, charge or investigation has been filed or is pending or threatened against the Company under the United States Civil Rights Acts of 1866 and 1964, the United States Equal Pay Act, ADEA, ADA, FMLA and FLSA, ERISA or any other federal Law or comparable state fair employment practices act or foreign Law;

(j) if the Company is a federal or state contractor obligated to develop and maintain an affirmative action plan, no discrimination claim, show cause notice, conciliation proceeding, sanction or debarment proceeding has been threatened or filed or is pending with the Office of Federal Contract Compliance Programs or any other federal agency or any comparable state or foreign agency or court and no desk audit or on-site review is in progress;

(k) no citation has been issued by OSHA against the Company and no notice of contest, claim, complaint, charge, investigation, or other administrative enforcement proceeding involving the Company has been filed or is pending or threatened against the Company under OSHA or any other applicable Law relating to occupational safety and health;

(l) no workers' compensation or retaliation claim, complaint, charge or investigation has been filed or is pending against the Company;

(m) no investigation or citation of the Company has occurred and no enforcement proceeding has been initiated or is pending or threatened under federal or foreign immigration Law;

(n) the Company has not taken any action that could constitute a "mass layoff," "mass termination,"or"plant closing"within the meaning of WARN or otherwise trigger notice requirements or liability under any federal, local, state or foreign plant closing notice or collective dismissal law;

(o) no wrongful discharge, retaliation, libel, slander or other claim, complaint, charge or investigation that arises out of the employment relationship between the Company and any of its employees has been filed or is pending or threatened against the Company under any applicable Law;

(p) the Company has maintained and currently maintains adequate insurance as required by applicable Law with respect to workers' compensation claims and unemployment benefits claims;

(q) the Company is in compliance with all applicable Labor Laws;

(r) the Company is not liable for any liability, judgement, decree, order, arrearage of wages or taxes, fine or penalty for failure to comply with any Labor Law;

(s) the Company has provided the Purchaser with a copy of the policy of the Company for providing leaves of absence under FMLA and Schedule 4.16 identifies (i) each employee who is eligible to request FMLA leave and the amount of FMLA leave utilized by each such employee during the current leave year, (ii) each employee who shall be on FMLA leave on the Closing Date and such employee's job title and description, salary and benefits and (iii) each employee who has requested FMLA leave to begin following the Closing Date, a description of the leave so requested and a copy of all notices provided to such employee regarding such leave; and

(t) the Company has paid or accrued all current assessments under workers' compensation legislation, and the Company has not been subject to any special or penalty assessment under such legislation that has not been paid.

Section 4.17 Insurance Policies. Schedule 4.17 contains a complete and correct list of all insurance policies carried by or for the benefit of the Company, specifying the insurer, the amount of and nature of coverage, the risk insured against, the deductible amount (if any) and the date through which coverage shall continue by virtue of premiums already paid. The Company maintains insurance with reputable insurers for the business and assets of the Company against all risks normally insured against, and in amounts normally carried, by Persons of similar size to the Company engaged in lines of business similar to the Business, and such coverage is sufficient. All insurance policies and bonds with respect to the business and assets of the Company are in full force and effect and shall be maintained by the Company in full force and effect as they apply to any matter, action or event relating to the Company occurring through the Closing Date and the Company has not reached or exceeded its policy limits for any insurance policy in effect at any time during the past five years.

Section 4.18 Environmental, Health and Safety Matters. Except as set forth on Schedule 4.18:

(a) the Company possesses all permits and approvals required under, and is in full compliance with, all Environmental Laws, and the Company is in compliance with all applicable limitations, restrictions, conditions, standards, prohibitions, requirements, obligations, schedules and timetables contained in all Environmental Laws or contained in any other Law, or any notice or demand letter issued thereunder;

(b) the Company has not received notice of actual or threatened liability under CERCLA or any similar foreign, state or local Law from any Governmental Entity or any third party and there is no fact or circumstance that could form the basis for the assertion of any claim against the Company under any Environmental Law, including CERCLA or any similar local, state or foreign Law with respect to any on-site or off-site location;

(c) the Company has not entered into or agreed to enter into, and the Company does not contemplate entering into, any consent decree or order, and the Company is not subject to any judgment, decree or judicial or administrative order relating to compliance with, or the cleanup of Hazardous Materials under, any applicable Environmental Law;

(d) the Company has not been alleged to be in violation of, and has not been subject to any administrative or judicial proceeding pursuant to, applicable Environmental Laws either now or any time during the past five years;

(e) the Company is not subject to any claim, obligation, liability, loss, damage or expense of any kind or nature whatsoever, contingent or otherwise, incurred or imposed or based upon any provision of any Environmental Law or arising out of any act or omission of the Company, or the Company's employees, agents or representatives or arising out of the ownership, use, control or operation by the Company of any plant, facility, site, area or property (including any plant, facility, site, area or property currently or previously owned or leased by the Company) from which any Hazardous Material was Released; [**Add additional Environmental Representations as appropriate**]

Section 4.19 Intellectual Property. Schedule 4.19 contains a list of all Company Registered Intellectual Property.

(a) No Company Intellectual Property or product or service of the Business related to Company Intellectual Property is subject to any proceeding or outstanding decree, order, judgment, agreement or stipulation (i) restricting in any manner the use, transfer or licensing thereof by the Company or (ii) that may affect the validity, use or enforceability of the Company Intellectual Property or any such product or service. Each item of Company Registered Intellectual Property is valid and subsisting. All necessary registration, maintenance and renewal fees currently due in connection with Company Registered Intellectual Property have been made and all necessary documents, recordations and certifications in connection with such Company Registered Intellectual Property have been filed with the relevant patent, copyright, trademark or other authorities in the United States or foreign jurisdictions, as the case may be, for the purpose of maintaining such Company Registered Intellectual Property.

(b) The Company owns and has good and exclusive title to, or has licenses (sufficient for the conduct of the Business as currently conducted and as proposed to be conducted) to, each item of Company Intellectual Property, free and clear of any Lien (excluding licenses and related restrictions); and the Company is the exclusive owner or exclusive licensee of all trademarks and service marks, trade names and domain names used in connection with and material to the operation or conduct of the Business, including the sale of any products or the provision of any services by the Business, free and clear of all Liens.

(c) The Company owns exclusively and has good title to all copyrighted works used in the Business that (i) are products of the Company or (ii) the Company otherwise expressly purports to own, free and clear of all Liens. Schedule 4.19(c) lists all works of original authorship used in the Business and prepared by or on behalf of the Company (including software programs) by title, version number, author(s) and publication date (if any), regardless of whether the Company has obtained or is seeking a copyright registration for such works.

(d) To the extent that any Company Intellectual Property has been developed or created by a third party for the Company, the Company has a written agreement with such third party with respect thereto and the Company thereby either (i) has obtained ownership of and is the exclusive owner of, or (ii) has obtained a license (sufficient for the conduct of the Business as currently conducted and as proposed to be conducted) to, all of such third party's Intellectual Property in such work, material or invention by operation of law or by valid assignment, to the fullest extent it is legally possible to do so.

(e) Schedule 4.19(e) lists all contracts, licenses and agreements to which the Company is a party (i) with respect to Company Intellectual Property licensed or transferred to any third party (other than end-user licenses in the ordinary course of business) or (ii) pursuant to which a third party has licensed or transferred any Company Intellectual Property to the Company.

(f) The operation of the Business as it is currently conducted and as proposed to be conducted, including the Company's design, development, marketing and sale of the products or services of the Company (including with respect to products currently under development), has not, does not and shall not infringe or misappropriate in any manner the Intellectual Property of any third party or, to the Knowledge of the Company, constitute unfair competition or trade practices under the Laws of any jurisdiction.

(g) The Company has no Knowledge of, and has not received written notice of or any other overt threat from any third party, that the operation of the Business as it is currently conducted and as proposed to be conducted, or any act, product or service of the Business, infringes or misappropriates the Intellectual Property of any third party or constitutes unfair competition or trade practices under the Laws of any jurisdiction.

(h) To the Knowledge of the Company, no Person has or is infringing or misappropriating any Company Intellectual Property.

(i) The Company has taken reasonable steps to protect the rights of the Company in the Confidential Information and any trade secret or confidential information of third parties used in the Business, and, without limiting the generality of the foregoing, the Company has enforced a policy requiring each employee and contractor to execute a proprietary information/confidentiality agreement in substantially the form provided to the Purchaser, and, except under confidentiality obligations, there has not been any disclosure by the Company of any Confidential Information or any such trade secret or confidential information of third parties.

Section 4.20 Software.

(a) Schedule 4.20(a) sets forth a true and complete list of: (i) the Company Proprietary Software, (ii) the Company Licensed Software and (iii) all technical and restricted materials relating to the acquisition, design, development, use or maintenance of computer code program documentation and materials used in connection with the Business.

(b) The Company has all right, title and interest in and to all intellectual property rights in the Company Proprietary Software. The Company has developed the Company Proprietary Software through its own efforts, as described in Section 4.20(d), and for its own account, and the Company Proprietary Software is free and clear of all Liens. The use of the Company Software does not breach any term of any license or other contract between the Company and any third party. The Company is in compliance with the terms and conditions of all license agreements in favor of the Company relating to the Company Licensed Software.

(c) The Company Proprietary Software does not infringe any patent, copyright or trade secret or any other intellectual property right of any third party. The source code for the Company Proprietary Software has been maintained in confidence.

(d) The Company Proprietary Software was: (i) developed by the Company's employees working within the scope of their employment at the time of such development; (ii) developed by agents, consultants, contractors or other Persons who have executed appropriate instruments of assignment in favor of the Company as assignee that have conveyed to the Company ownership of all of its intellectual property rights in the Company Proprietary Software; or (iii) acquired by the Company in connection with acquisitions in which the Company obtained appropriate representations, warranties and indemnities from the transferring party relating to the title to the Company Proprietary Software. The Company has not received notice from any third party claiming any right, title or interest in the Company Proprietary Software.

(e) The Company has not granted rights in the Company Software to any third party.

Section 4.21 Transactions with Affiliates. Except as set forth on Schedule 4.21, no officer or director of the Company, no Person with whom any such officer or director has any direct or indirect relation by blood, marriage or adoption, no entity in which any such officer, director or Person owns any beneficial interest (other than a publicly held corporation whose stock is traded on a national securities exchange or in the over-the-counter market and less than five percent of the stock of which is beneficially owned by all such officers, directors and Persons in the aggregate), no Affiliate of any of the foregoing and no current or former Affiliate of the Company has any interest in: (a) any contract, arrangement or understanding with, or relating to, the Business, the Assets or the Assumed Liabilities; (b) any loan, arrangement, understanding, agreement or contract for or relating to the Business or the Assets; or (c) any property (real, personal or mixed), tangible or intangible, used or currently intended to be used by the Company. Schedule 4.21 also sets forth a complete list of all accounts receivable, notes receivable and other receivables and accounts payable owed to or due from any Affiliate of the Company to the Company.

Section 4.22 Undisclosed Payments. Neither the Company nor the officers or directors of the Company, nor anyone acting on behalf of any of them, has made or received any payment not correctly categorized and fully disclosed in the Company's books and records in connection with or in any way relating to or affecting the Company or the Business.

Section 4.23 Customer and Supplier Relations. Schedule 4.23 contains a complete and accurate list of the names and addresses of the Customers. The Company maintains good relations with each of its Customers and, to the Knowledge of the Company, no event has occurred that could materially and adversely affect the Company's relations with any such Customer. Except as set forth on Schedule 4.23, no Customer (or former Customer) during the prior 12 months has canceled, terminated or made any threat to cancel or otherwise terminate any of such Customer's contracts with the Company or to decrease such Customer's usage of the Company's services or products. The Company has not received any notice or has no Knowledge to the effect that any current customer or supplier may terminate or materially alter its business relations with the Company, either as a result of the transactions contemplated hereby or otherwise.

Section 4.24 Notes and Accounts Receivable.

(a) Notes. All notes receivable of the Company owing by any director, officer or employee of the Company or by the Shareholder have been paid in full prior to the date hereof or shall have been paid in full prior to the Closing Date.

(b) Accounts Receivable. The Company has delivered to the Purchaser a true and complete schedule of the Receivables showing the amount of each Receivable and an aging of amounts due thereunder, which schedule is true and complete as of that date. Except as set forth on Schedule 4.24(b), to the Knowledge of the Company, the debtors to which the Receivables relate are not in or subject to a bankruptcy or insolvency proceeding and none of the Receivables have been made subject to an assignment for the benefit of creditors. Except as set forth on Schedule 4.24(b), all accounts receivables that are reflected on the [audited/unaudited] balance sheet of the Company at [DATE] (and that shall be reflected on the Final Working Capital Statement) (net of any reserves shown thereon, which reserves shall be established in accordance with the past practices of the Company and shall not be in excess of $_____) (i) are valid, existing and collectible in a manner consistent with the Company's past practice without resort to legal proceedings or collection agencies, (ii) represent monies due for goods sold and delivered or services rendered in the ordinary course of business and (iii) are not subject to any refund or adjustment or any defense, right of set-off, assignment, restriction, security interest or other Lien. Except as set forth on Schedule 4.24(b), all such Receivables are current and there are no disputes regarding the collectibility of any such Receivables. The Company has not factored any of its Receivables.

(c) Accounts Payable. The accounts payable of the Company reflected on the [audited/unaudited] balance sheet of the Company at

[DATE] (or that are reflected on the Final Working Capital Statement) arose from *bona fide* transactions in the ordinary course of business.

Section 4.25 Licenses. Schedule 4.25 is a true and complete list of all Licenses held by the Company. The Company owns or possesses all Licenses that are necessary to enable it to carry on the Business as presently conducted. All Licenses are valid, binding and in full force and effect. The execution, delivery and performance hereof and the consummation of the transactions contemplated hereby shall not adversely affect any License. The Company has taken all necessary action to maintain each License, except where the failure to so act shall not have an adverse effect on the Company or the Business. No loss or expiration of any License is threatened, pending or reasonably foreseeable (other than expiration upon the end of any term).

Section 4.26 Ethical Practices. Neither the Company nor any representative thereof has offered or given, and the Company has no Knowledge of any Person that has offered or given on its behalf, anything of value to: (i) any official of a Governmental Entity, any political party or official thereof or any candidate for political office; (ii) any customer or member of any Governmental Entity; or (iii) any other Person, in any such case while knowing or having reason to know that all or a portion of such money or thing of value may be offered, given or promised, directly or indirectly, to any customer or member of any Governmental Entity or any candidate for political office for the purpose of the following: (x) influencing any action or decision of such Person, in such Person's official capacity, including a decision to fail to perform such Person's official function; (y) inducing such Person to use such Person's influence with any Governmental Entity to affect or influence any act or decision of such Governmental Entity to assist the Company in obtaining or retaining business for, with, or directing business to, any Person; or (z) where such payment would constitute a bribe, kickback or illegal or improper payment to assist the Company in obtaining or retaining business for, with, or directing business to, any Person.

Section 4.27 Product and Service Warranties. Except as set forth on Schedule 4.27, the Company does not make any express warranty or guaranty as to goods sold, or services provided by, the Business, and there is no pending or, to the Knowledge of the Company, threatened claim alleging any breach of any such warranty or guaranty. Except as set forth on Schedule 4.27 (attached to which are copies of all such warranties), the Company has no exposure to, or liability under, any such warranty (a) beyond that which is typically assumed in the ordinary course of business by Persons engaged in businesses comparable in size and scope to the Business or (b) that would have an adverse effect on the Business or the Assets.

Section 4.28 Bank Accounts. [Note: This Section 4.28 applies only if Section 2.3(f) is deleted to include cash, cash equivalents or marketable securities as Assets.] Schedule 4.28 sets forth a true, correct and complete list and description of the Company's bank accounts, lock box accounts and other accounts maintained by or for the benefit of the Company (the "Bank Accounts").

Section 4.29 Brokers, Finders and Investment Bankers. Except as set forth on Schedule 4.29, neither the Company, nor any officer, member, director or employee of the Company nor any Affiliate of the Company, has employed any broker, finder or investment banker or incurred any liability for any investment banking fees, financial advisory fees, brokerage fees or finders' fees in connection with the transactions contemplated hereby.

Section 4.30 Disclosure.

(a) No representation, warranty or covenant made by the Company or the Shareholder in this Agreement, any Shareholder Ancillary Document or Company Ancillary Document contains an untrue statement of a material fact or omits to state a material fact required to be stated herein or therein or necessary to make the statements contained herein or therein not misleading. The financial projections relating to the Business delivered to the Purchaser are made in good faith and are based upon reasonable assumptions, and the Company is not aware of any fact or set of circumstances that could lead it to believe that such projections are incorrect or misleading in any material respect.

(b) Prior to the execution hereof, the Company has delivered to the Purchaser true and complete copies of the Assumed Contracts, all documents evidencing any of the Intellectual Property or any Lien on any Asset, and all other documents and instruments identified or referred to in the Schedules. Such delivery shall not alone constitute adequate disclosure of those facts required to be disclosed on any Schedule, and notice of their contents (other than by express reference on a Schedule) shall in no way limit the Company's or the Shareholder's other obligations or the Purchaser's other rights hereunder.

[Note: Add any other appropriate representations specific to business being acquired, etc.]

ARTICLE V
REPRESENTATIONS AND WARRANTIES OF PURCHASER

The Purchaser hereby represents and warrants to the Company and the Shareholder as follows:

Section 5.1 Organization. The Purchaser is a corporation duly organized, validly existing and in good standing under the laws of the jurisdiction set forth in the introductory paragraph hereof as its jurisdiction of incorporation and has all requisite corporate power and authority to own, lease and operate its properties and to carry on its business as now being conducted.

Section 5.2 Authorization. The Purchaser has full corporate power and authority to execute and deliver this Agreement and the Purchaser Ancillary Documents, to perform its obligations hereunder and thereunder and to consummate the transactions contemplated hereby and thereby. The execution and delivery of this Agreement and the Purchaser Ancillary Documents by the Purchaser, the performance by the Purchaser of its obligations hereunder and thereunder, and the consummation of the transactions provided for herein and therein have been duly and validly authorized by all necessary corporate action on the part of the Purchaser. This Agreement has been and, as of the Closing Date, the Purchaser Ancillary Documents shall be, duly executed and delivered by the Purchaser and do or shall, as the case may be, constitute the valid and binding agreements of the Purchaser, enforceable against the Purchaser in accordance with their respective terms, subject to applicable bankruptcy, insolvency and other similar laws affecting the enforceability of creditors' rights generally, general equitable principles and the discretion of courts in granting equitable remedies.

Section 5.3 Absence of Restrictions and Conflicts. The execution, delivery and performance of this Agreement and the Purchaser Ancillary Documents, the consummation of the transactions contemplated hereby and thereby and the fulfillment of, and compliance with, the terms and conditions hereof this Agreement and thereof do not or shall not (as the case may be), with the passing of time or the giving of notice or both, violate or conflict with, constitute a breach of or default under, result in the loss of any benefit under, or permit the acceleration of any obligation under, (a) any term or provision of the charter documents of the Purchaser, (b) any contract to which the Purchaser is a party, (c) any judgment, decree or order of any Governmental Entity to which the Purchaser is a party or by which the Purchaser or any of its properties is bound or (d) any statute, law, rule or regulation applicable to the Purchaser, except for compliance with the applicable requirements of the HSR Act.

ARTICLE VI
CERTAIN COVENANTS AND AGREEMENTS

Section 6.1 Conduct of Business by the Company. For the period commencing on the date hereof and ending on the Closing Date, the Company shall, except as expressly required hereby and except as otherwise consented to in advance in writing by the Purchaser:

(a) conduct its businesses in the ordinary course on a basis consistent with past practice and not engage in any new line of business or enter into any agreement, transaction or activity or make any commitment with respect to the Business or the Assets, except those in the ordinary course of business and not otherwise prohibited under this Section 6.1;

(b) use its best efforts to preserve intact the goodwill and business organization of the Company, keep the officers and employees of the Company available to the Purchaser and preserve the relationships and goodwill of the Company with customers, distributors, suppliers, employees and other Persons having business relations with the Company;

(c) maintain its existence and good standing in its jurisdiction of organization and in each jurisdiction in which the ownership or leasing of its property or the conduct of its business requires such qualification;

(d) duly and timely file or cause to be filed all reports and returns required to be filed with any Governmental Entity and promptly pay or cause to be paid when due all Taxes, assessments and governmental charges, including interest and penalties levied or assessed, unless diligently contested in good faith by appropriate proceedings;

(e) maintain in existing condition and repair (ordinary wear and tear excepted), consistent with past practices, all buildings, offices, shops and other structures located on the Real Property, and all equipment, fixtures and other tangible personal property located on the Real Property;

(f) not dispose of or permit to lapse any right to the use of any patent, trademark, trade name, service mark, license or copyright of the Company (including any of the Company Intellectual Property), or dispose of or disclose to any Person, any trade secret, formula, process, technology or know-how of the Company not heretofore a matter of public knowledge;

(g) not (i) sell any Asset, other than finished goods sold in the ordinary course of business, (ii) create, incur or assume any indebtedness secured by the Assets, (iii) grant, create, incur or suffer to exist any Lien on the Assets that did not exist on the date hereof, (iv) incur any liability or obligation (absolute, accrued or contingent), except in the ordinary course of business consistent with past practice, (v) write-off any guaranteed check, note or account receivable, except in the ordinary course of business consistent with past practice, (vi) write-down the value of any asset or investment (including any Asset) on the books or records of the Company, except for depreciation and amortization in the ordinary course of business and consistent with past practice, (vii) cancel any debt or waive any claim or right, (viii) make any commitment for any capital expenditure to be made on or following the date hereof in excess of $_____ in the case of any single expenditure or $_____ in the case of all capital expenditures or (ix) enter into any material contract or agreement without the written consent of the Purchaser;

[Add additional Affirmative Covenants and Negative Covenants as appropriate]

In connection with the continued operation of the Business during the period commencing on the date hereof and ending on the Closing Date, the Company shall confer in good faith on a regular and frequent basis with the Purchaser regarding operational matters and the general status of ongoing operations of the Company. The Company hereby acknowledges that the Purchaser does not and shall not waive any right it may have hereunder as a result of such consultations. The Company shall not take any action that would, or that could reasonably be expected to, result in any representation or warranty of the Company set forth herein to become untrue.

Section 6.2 Inspection and Access to Information. During the period commencing on the date hereof and ending on the Closing Date, the Company shall (and shall cause its officers, directors, employees, auditors and agents to) provide the Purchaser and its accountants, investment bankers, counsel, environmental consultants and other authorized representatives full access, during reasonable hours and under reasonable circumstances, to any and all of its premises, employees (including executive officers), properties, contracts, commitments, books, records and other information (including Tax Returns filed and those in preparation) and shall cause its officers to furnish to the Purchaser and its authorized representatives, promptly upon request therefore, any and all financial, technical and operating data and other information pertaining to the Company and the Business and otherwise fully cooperate with the conduct of due diligence by the Purchaser and its representatives.

Section 6.3 Notices of Certain Events. The Company shall promptly notify the Purchaser of:

(a) any change or event that, individually or in the aggregate, have had or could reasonably be expected to have a Material Adverse Effect on the Business, the Assets or the Assumed Liabilities or otherwise result in any representation or warranty of the Company hereunder being inaccurate in any material respect;

(b) any notice or other communication from any Person alleging that the consent of such Person is or may be required in connection with the transactions contemplated hereby;

(c) any notice or other communication from any Governmental Entity in connection with the transactions contemplated hereby;

(d) any action, suit, claim, investigation or proceeding commenced or, to its Knowledge, threatened against, relating to or involving or otherwise affecting the Company or the Business that, if pending on the date hereof, would have been required to have been disclosed pursuant to Section 4.10 or that relate to the consummation of the transactions contemplated hereby; and

(e) (i) the damage or destruction by fire or other casualty of any Asset or part thereof or (ii) any Asset or part thereof becoming the subject of any proceeding (or, to the Knowledge of the Company, threatened proceeding) for the taking thereof or of any right relating thereto by condemnation, eminent domain or other similar governmental action.

The Company hereby acknowledges that the Purchaser does not and shall not waive any right it may have hereunder as a result of such notifications.

Section 6.4 Interim Financials. As promptly as practicable following each regular accounting period subsequent to the end of the most recent fiscal year and prior to the Closing Date, the Company shall deliver to the Purchaser periodic financial reports in the form that it customarily prepares for its internal purposes concerning the Business and, if available, unaudited statements of the financial position of the Business as of the last day of each accounting period and consolidated statements of income and changes in financial position of such entities for the period then ended. The Company covenants that such interim statements (i) shall present fairly the financial condition of the Business as of their respective dates and the related results of their respective operations for the respective periods then ended, and (ii) shall be prepared on a basis consistent with prior interim periods.

Section 6.5 No Solicitation of Transactions. Neither the Company nor any of its Affiliates shall, directly or indirectly, through any officer, director, manager or agent of any of them or otherwise, initiate, solicit or encourage (including by way of furnishing non-public information or assistance), or enter into negotiations of any type, directly or indirectly, or enter into a confidentiality agreement, letter of intent or purchase agreement, merger agreement or other similar agreement with any Person other than the Purchaser with respect to a sale of all or any substantial portion of the Assets, or a merger, consolidation, business combination, sale of all or any substantial portion of the capital stock of the Company, or the liquidation or similar extraordinary transaction with respect to the Company. The Company shall notify the Purchaser orally (within one Business Day) and in writing (as promptly as practicable) of all relevant terms of any inquiry or proposal by a third party to do any of the foregoing that the Company or any of its Affiliates or any of their respective officers, directors, partners, managers, employees, investment bankers, financial advisors, attorneys, accountants or other representatives may receive relating to any of such matters. In the event such inquiry or proposal is in writing, the Company shall deliver to the Purchaser a copy of such inquiry or proposal together with such written notice.

Section 6.6 Reasonable Efforts; Further Assurances; Cooperation. Subject to the other provisions hereof, each Party shall each use its reasonable, good faith efforts to perform its obligations hereunder and to take, or cause to be taken, and do, or cause to be done, all things necessary, proper or advisable under applicable Law to obtain all consents required as described on Schedule 4.12 and all regulatory approvals and to satisfy all conditions to its obligations hereunder and to cause the transactions contemplated herein to be effected as soon as practicable, but in any event on or prior to the Expiration Date, in accordance with the terms hereof and shall cooperate fully with each other Party and its officers, directors, employees, agents, counsel, accountants and other designees in connection with any step required to be taken as a part of its obligations hereunder, including the following:

(a) Each Party promptly shall make its filings and submissions and shall take all actions necessary, proper or advisable under applicable Laws to obtain any required approval of any Governmental Entity with jurisdiction over the transactions contemplated hereby (except that the Purchaser shall have no obligation to take or consent to the taking of any action required by any such Governmental Entity that could adversely affect the Business, the Assets or the transactions contemplated by this Agreement or the Purchaser Ancillary Documents). Each Party shall furnish all information required for any application or other filing to be made pursuant to any applicable Law in connection with the transactions contemplated hereby.

(b) In the event any claim, action, suit, investigation or other proceeding by any Governmental Entity or other Person is commenced that questions the validity or legality of the Acquisition or any other transaction contemplated hereby or seeks damages in connection therewith, the Parties shall (i) cooperate and use all reasonable efforts to defend against such claim, action, suit, investigation or other proceeding, (ii) in the event an injunction or other order is issued in any such action, suit or other proceeding, use all reasonable efforts to have such injunction or other order lifted, and (iii) cooperate reasonably regarding any other impediment to the consummation of the transactions contemplated hereby.

(c) The Company shall give all notices to third parties and use its best efforts (in consultation with the Purchaser) to obtain all third-party consents (i) necessary, proper or advisable to consummate the transactions contemplated hereby, (ii) required to be given or obtained, including those required to be given or obtained on Schedule 4.12 and the other Schedules, (iii) required to avoid a breach of or default under any Assumed Contract in connection with the consummation of the transactions contemplated hereby or (iv) required to prevent a Material Adverse Effect, whether prior to, on or following the Closing Date.

(d) Each Party shall give prompt notice to the other Parties of (i) the occurrence, or failure to occur, of any event that the occurrence or failure of which would be likely to cause any representation or warranty of the Company, the Shareholder or the Purchaser, as the case may be, contained herein to be untrue or inaccurate at any time from the date hereof to the Closing Date or that shall or may result in the failure to satisfy any condition specified in Article VII and (ii) any failure of the Company, the Shareholder or the Purchaser, as the case may be, to comply with or satisfy any covenant, condition or agreement to be complied with or satisfied by any of them hereunder. Each of the Company and the Shareholder hereby acknowledges that the Purchaser does not and shall not waive any right it may have hereunder as a result of such notifications.

Section 6.7 Consents. The Company shall, during the remaining term of each Non-Assignable Contract, use all commercially available efforts to (a) obtain the consent of the third parties required thereunder, (b) make the benefit of such Non-Assignable Contract available to the Purchaser so long as the Purchaser fully cooperates with the Company and promptly reimburses the Company for all payments made by the Company (with the prior approval of the Purchaser) in connection therewith and (c) enforce, at the request of the Purchaser and at the expense and for the account of the Purchaser, any right of the Company arising from such Non-Assignable Contract against the other party or parties thereto (including the right to elect or terminate any such Non-Assignable Contract in accordance with the terms thereof). The Company shall not take any action or suffer any omission that could limit, restrict or terminate in any material respect the benefits to the Purchaser of such Non-Assignable Contract unless, in good faith and after consultation with and prior written notice to the Purchaser, the Company is (i) ordered orally or in writing to do so by a Governmental Entity of competent jurisdiction or (ii) otherwise required to do so by Law; provided that if any such order is appealable, the Company shall, at the Purchaser's cost and expense, take such actions as are requested by the Purchaser to file and pursue such appeal and to obtain a stay of such order. With respect to any such Non-Assignable Contract as to which the necessary approval or consent for the assignment or transfer to the Purchaser is obtained following the Closing, the Company shall transfer such Non-Assignable Contract to the Purchaser by execution and delivery of an instrument of conveyance reasonably satisfactory to the Purchaser and the Company within three Business Days following receipt of such approval or consent. Notwithstanding the foregoing, the Company shall not be indemnified to the extent of any losses that result from (i) the Company's failure to take any lawful action in accordance with the Purchaser's reasonable instructions or (ii) the Company's gross negligence or willful misconduct.

Section 6.8 Public Announcements. Subject to its legal obligations (including requirements of stock exchanges and other similar regulatory bodies), each Party shall consult with the other Parties with respect to the timing and content of all announcements regarding any aspect hereof or the transactions contemplated hereby to the financial community, Governmental Entities, employees, customers or the general public and shall use reasonable efforts to agree upon the text of any such announcement prior to its release.

Section 6.9 Supplements to Schedules. From time to time up to the Closing, the Company and the Shareholder shall promptly supplement or amend the Schedules that they have delivered with respect to any matter first existing or occurring following the date hereof that (a) if existing or occurring at or prior to the date hereof, would have been required to be set forth or described in the Schedules, or (b) is necessary to correct any information in the Schedules that has been rendered inaccurate thereby. No supplement or amendment to any Schedule shall have any effect for the purpose of determining satisfaction of the conditions set forth in Section 7.2 or the obligations of the Company and the Shareholder under Section 10.1(c).

Section 6.10 Employees.

[Note: This provision will vary based upon the policies of the Purchaser and the business terms struck by the Parties.]

(a) Transferred Employees. On the Closing Date effective as of the Closing, the Company shall terminate all of its employees, except as otherwise provided in this Section 6.10. Commencing on the Closing Date, the Purchaser shall offer employment, on an "at will" basis, to **[all of the employees of the Company who are "actively at work" on the Closing Date]** ("Potential Transferred Employees"). Potential Transferred Employees who accept such offer are, as of the time they first perform services for the Purchaser, referred to herein as the "Transferred Employees". The Purchaser shall have no obligation of any kind to offer employment or otherwise with respect to any employee of the Company who is not a Potential Transferred Employee and each such employee shall remain an employee of the Company unless otherwise agreed in writing by the Purchaser. For purposes hereof, "actively at work" means: (i) any employee who has averaged a minimum of 30 hours per week in a permanent position in the three months prior to the Closing Date; (ii) any employee absent on the Closing Date due to the FMLA or similar state Laws; (iii) any employee absent on the Closing Date due to maternity leave under the Company's maternity leave policy; (iv) any employee absent on the Closing Date due to military duty; (v) any employee absent on the Closing Date due to jury duty; and (vi) any employee absent on the Closing Date due to vacation or personal days consistent with the Company's employment policies.

(b) COBRA Coverage. The Company shall be solely responsible for offering and providing any COBRA Coverage with respect to any "qualified beneficiary" who is covered by a Company Benefit Plan that is a "group health plan" and who experiences a "qualifying event" on or prior to the Closing Date. The Purchaser shall be solely responsible for offering and providing any COBRA Coverage required with respect to any Transferred Employee (or other qualified beneficiary) who becomes covered by a group health plan sponsored or contributed to by the Purchaser and who experience a qualifying event following the Closing Date. For purposes hereof, each of "qualified beneficiary", "group health plan" and "qualifying event" shall have the meaning ascribed thereto in Section 4980B of the Code.

(c) Information. The Company shall provide the Purchaser all information relating to each Potential Transferred Employee as the Purchaser may reasonable require in connection with its employment of such individuals, including initial employment dates, termination dates, reemployment dates, hours of service, compensation and tax withholding history in a form that shall be usable by the Purchaser and such information shall be true and correct in all respects.

Section 6.11 Taxes; Expenses. Any Taxes or recording fees payable as a result of the Acquisition or any other action contemplated hereby shall be paid by the Company. The Parties shall cooperate in the preparation, execution and filing of all returns, questionnaires, applications and other documents regarding Taxes and all transfer, recording, registration and other fees that become payable in connection with the transactions contemplated hereby that are required or permitted to be filed at or prior to the Closing.

Section 6.12 Insurance. If requested by the Purchaser, the Company and the Shareholder shall in good faith cooperate with the Purchaser and take all actions reasonably requested by the Purchaser that are necessary or desirable to permit the Purchaser to have available to it following the Closing the benefits (whether direct or indirect) of the insurance policies maintained by or on behalf of the Company that are currently in force. All costs relating to the actions described in this Section 6.12 shall be borne by the Purchaser.

Section 6.13 Non-Competition.

(a) Confidential Information. The Company and the Shareholder shall hold in confidence at all times following the date hereof all Confidential Information and shall not disclose, publish or make use of Confidential Information at any time following the date hereof without the prior written consent of the Purchaser.

(b) Noncompetition.

(i) Each of the Company and the Shareholder hereby acknowledges that (A) the Company conducts Business throughout the Territory and (B) to protect adequately the interest of the Purchaser in the business of the Company, it is essential that any noncompete covenant with respect thereto cover all of the Business and the entire Territory.

(ii) The Company and the Shareholder shall not, during the Noncompete Period, in any manner, directly or indirectly or by assisting any other Person, engage in, have an equity or profit interest in, or render services (of an executive, marketing, manufacturing, research and development, administrative, financial, consulting or other nature) to any Person that conducts any of the Business in the Territory.

(c) Nonsolicitation. The Company and the Shareholder shall not, prior to the second anniversary of the Closing Date, in any manner, directly or indirectly or by assisting any other Person, recruit or hire away or attempt to recruit or hire away, on any of their behalves or on behalf of any other Person, any Transferred Employee.

(d) Severability. In the event a judicial or arbitral determination is made that any provision of this Section 6.13 constitutes an unreasonable or otherwise unenforceable restriction against the Company or the Shareholder, the provisions of this Section 6.13 shall be rendered void only to the extent that such judicial or arbitral determination finds such provisions to be unreasonable or otherwise unenforceable with respect to the Company or the Shareholder. In this regard, any judicial authority construing this Agreement shall be empowered to sever any portion of the Territory, any prohibited business activity or any time period from the coverage of this Section 6.13 and to apply the provisions of this Section 6.13 to the remaining portion of the Territory, the remaining business activities and the remaining time period not so severed by such judicial or arbitral authority. Moreover, notwithstanding the fact that any provision of this Section 6.13 is determined not to be specifically enforceable, the Purchaser shall nevertheless be entitled to recover monetary damages as a result of the breach of such provision by the Company or the Shareholder. The time period during which the prohibitions set forth in this Section 6.13 shall apply shall be tolled and suspended for a period equal to the aggregate time during which the Company or the Shareholder violates such prohibitions in any respect.

(e) Injunctive Relief. Any remedy at law for any breach of the provisions contained in this Section 6.13 shall be inadequate and the Purchaser shall be entitled to injunctive relief in addition to any other remedy the Purchaser might have hereunder.

Section 6.14 Name Change. Simultaneously with the Closing, the Company shall change its corporate name to remove any reference to the name "[NAME]" or any other trade name used in the Business. As promptly as practicable following the Closing, the Company shall file in all jurisdictions in which it is qualified to do business all documents necessary to reflect such change of name or to terminate its qualification therein. In connection with enabling the Purchaser, at or as soon as practicable following the Closing, to use the current corporate name of the Company, the Company shall, at or prior to the Closing, execute and deliver to the Purchaser all consents related to such change of name as may be requested by the Purchaser, and shall otherwise cooperate with the Purchaser.

Section 6.15 Risk of Loss. The risk of loss with respect to the Assets shall remain with the Company until the Closing. Until the Closing, the Company shall maintain in force all the policies of property damage insurance under which any Asset is insured. In the event prior to the Closing any Asset is lost, damaged or destroyed and such loss, damage or destruction would likely result in a Material Adverse Effect, then:

(a) the Purchaser may terminate this Agreement in accordance with the provisions of Section 9.1(d); or

(b) the Purchaser may require the Company to assign to the Purchaser the proceeds of any insurance payable as a result of the occurrence of such loss, damage or destruction and to reduce the Purchase Price by the amount of the replacement cost of the Assets that were lost, damaged or destroyed less the amount of any proceeds of insurance payable as a result of the occurrence.

Section 6.16 Customer Visits. During the period commencing on the date hereof and ending on the Closing Date, and subject to such reasonable limitations as the Shareholder shall deem necessary, the Shareholder shall permit, and shall cause the Company to permit, the Purchaser to discuss and meet, and shall cooperate in such discussions and meetings, with any customer of the Company that the Purchaser so requests. A senior executive of the Company, reasonably satisfactory to the Purchaser, shall accompany the Purchaser's representative to such meeting and shall participate with the Purchaser's representative in any such discussions. Furthermore, the Shareholder shall cooperate with the Purchaser in the preparation of a presentation to such customers with respect to the Acquisition.

ARTICLE VII
CONDITIONS TO CLOSING

Section 7.1 Conditions to Each Party's Obligations. The respective obligations of each Party to effect the transactions contemplated hereby shall be subject to the expiration or termination of the waiting period applicable to the consummation of the Acquisition under the HSR Act.

Section 7.2 Conditions to Obligations of the Purchaser. The obligations of the Purchaser to consummate the transactions contemplated hereby shall be subject to the fulfillment at or prior to the Closing of each of the following additional conditions:

(a) Injunction. There shall be no effective injunction, writ or preliminary restraining order or any order of any nature issued by a Governmental Entity of competent jurisdiction to the effect that the Acquisition may not be consummated as provided herein, no proceeding or lawsuit shall have been commenced by any Governmental Entity for the purpose of obtaining any such injunction, writ or preliminary restraining order and no written notice shall have been received from any Governmental Entity indicating an intent to restrain, prevent, materially delay or restructure the transactions contemplated hereby, in each case where the Closing would (or would be reasonably likely to) result in a material fine or penalty payable by the Purchaser or any of its Affiliates or to impose any restraint or restriction on Purchaser's operation of the Business following the Closing.

(b) Governmental Consents. All consents, approvals, orders or authorizations of, or registrations, declarations or filings with, all Governmental Entities required in connection with the execution, delivery or performance hereof shall have been obtained or made, except where the failure to have obtained or made any such consent, approval, order, authorization, registration, declaration or filing would not result in a material fine or penalty payable by the Purchaser or any of its Affiliates or any adverse effect on the assets, liabilities, results of operations, business or prospects of the Business following the Closing.

(c) Representations and Warranties. The representations and warranties of the Company and the Shareholder set forth in Article IV shall have been true and correct in all material respects as of the date hereof and shall be true and correct in all material respects as of the Closing Date as though made on and as of the Closing Date, except that those representations and warranties that by their terms are qualified by materiality shall be true and correct in all respects.

(d) Performance of Obligations of the Company. The Company and the Shareholder shall have performed in all material respects all covenants and agreements required to be performed by each of them hereunder at or prior to the Closing.

(e) No Material Adverse Effect. Between the date hereof and the Closing Date, there shall not have occurred (nor shall the Purchaser have become aware of) any Material Adverse Effect [or any development likely to result in a Material Adverse Effect];

(f) Company Certificate. The President and Chief Financial Officer of the Company shall have executed and delivered to the Purchaser a certificate as to compliance with the conditions set forth in Sections 7.2(b), (c), (d) and (e).

(g) Shareholder Certificate. The [authorized officers of the] Shareholder shall have executed and delivered to the Purchaser a certificate as to compliance with the conditions set forth in Sections 7.2(b), (c) and (d).

(h) Consents. The Company shall have obtained and delivered to the Purchaser the written consents (or waivers with respect thereto) as described on Schedule 4.12 (all such consents and waivers shall be in full force and effect).

(i) [Release of Liens. The Company shall have delivered to the Purchaser satisfactory evidence that all Liens affecting the Assets have been released.]

(j) [Purchaser Approvals. The Purchaser shall have received all necessary internal approvals of the transactions contemplated hereby.]

(k) [Estoppel and Consent Certificates. The Company shall have delivered to the Purchaser an Estoppel and Consent Certificate substantially in the form attached as Exhibit 7.2(k), executed by the landlord of each Leased Real Property;]

(l) [Title Commitment. The Purchaser shall have been able to obtain at its expense a commitment for a title insurance policy or policies in form and substance and at rates satisfactory to the Purchaser ensuring the Purchaser that at the Closing it shall acquire good, marketable and insurable title to the Owned Real Property, subject only to Permitted Liens. The Company shall have executed and delivered such owner's affidavits (in customary form) as are necessary to enable the Purchaser to obtain any such title insurance policy or policies.]

(m) Environmental Reports. The Company, at its sole cost and expense, shall have delivered to the Purchaser a Phase I environmental report with respect to each parcel included in the Owned Real Property, which report shall be reasonably satisfactory to the Purchaser.

(n) Opinion of Company's Counsel. The Purchaser shall have received an opinion of [NAME], counsel to the Company and the Shareholder, dated the Closing Date, substantially in the form attached as Exhibit 7.2(n).

(o) Ancillary Documents. The Company shall have delivered, or caused to be delivered, to the Purchaser the following:

(i) executed deeds, bills of sale, instruments of assignment, certificates of title and other conveyance documents, dated as of the Closing Date, transferring to the Purchaser all of the Company's right, title and interest in and to the Assets, together with possession of the Assets, including the Bill of Sale (the "Bill of Sale") substantially in the form of Exhibit 7.2(q)(i);

(ii) documents evidencing the assignment of the Assumed Contracts and the assignment of any assignable Licenses, including the Assignment and Assumption Agreement (the "Assignment and Assumption Agreement") substantially in the form of Exhibit 7.2(q)(ii);

(iii) a certificate by the Secretary or any Assistant Secretary of the Company, dated the Closing Date, as to (1) the good standing of the Company in its jurisdiction of incorporation and in each other jurisdiction where it is qualified to do business, (2) no amendments to the Company's charter documents and (3) the effectiveness of the resolutions of the board of directors and the Shareholder authorizing the execution, delivery and performance hereof by the Company passed in connection herewith and the transactions contemplated hereby; and

(iv) all other documents required to be entered into by the Company and the Shareholder pursuant hereto or reasonably requested by the Purchaser to convey the Assets to the Purchaser or to otherwise consummate the transactions contemplated hereby.

(p) FIRPTA Affidavit. The Company shall have delivered to the Purchaser a non-foreign affidavit dated as of the Closing Date and in form and substance required under the Treasury Regulations issued under Section 1445 of the Code so that the Purchaser is exempt from withholding any portion of the Purchase Price thereunder.

Section 7.3 Conditions to Obligations of the Company. The obligations of the Company and the Shareholder to consummate the transactions contemplated hereby shall be subject to the fulfillment at or prior to the Closing of each of the following additional conditions:

(a) Injunction. There shall be no effective injunction, writ or preliminary restraining order or any order of any nature issued by a Governmental Entity of competent jurisdiction to the effect that the Acquisition may not be consummated as provided herein, no proceeding or lawsuit shall have been commenced by any Governmental Entity for the purpose of obtaining any such injunction, writ or preliminary restraining order and no written notice shall have been received from any Governmental Entity indicating an intent to restrain, prevent, materially delay or restructure the transactions contemplated hereby, in each case where the Closing would (or would be reasonably likely to) result in a material fine or penalty payable by the Company or a material restriction on the Company's operations as a result of such matter.

(b) Governmental Consents. All consents, approvals, orders or authorizations of, or registrations, declarations or filings with, any Governmental Entity required in connection with the execution, delivery or performance hereof shall have been obtained or made, except where the failure to have obtained or made any such consent, approval, order, authorization, registration, declaration or filing would not result in a material fine or penalty payable by the Company or a material restriction on the Company's operations.

(c) Representations and Warranties. The representations and warranties of the Purchaser set forth in Article V shall have been true and correct in all material respects as of the date hereof and shall be true and correct in all material respects as of the Closing Date as though made on and as of the Closing Date, except that those representations and warranties that by their terms are qualified by materiality shall be true and correct in all respects.

(d) Performance of Obligations by the Purchaser. The Purchaser shall have performed in all material respects all covenants and agreements required to be performed by it hereunder on or prior to the Closing Date.

(e) Certificates. The Purchaser shall have delivered to the Company a certificate of an authorized officer as to compliance with the conditions set forth in Sections 7.3(b) and (c).

(f) **[Opinion of Purchaser's Counsel. The Company shall have received an opinion of [NAME], counsel to the Purchaser, dated the Closing Date, substantially in the form attached hereto as Exhibit 7.3(f).]**

(g) Ancillary Documents. The Purchaser shall have delivered, or caused to be delivered, to the Company and the Shareholder the following:

(i) documents evidencing the assumption of the Assumed Contracts the acceptance of the Assignable Licenses and the Assumed Liabilities, including the Assignment and Assumption Agreement;

(ii) a certificate by the Secretary or any Assistant Secretary of the Purchaser, dated the Closing Date, as to (1) the good standing of the Purchaser in its jurisdiction of incorporation and (2) the effectiveness of the resolutions of the board of directors of the Purchaser or committee thereof authorizing the execution, delivery and performance hereof by the Purchaser passed in connection herewith and the transactions contemplated hereby;

(iii) the Holdback Note; and

(iv) all other documents required to be entered into or delivered by the Purchaser at or prior to the Closing pursuant hereto.

ARTICLE VIII
CLOSING

The Closing shall occur within five Business Days following the satisfaction or waiver of the conditions set forth in Article VII, or on such other date as the Parties may agree. The Closing shall take place at the offices of _____, [ADDRESS], or at such other place as the Parties may agree.

<h2 style="text-align:center">ARTICLE IX
TERMINATION</h2>

Section 9.1 Termination. This Agreement may be terminated:

(a) in writing by mutual consent of the Parties;

(b) by written notice from the Company to the Purchaser, in the event the Purchaser (i) fails to perform in any material respect any of its agreements contained herein required to be performed by it at or prior to the Closing or (ii) materially breaches any of its representations and warranties contained herein, which failure or breach is not cured within 10 days following the Company having notified the Purchaser of its intent to terminate this Agreement pursuant to this Section 9.1(b);

(c) by written notice from the Purchaser to the Company, in the event either the Company or the Shareholder (i) fails to perform in any material respect any of its agreements contained herein required to be performed by it at or prior to the Closing or (ii) materially breaches any of its representations and warranties contained herein, which failure or breach is not cured within 10 days following the Purchaser having notified the Company of its intent to terminate this Agreement pursuant to this Section 9.1(c);

(d) by written notice from the Purchaser to the Company under the circumstances described in Section 6.15; or

(e) by written notice by the Company to the Purchaser or the Purchaser to the Company, as the case may be, in the event the Closing has not occurred on or prior to [DATE] (the "Expiration Date") for any reason other than delay or nonperformance of the Party seeking such termination.

Section 9.2 Specific Performance and Other Remedies. Each Party hereby acknowledges that the rights of each Party to consummate the transactions contemplated hereby are special, unique and of extraordinary character and that, in the event that any Party violates or fails or refuses to perform any covenant or agreement made by it herein, the non-breaching Party may be without an adequate remedy at law. In the event that any Party violates or fails or refuses to perform any covenant or agreement made by such Party herein, the non-breaching Party or Parties may, subject to the terms hereof and in addition to any remedy at law for damages or other relief, institute and prosecute an action in any court of competent jurisdiction to enforce specific performance of such covenant or agreement or seek any other equitable relief.

Section 9.3 Effect of Termination. In the event of termination of this Agreement pursuant to this Article IX, this Agreement shall forthwith become void and there shall be no liability on the part of any Party or its partners, officers, directors or stockholders, except for obligations under Section 6.8 (Public Announcements), Section 11.1 (Notices), Section 11.5 (Controlling Law; Amendment), Section 11.6 (Consent to Jurisdiction, Etc.) and Section 11.14 (Transaction Costs) and this Section 9.3, all of which shall survive the Termination Date. Notwithstanding the foregoing, nothing contained herein shall relieve any Party from liability for any breach hereof.

ARTICLE X
INDEMNIFICATION

Section 10.1 Indemnification Obligations of the Company and Shareholder. The Company and the Shareholder shall, jointly and severally, indemnify, defend and hold harmless the Purchaser Indemnified Parties from, against, and in respect of, any and all claims, liabilities, obligations, damages, losses, costs, expenses, penalties, fines and judgments (at equity or at law, including statutory and common) and damages whenever arising or incurred (including amounts paid in settlement, costs of investigation and reasonable attorneys' fees and expenses) arising out of or relating to:

(a) any liability or obligation of the Company or the Shareholder of any nature whatsoever, except the Assumed Liabilities;

(b) events or circumstances occurring or existing with respect to the ownership, operation and maintenance of the Business and the Assets on or prior to the Closing Date;

(c) any breach or inaccuracy of any representation or warranty made by the Company or the Shareholder in this Agreement, the Company Ancillary Documents or the Shareholder Ancillary Documents (for purposes of this Section 10.1(c), such representations and warranties shall be read without reference to materiality, Material Adverse Effect or similar monetary and non-monetary qualifications);

(d) any breach of any covenant, agreement or undertaking made by the Company or the Shareholder in this Agreement, the Company Ancillary Documents or the Shareholder Ancillary Documents;

(e) any fraud, willful misconduct or bad faith of the Company or the Shareholder in connection with this Agreement, the Company Ancillary Documents or the Shareholder Ancillary Documents;

(f) [any provision of any Environmental Law and arising out of, or relating to, (i) any act or omission of the Company or its employees, agents or representatives or (ii) the ownership, use, control or operation on or prior to the Closing Date of any real property, plant, facility, site, area or property used in the Business (whether currently or previously owned or leased by the Company), including arising from any Release of any Hazardous Material or off-site shipment of any Hazardous Material at or from such real property, plant, facility, site, area or property;] or

(g) non-compliance by the Parties with any applicable bulk sales Law.

[Add others as applicable]

The claims, liabilities, obligations, losses, damages, costs, expenses, penalties, fines and judgments of the Purchaser Indemnified Parties described in this Section 10.01 as to which the Purchaser Indemnified Parties are entitled to indemnification are collectively referred to as "Purchaser Losses."

Section 10.2 Indemnification Obligations of the Purchaser. The Purchaser shall indemnify and hold harmless the Company Indemnified Parties from, against and in respect of any and all claims, liabilities, obligations, losses, damages, costs, expenses, penalties, fines and judgments (at equity or at law, including statutory and common) and damages whenever arising or incurred (including amounts paid in settlement, costs of investigation and reasonable attorneys' fees and expenses) arising out of or relating to:

(a) the Purchaser's failure to perform, discharge or satisfy the Assumed Liabilities;

(b) any breach or inaccuracy of any representation or warranty made by the Purchaser in this Agreement or in any Purchaser Ancillary Document;

(c) any breach of any covenant, agreement or undertaking made by the Purchaser in this Agreement or in any Purchaser Ancillary Document; or

(d) any fraud, willful misconduct or bad faith of the Purchaser in connection with this Agreement or the Purchaser Ancillary Documents.

The claims, liabilities, obligations, losses, damages, costs, expenses, penalties, fines and judgments of the Company Indemnified Parties described in this Section 10.2 as to which the Company Indemnified Parties are entitled to indemnification are collectively referred to as "Company Losses."

Section 10.3 Indemnification Procedure. [Add specific procedure]

Section 10.4 Claims Period. The Claims Periods hereunder shall begin on the date hereof and terminate as follows: [**Add as specific to transaction**]

Section 10.5 Liability Limits. [**Add as specific to transaction**]

ARTICLE XI
MISCELLANEOUS PROVISIONS

Section 11.1 Notices. All notices, communications and deliveries hereunder shall be made in writing signed by or on behalf of the Party making the same, shall specify the Section pursuant to which it is given or being made, and shall be delivered personally or by next day courier (with evidence of delivery and postage and other fees prepaid) as follows: or to such other representative or at such other address of a party as such party may furnish to the other parties in writing. Any such notice, communication or delivery shall be deemed given or made (a) on the date of delivery, if delivered in person, (b) on the first Business Day following delivery to a overnight courier service or (c) on the fifth Business Day following it being mailed by registered or certified mail.

Section 11.2 Schedules and Exhibits. The Schedules and Exhibits are hereby incorporated into this Agreement and are hereby made a part hereof as if set out in full herein.

Section 11.3 Assignment; Successors in Interest. No assignment or transfer by any Party of such Party's rights and obligations hereunder shall be made except with the prior written consent of the other Parties; provided that the Purchaser shall, without the obligation to obtain the prior written consent of any other Party, be entitled to assign this Agreement or all or any part of its rights or obligations hereunder to one or more Affiliates of the Purchaser. This Agreement shall be binding upon and shall inure to the benefit of the Parties and their respective successors and permitted assigns, and any reference to a Party shall also be a reference to the successors and permitted assigns thereof.

Section 11.4 Captions. The titles, captions and table of contents contained herein are inserted herein only as a matter of convenience and for reference and in no way define, limit, extend or describe the scope of this Agreement or the intent of any provision hereof.

Section 11.5 Controlling Law; Amendment. This Agreement shall be governed by and construed and enforced in accordance with the internal Laws of the State of _____ without reference to its choice of law rules. This Agreement may not be amended, modified or supplemented except by written agreement of the Parties.

Section 11.6 Consent to Jurisdiction, Etc. Each Party hereby irrevocably agrees that any Legal Dispute [may be brought in] [shall be brought only to the exclusive jurisdiction of] the courts of the State of _____ or the federal courts located in the State of _____, and each Party hereby consents to the jurisdiction of such courts (and of the appropriate appellate courts therefrom) in any such suit, action or proceeding and irrevocable waives, to the fullest extent permitted by law, any objection that it may now or hereafter have to the laying of the venue of any such suit, action or proceeding in any such court or that they any such suit, action or proceeding that is brought in any such court has been brought in an inconvenient forum. During the period a Legal Dispute that is filed in accordance with this Section 11.6 is pending before a court, all actions, suits or proceedings with respect to such Legal Dispute or any other Legal Dispute, including any counterclaim, cross-claim or interpleader, shall be subject to the exclusive jurisdiction of such court. Each Party hereby waives, and shall not assert as a defense in any Legal Dispute, that (a) such Party is not subject thereto, (b) such action, suit or proceeding may not be brought or is not maintainable in such court, (c) such Party's property is exempt or immune from execution, (d) such action, suit or proceeding is brought in an inconvenient forum or (e) the venue of such action, suit or proceeding is improper. A final judgment in any action, suit or proceeding described in this Section 11.6 following the expiration of any period permitted for appeal and subject to any stay during appeal shall be conclusive and may be enforced in other jurisdictions by suit on the judgment or in any other manner provided by applicable Laws.

Section 11.7 Severability. Any provision hereof that is prohibited or unenforceable in any jurisdiction shall, as to such jurisdiction, be ineffective to the extent of such prohibition or unenforceability without invalidating the remaining provisions hereof, and any such prohibition or unenforceability in any jurisdiction shall not invalidate or render unenforceable such provision in any other jurisdiction. To the extent permitted by Law, each Party hereby waives any provision of law that renders any such provision prohibited or unenforceable in any respect.

Section 11.8 Counterparts. This Agreement may be executed in two or more counterparts, each of which shall be deemed an original, and it shall not be necessary in making proof of this Agreement or the terms hereof to produce or account for more than one of such counterparts.

Section 11.9 Enforcement of Certain Rights. Nothing expressed or implied herein is intended, or shall be construed, to confer upon or give any Person other than the Parties, and their successors or permitted assigns, any right, remedy, obligation or liability under or by reason of this Agreement, or result in such Person being deemed a third-party beneficiary hereof.

Section 11.10 Waiver. Any agreement on the part of a Party to any extension or waiver of any provision hereof shall be valid only if set forth in an instrument in writing signed on behalf of such Party. A waiver by a Party of the performance of any covenant, agreement, obligation, condition, representation or warranty shall not be construed as a waiver of any other covenant, agreement, obligation, condition, representation or warranty. A waiver by any Party of the performance of any act shall not constitute a waiver of the performance of any other act or an identical act required to be performed at a later time.

Section 11.11 Integration. This Agreement and the documents executed pursuant hereto supersede all negotiations, agreements and understandings among the Parties with respect to the subject matter hereof (except for that certain Confidentiality Agreement, dated as of [DATE], by and between the Purchaser and the Company) and constitute the entire agreement among the Parties with respect thereto.

Section 11.12 Compliance with Bulk Sales Laws. Each Party hereby waives compliance by the Parties with the "bulk sales," "bulk transfers" or similar Laws and all other similar Laws in all applicable jurisdictions in respect of the transactions contemplated by this Agreement.

Section 11.13 Cooperation Following the Closing. Following the Closing, each Party shall deliver to the other Parties such further information and documents and shall execute and deliver to the other Parties such further instruments and agreements as any other Party shall reasonably request to consummate or confirm the transactions provided for herein, to accomplish the purpose hereof or to assure to any other Party the benefits hereof.

Section 11.14 Transaction Costs. Except as provided above or as otherwise expressly provided herein, (a) the Purchaser shall pay its own fees, costs and expenses incurred in connection herewith and the transactions contemplated hereby, including the fees, costs and expenses of its financial advisors, accountants and counsel, and (b) the Company and the Shareholder shall pay the fees, costs and expenses of the Company and the Shareholder incurred in connection herewith and the transactions contemplated hereby, including the fees, costs and expenses of their financial advisors, accountants and counsel.

[Note: Add any other applicable miscellaneous provisions.]

IN WITNESS WHEREOF, the Parties have caused this Agreement to be duly executed, as of the date first above written.

[PURCHASER]

By: _____

Name: _____

Title: _____

[COMPANY]

By: _____

Name: _____

Title: _____

[SHAREHOLDER]

By: _____

Name: _____

Title: _____

Index

Boldface numbers indicate illustrations; *t* indicates a table.

Bob Stefanowski, **CPA, CMA, CFE,** is the president and CEO of GE Commercial Finance's Global Media and Communications unit, which provides debt and financing solutions to the telecommunications, media, cable, and publishing industries. He is also an adjunct professor of finance at New York University's Stern School of Business, specializing in M&A.